An Account of the Baptist Churches of Shropshire and the surrounding Areas

Michael J. Collis

Michael J. Collis
25 October 2008

First published by the Shropshire Group of Baptist Churches,
Heart of England Baptist Association in 2008
Forest Lodge, Sarn, Newtown, Powys, SY16 4EU

ISBN 978-0-9560329-0-4

Typography: Arthur Pallett

Printed in Great Britain by Imprint, New Road,
Newtown, SY16 1BD, Powys

To the memory
of
GEORGE RICHARD ROBERTS
21st October 1906 – 7th January 1996
Baptist Lay Preacher
and
Deacon Emeritus of Claremont Baptist Church
Claremont Street
Shrewsbury

Index of Contents

Foreword

The story of non-conformity in Britain has, historically, much to say about those who embraced Baptist teaching and forms of worship. Nearly 400 years have passed since Baptists first met together in Spitalfields, Southwark, in 1611, and soon Baptists were to be found fanned out across the nation. Included amongst those early Baptists were those who met in Shropshire, and it is their story that unfolds as this book relates.

It is a fascinating story of sometimes small, informal groups of dissenters meeting in homes or hired rooms in villages and hamlets as well as in larger towns. On the other hand there are the larger welt established churches meeting in their own buildings. It is the story of advance and regress, of division and amalgamation, of ministries long and short, of pious endeavour and gospel strategy, and of courage, sacrifice and the will to see Christ's Kingdom come.

No single volume can tell the whole story, but the original notes written by Mr. George Roberts who probably knew the Baptist Churches of Shropshire and the border counties area as much as any man, have gone a long way to making this volume possible. For some sixty years he was a lay preacher nourished in the Scriptures, who faithfully imparted the Good News to congregations large and small. In addition he was variously, Deacon, Treasurer, Secretary and Deacon Emeritus of Claremont, Shrewsbury.

When the Shropshire Group of Baptist Churches decided to produce a book based upon George Roberts's notes it was to the Rev. Dr. Michael Collis, Minister of Sarn Baptist Church, they turned. He has since done a tremendous amount of research, and diligently and painstakingly from a large number of sources, pieced together the story. The text has been enhanced by numerous photographs, prints, maps, diagrams and charts, and to him and all who assisted him, the reader must owe a deep debt of gratitude, In these pages are found the most comprehensive compilation of information yet produced concerning Baptists in Shropshire, and is a mine of information.

Our forebears in the faith were men and women of religious conviction, deep commitment and visionary outlook, and we do well in the 21st Century in applying those same virtues as we add further pages to the ongoing worship, work and witness of Baptists in Shropshire and beyond.

Rev. J. Alan L. Edwards
Heart of England Baptist Association, Pastoral Minister for Shropshire

Abbreviations

art.	article
BCRL	Birmingham Central Reference Library
BDE	Timothy Larsen (ed.), *Biographical Dictionary of Evangelicals,* Leicester & Downers Grove, Illinois, 2003
Beds.	Bedfordshire
Berks.	Berkshire
BH	*The Baptist Handbook*
BMag	*The Baptist Magazine*
BMan	*The Baptist Manual*
Boase	Frederic Boase, *Modern English Biography,* 6 volumes, 1892-1921, reprinted 1965.
Brecs.	Breconshire (Brecknockshire)
Breed	Geoffrey R. Breed, *Particular Baptists in Victorian England and their Strict Communion Organizations,* Didcot, 2003
BQ	*The Baptist Quarterly*
Bucks.	Buckinghamshire
BU Directory	*The Baptist Union Directory*
BU Proc	*Account of the Proceedings of the Baptist Union*
c.	circa (about)
CYB	*Congregational Year Book*
d.	died
DEB	Donald M. Lewis (ed.), *The Blackwell Dictionary of Evangelical Biography 1730-1860,* 2 volumes, Oxford, 1995
Denbs.	Denbighshire
DWB	*Dictionary of Welsh Biography down to 1940,* 1959
DWL	Dr. Williams's Library, London
E.	English-speaking
ed.	Editor(s), edited by
EV	*The Earthen Vessel*
FIEC	The Fellowship of Independent Evangelical Churches
fl.	floruit [flourished]
Flints.	Flintshire
GH	*The Gospel Herald*
Glam.	Glamorganshire
Glos.	Gloucestershire
gol.	golygydd (editor)
Hayden	Roger Hayden, *Continuity and Change: Evangelical Calvinism among eighteenth-century Baptist ministers trained at Bristol Academy, 1690-1791,* The Author and the Baptist Historical Society, 2006
Hants.	Hampshire
Herefs.	Herefordshire
Herts.	Hertfordshire
Lancs.	Lancashire
m.	married
Meir.	Meirioneth
Middx.	Middlesex
Mon.	Monmouthshire
Mont.	Montgomeryshire
Northants	Northamptonshire
Notts.	Nottinghamshire
NLW	National Library of Wales
ODNB	*Oxford Dictionary of National Biography from the earliest times until the year 2000*
Oxon.	Oxfordshire
PRO	Public Record Office
RCAHMW	Royal Commission of the Ancient and Historical Monuments of Wales
RCHME	Royal Commission of the Historical Monuments of England
Rads.	Radnorshire
RPC	Regent's Park College, Oxford
SA	Shropshire Archives (formerly Shropshire Records and Research Centre), Shrewsbury
Salop	Shropshire
Staffs.	Staffordshire
SSMR	Shropshire Sites and Monuments Record
tt.	tudalennau (pages)
UBCLL	*Undeb Bedyddwyr Cymru Llawlyfr [The Baptist Union of Wales Handbook]*
URC	United Reformed Church in the United Kingdom
URCYB	*United Reformed Church Year Book*
VCH	*Victoria History of the Counties of England*
Warks.	Warwickshire
Wilts.	Wiltshire
Worcs.	Worcestershire
Yorks.	Yorkshire

Preface

R.F. Skinner in his book *Nonconformity in Shropshire* has traced the growth of Nonconformity in the county in the period 1662-1816. Although several chapel histories have been written, there has been no overall account of the history of the Baptist churches of Shropshire and those in the neighbouring counties with which they have been associated. The present publication seeks to set the story of these churches in the wider context of Baptist life in England and Wales.

Mr. George Roberts compiled notes about many of the Baptist chapels in Shropshire and the surrounding areas and his manuscript was typed as a Microsoft® Word Document by Mr. Clifford Challinor. When I was asked to edit the manuscript, I sent the manuscript to the churches for checking and, where necessary, for bringing the information up to date. All but one of the churches replied. The need for further research has delayed the publication of this book.

I wish to express my thanks to all those who have made helpful comments on the articles relating to their churches. Amongst those providing information and answering my many queries are: Rev. Alan Betteridge, Mr. Paul Bellingham, Mr. David Buckingham, Mrs. Janice V. Cox, Mr. Colin Dyke (Church Secretary, Upton Baptist Church, Chester), Miss Meinir George (formerly Office Manager, The Baptist Union of Wales, Swansea), Rev. Patrick Goodland, Rev. Martin Graham (Kington Baptist Church), Mrs. Mary Humphreys (Church Secretary, Norton Street Baptist Church, Knighton), Mrs. Susan Mills (Librarian, Regent's Park College), Rev. Dr. Hughes Matthews (formerly Principal, Cardiff Baptist College), Dr. Richard K. Moore (Hon. Archivist, Baptist Theological College of Western Australia), Mr. Jonathan Morgan (Archivist, Dr. William's Library), Mrs. Ruth Ludgate (Hoole Baptist Church, Chester), Mr. Chris Moore, Mr. Tony Peake, Mrs. Judy Powles (Librarian, Spurgeon's College), Mrs. Daphne Thomas, Dr. Sylvia Watts (St. Andrew's Archive Group, Shifnal), and Rev. Dennis and Mrs. Rhoda Weller. Help has been given by the staff of the Royal Commission on the Ancient and Historical Monuments of Wales, the Cheshire, Herefordshire, and Shropshire Record Offices, the Public Record Office, Powys Library Headquarters, and Llandrindod, Newtown, Craven Arms and Highley Libraries.

I am grateful for the loan of the Minute Books of the Baptist churches at Donnington Wood, Market Drayton, Pontesbury, and Welshpool, and also those of the Shropshire Baptist Association. The early Minute Books of Market Drayton Baptist Church and those of the Shropshire Baptist Association have now been deposited in Shropshire Archives. Mr. Mike Brain (Church Secretary, Chester Street Baptist Church, Wrexham), Mr. and Mrs. Henry Pritchard (Broseley Baptist Church), and Rev. Dennis Weller have loaned chapel histories and other documents. Mrs. Clarice Thomas lent me her MSS history of the Baptist Church, Cwmgwyn (subsequently published as *A History of Cwmgwyn 1900-2000: A Chapel and its People,* Felindre, 2005) and Mr. W. G. Newell lent me the MSS of his forthcoming book *Baptist Church Dawley: an Account of the first 150 Years.*

My thanks are also due to:

Mesdames Florence Banks and Hilda Foster, and Revs Jonathan Booth, Peter Egginton and Stanley Woods for their personal recollections of Highley Chapel

The late Mr. Vivian Davies, Y Drenewydd, Mrs. Nelda Foster, Llandrindod, and Rev. Leonard Parry Jones, Ceri, for translating articles written in Welsh

Mr. Frank Law for information about Mr. Thomas Brocas and the wills of Rev. and Mrs. John Palmer and Rev. Thomas Harrisson

Mrs. Carrie White, Snowfield, Ceri, for information about the Dissenting Registrations for Montgomeryshire and Shropshire.

My wife, Anne Collis, drew the sketch maps showing Baptist Places of Worship in Shropshire and the Welsh Borders, as well as taking many photographs for this book. Other photographs were provided by Mrs. Mary Blount, Mr. David Buckingham, Mr. Richard Camp, Mrs. Janice Cox, Rev. Alan Edwards, Mr. Edwin Green, Rev. Ron Lycett, Mr. W. G. Newell, Mr. David Oakley, Dr. Trevor Pryce-Jones, Rev. Ivor Waddelow, the late Mr. Sidney Watkin, and also by the author. Mr. H. Keith Morris, of Eight Mile Plains, Queensland, Australia, provided me with a copy of the lithograph of the baptism by Rev. Thomas Morris in River Ebbw in 1843. My son, Justin Collis, gave me invaluable help in converting photographs into JPG format, and in many other ways.

Rev. Geoffrey R. Breed has provided biographical information about Baptist ministers. The following have also provided me with biographical information: Mrs. Elizabeth Heathcott (Rev. Richard Pryce Jones), Miss Helen Jones and Mr. Christopher Withers (Rev. Benjamin Withers), Mr. M. McDonagh and Rev. Maggie Rich (Rev. Alexander Leitch), Mrs. Gillian Milne (Rev. Charles Henry Doughty), Mr. H. Keith Morris (Rev. Thomas Morris), Mr. Stephen Gabb and Ms. Pat Royall (Rev. Frederick Hemus), and Mrs. Ellen Squires (Rev. Thomas Smith Bristow).

I am grateful to Mrs. Anne Collis, Rev. Geoffrey Breed and Rev. Alan Edwards, for reading the text and their helpful comments. They are not responsible for any errors that remain.

The present book is by no means a definitive history of Baptist work in Shropshire but it is hoped that its publication will stimulate further research.

Michael J. Collis — December 2007

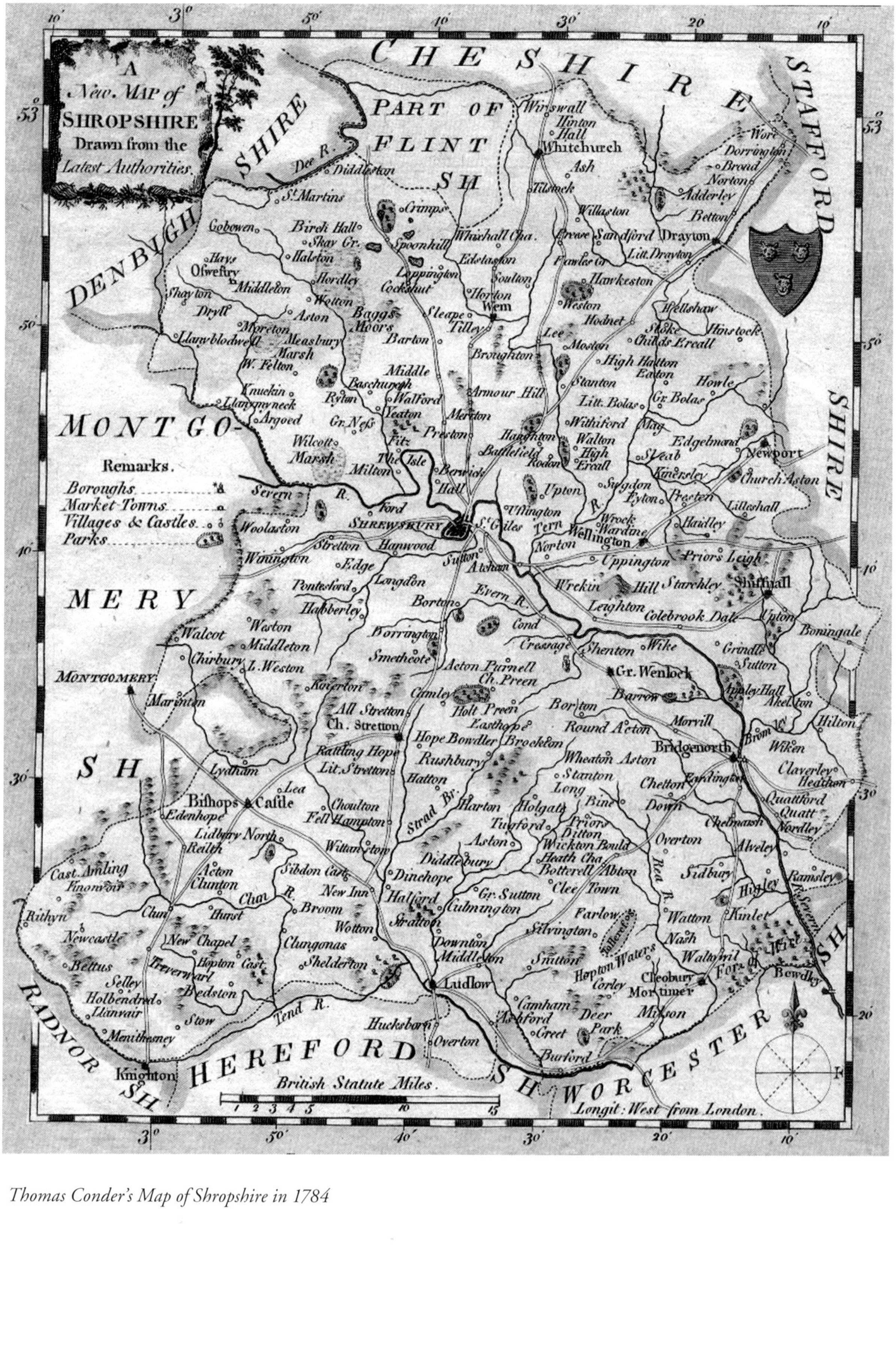

Thomas Conder's Map of Shropshire in 1784

Introduction

Shropshire (or Salop as it was often known) was at the end of the eighteenth-century predominantly a rural county, although the Coalbrookdale and Ironbridge locality was the leading iron-producing area in Great Britain.

Since 1840 there have been changes to the boundaries of Shropshire. For instance, Hales Owen (now spelt Halesowen) and Oldbury were incorporated into Worcestershire in 1844. In 1974 the counties adjoining Shropshire were as follows: starting in the north was Cheshire, and then working clockwise was Staffordshire in the east, Worcestershire in the southeast, Herefordshire in the south, Radnorshire in the southwest, Montgomeryshire in the west and Denbighshire in the northwest. A small-detached portion of Flintshire was also located in the northwest between Denbighshire and Cheshire. In 1974 the counties of Breconshire, Montgomeryshire and Radnorshire merged to form the new county of Powys. In Commonwealth times there were Baptist societies in Shropshire at Bridgnorth, Ellesmere, Ludlow and Shrewsbury and by 1669 there was a Baptist society at Stoke upon Tern. However, the story of Baptists in the county needs to be seen in the context of the development of Baptist churches elsewhere in England and Wales.

Baptists in England and Wales

The first Baptist church in England met in London at Spitalfields in Southwark, from 1611. Guy's Hospital now stands on this site. Thomas Helwys formed this on his return from Amsterdam where he had fled to avoid persecution. It was the first of a number of Baptist churches, which were found chiefly in Kent, and other pockets of rural England. They called themselves by titles such as 'Churches of Christ' or 'Churches of God, who walk according to the commands of Jesus Christ'. Later they were termed 'General Baptist' or 'Arminian' from the name of the Dutch theologian Jacob Arminius, because they believed in *general re-demption*, holding that the salvation, which Christ secured on the cross, was for all people who were capable of receiving saving faith. They were distin-

A Topographical Account of Shropshire from Pigot's & Co's *British Atlas comprising the Counties of England* (1840)

SALOP is an inland county, bounded on the north by Cheshire and part of Flintshire; on the east by Staffordshire; on the south by the counties of Radnor, Hereford and Worcester; and on the west by those of Denbigh and Montgomery.

SOIL, CLIMATE, and AGRICULTURAL PRODUCE. – Few counties are possessed of a greater variety of soil, or are more diversified in appearance: divided into nearly two equal parts by the Severn, its south portion assumes the mountainous character exhibited by the counties of Montgomery and Denbigh; while the north approaches the resemblance of a level, agreeably relieved by a few simple hills and romantic valleys, finely wooded. The meadows on the side of the Severn are extremely fertile, being frequently enriched by the overflowing of that river, which is navigable in its whole course. The CLIMATE is considered highly salubrious; the air is pure, although in many parts it is sharp and piercing. The PRODUCTIONS of this county are various and valuable: the breed of cows and sheep deserve particular notice,- the former giving large quantities of milk, and much of the cheese sold under the denomination 'Cheshire' is produced from the dairies here; it is acknowledged that the sheep fed upon its hilly tracts afford some of the finest fleeces in the Kingdom. The whole county is in general well cultivated, yielding great quantities of grain; its southern borders producing excellent hops, and agreeably varied with fine, healthy orchards.

MINERALS AND MANUFACTURES. - Rich as this county is in the production of the field, the treasures extracted from it bowels are not of minor importance: lead iron, lime-stone, free-stone, pipe clay and coals are found in great abundance; and in the hundred of North Bradford are salt springs; while on the eastern side of the county are a number of extensive iron-works, that give employment to several hundred hands. The chief MANUFACTURES are porcelain and flannel, the former is of great excellence and in proportionate demand; the latter though somewhat reduced from its former importance is by no means reduced to insignificance. The principal manufacturing towns are Shrewsbury and Oswestry, for flannels; in the neighbourhood of the former town are large iron foundries, and it was here that the noble Menai Bridge was cast. In the parish of Madeley are also immense iron-works; the stupendous iron bridge that bestrides the Severn at this place was constructed from the furnaces here. At Coalport are china manufactories, of great extent and celebrity; at Bridgnorth, carpets and porcelain are manufactured; at Broseley, various descriptions of porcelain ware; at Hales Owen, nails and pearl buttons; and Ludlow and its vicinity derive considerable prosperity from its extensive malting trade.

Sketch Map of Shropshire showing Baptist Places of Worship
Shropshire County Boundaries as in 1840

guished from Particular or Calvinistic churches, which believed in *particular redemption* holding that Christ's salvation was only for the elect, those already known to God; they alone would be given the grace to respond to Christ in faith. The first Calvinistic Baptist church appeared in London in 1638 under the leadership of John Spilsbury. These churches were strong in London, the Midlands and the West Country. A much smaller group, the Seventh Day Baptists, was usually, though not invariably, Calvinistic in theology, and seems to have developed during the 1650s.

Both General and Particular Baptist churches had much in common. They alike were congregational in government and wished to be independent of any state interference. Their members were responsible for the appointment of their pastors and other officers. They sought to organise their life on the model of the New Testament, which was their authority in all matters of faith. This led to their rejection of paedobaptism (child baptism) as they claimed that scripture only recognised the baptism of believers. So they were sometimes called Anti-Paedobaptists.

Pulpit chair said to have been used by Vavasor Powell now at The Garth, Pantydwr

Baptist work in Wales can be traced back to back to 1646 and a mission of Hugh Evans, a native of Llan-hir (Llanyre), near Llandrindod. After spending sometime as a clothier's apprentice in Worcester, he moved to Coventry and joined a General Baptist church there. His concern for his native land led him to seek the help of Jeremy Ives, minister of the General Baptist church in Old Jewry. London. The two came to Wales, preaching for the most part in Radnorshire, where several Baptist fellowships were formed. The hope excited by these workers is reflected in the preface to the General Baptist Midland Confession of 1651, addressed partly to Wales. The English language was little used in Mid-Wales and so the Radnorshire Baptists were left without suitable literature in their own language. Spontaneity and 'openness to the Spirit' was a significant feature of General Baptist worship and so it is not surprising that when the Quakers came to the county, they were successful in making converts from these General Baptists.[1]

The Puritan leader Vavasor Powell, who was born at Cnwclas (Knucklas), Radnorshire, was an ardent evangelist and it is said that there were few places in Wales that he did not visit to preach the Gospel. We have a delightful picture of him preaching in Shropshire at Sweeney Hall, Oswestry,[2] by Richard Gough who was there:

> I have heard him pray and preach for four houres together in the dineing room att Sweeney, where many persons came to heare him: and when the people departed they had every one a quarter of a two-penny bun or cake, and every one had a glass of beere, of about halfe a pint.[3]

Powell founded over 20 churches and organized a system of itinerant preachers. For many years his followers were known as *Pobl Vavasor Powell*, the people of Vavasor Powell. For these churches he drew up a Calvinistic Confession of Faith.[4] He was baptized as a believer in 1655 but we do not know where his baptism took place. Two places have been suggested, namely, Olchon, near Abergavenny, and Rhual Park, near Mold. There is an open-air baptistery at Rhual but it was not built until 1685.[5] Powell preached at Garth Fawr Farm in Montgomeryshire and a field where he preached on the adjoining farm is known as the 'Pulpit Field'. On the last occasion he came to Brondrefawr in Radnorshire he had to flee when he received news of the approach of troops seeking to arrest him. He left behind his mobile pulpit, which was subsequently recovered and is now in Bwlchysarnau Baptist Chapel.[6] Powell's emphasis was on gathering congregations of Dissenters comprising both paedo-Baptists and

Rhual Park Baptistry – External View

Rhual Park Baptistry – Internal View

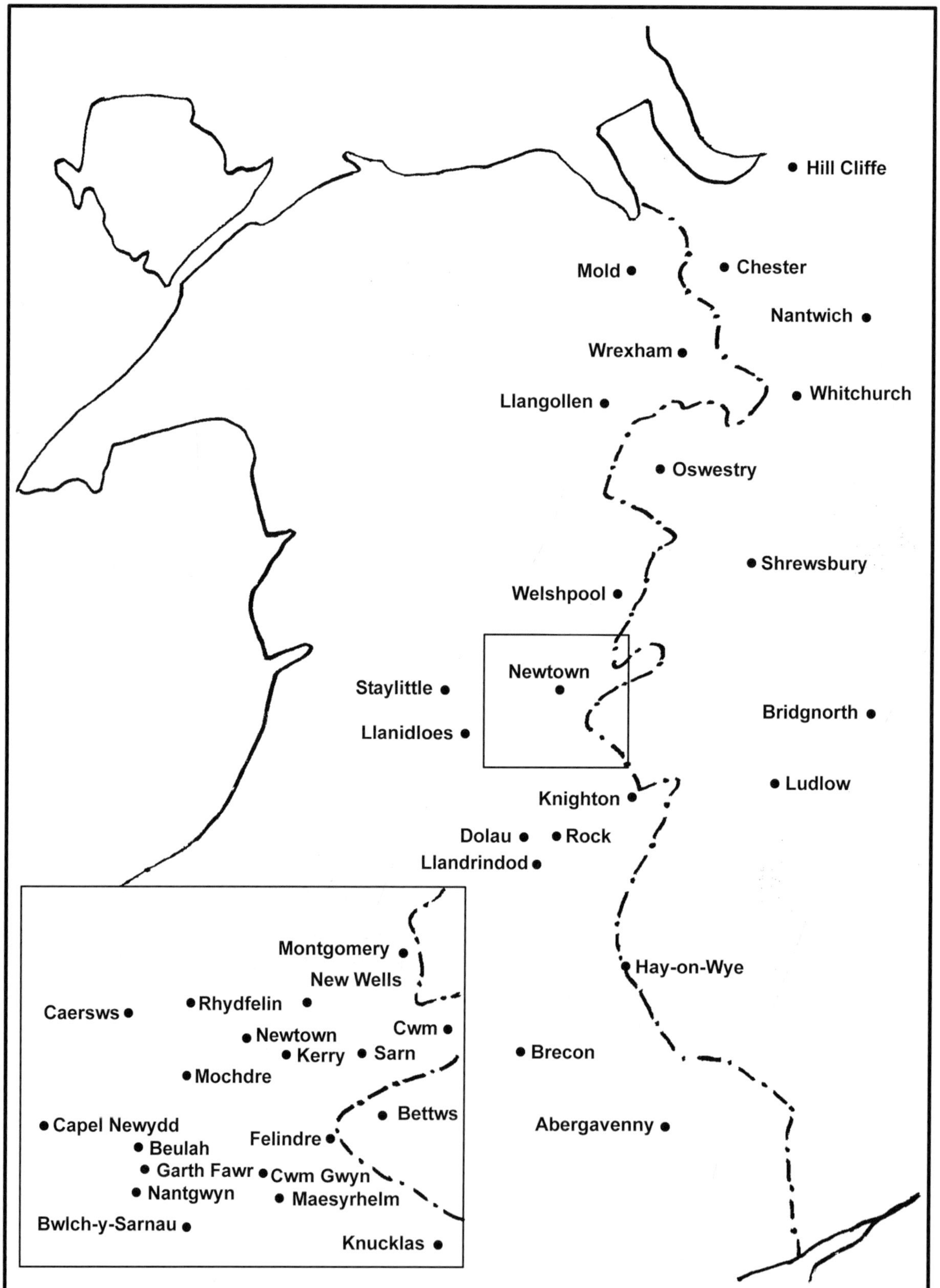

Sketch Map showing Baptist Chapels and Meeting Houses near the Welsh Border

Baptists, rather than forming specifically Baptist churches. His own church, the main gathering of which was at Llanbrynmair, Montgomeryshire, practised both infant and believers' baptism. Consequently, he did not have a long-term influence on the development of Baptist churches in the country. Powell spent much of the final decade of his life imprisoned in Shrewsbury, the Fleet and Caronne House, Lambeth, where he died, aged 53, in 1678. The first Particular Baptist church in Wales was formed in 1649 at Ilston, then in Glamorgan.[7] According

Ilston Memorial, Gower

to tradition the church met in the pre-Reformation Chapel of The Trinity in Ilston valley. From this church several churches were formed, including those at Hay and Abergavenny. Salem Baptist Chapel, Hay, has a plaque which states that it is 'The second oldest Nonconformist Chapel in Wales' with the Schoolroom dating from 1647. However, the building dates from 1815 when a fairly good (Welsh, *lled dda*) meeting-house was erected. The original church seems to have closed *c.* 1754 when Joshua Thomas, who supplied the church on two Sundays a month, left the town for Leominster. The cause was revived in 1813 and it was described as a new cause (*eglwys newydd*) when it was admitted to the South-Eastern Association in 1823.[8]

The church at Llanwenarth, near Abergavenny claims to be the oldest Baptist Fellowship now existing in Wales.[9] In Wrexham, Denbighshire, a Baptist church developed from the oldest Dissenting congregation in the town. Its minister, Rev. John Evans, became a Baptist in 1715.[10]

Particular Baptist meeting houses in Radnorshire were opened at Rock, near Pen-y-bont, in 1721 and Newbridge in 1760.[11] In 1792 a chapel was erected at Nantgwyn near the border of Radnorshire with Montgomeryshire. The Nantgwyn congregation, together with the small congregation at Capel Newydd (Newchapel) in the parish of Llanidloes, Montgomeryshire,[12] was received into the South-eastern Association as the Nantgwyn church in 1797.[13] The

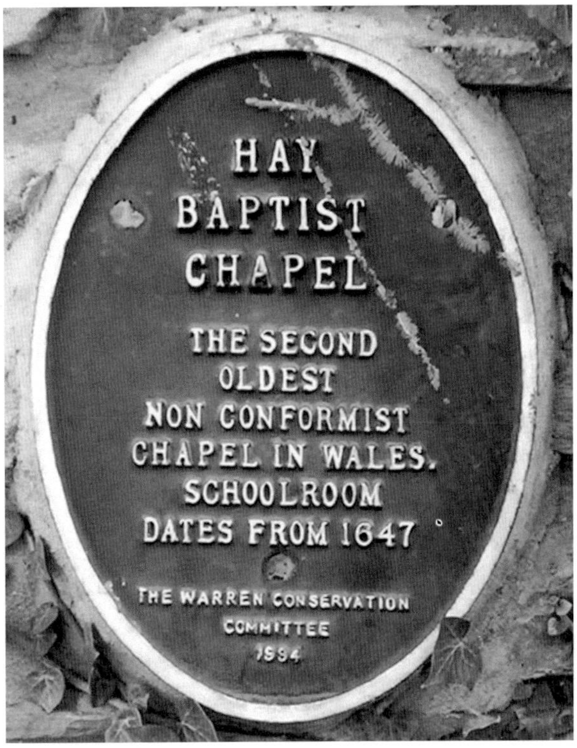

Plaque outside Hay Baptist Chapel

Hay Baptist Chapel School Room

congregation at Capel Newydd was a branch of the Nantgwyn church until about 1838 when it became an independent church. The chapel at Capel Newydd dates from 1815.[14]

With the help of David Evans, the minister of Dolau in Radnorshire, a church at Rhydfelin, near Newtown (then spelt *Y Drefnewydd* in Welsh), was formed in 1792.[15] A meeting-house was erected with a cottage for the use of the chapel keeper. From this church developed a separate congregation at Newtown.
The early Baptist meeting houses were simple buildings. They did not have baptisteries and so baptisms took place in the open air in streams and rivers and so were an occasion for public witness. For instance, the *Baptist Reporter* in 1845 contained the following report:

Earliest Nantgwyn Baptist Chapel as shown on an old postcard

Capel Newydd

> BAPTIZING IN THE RIVER EBBW.- This novel and picturesque ceremony was performed on sabbath-day, April 7, in the river Ebbw, adjacent to the Old Bridge on the Cardiff road, and the beautiful park of Sir Charles Morgan; when four females and four males were baptized and received into the baptist church by immersion. The Rev. J. Morris officiated.- *Bristol Mercury*

The minister referred in this report was not, in fact, 'Rev. J. Morris' but Rev. Thomas Morris of Newport, Commercial Road, who after he had built or enlarged ten chapels was known as 'Ten Chapel Tom.'

In the early days of Baptist life in Wales and, to a lesser extent in England, Baptists expressed their relationship to each other by means of a church covenant. The concept of a church covenant arose first among the English Separatists. A Separatist congregation was formed at Gainsborough, Lincolnshire, on the basis of a church covenant in 1606. Writing at a later date William Bradford wrote about the Gainsborough church,

> As the Lord's free people they joined themselves together by a covenant of the Lord into a church state, in the fellowship of the gospel to walk in all His ways, made known or to be made known unto them, according to their best endeavours whatever it should cost them, the Lord assisting them.[16]

The fundamental nature of a church covenant is illustrated by that adopted by the church at Hawkshead Hill in the Lake District in June 1678:

> First giving ourselves to the Lord and one another according to the will of God, promising by the help of divine Grace to walk as becometh Saints in the order of the Gospel.[17]

This covenant made clear that the members of the church committed themselves both to the Lord and to each other. Only at a later date did they find it necessary to specify the beliefs they held.
The eighteenth century Evangelical Revival led to the formation of the Wesleyan Methodist Church in England and the Calvinistic Methodist Church in Wales. In Wales the Revival is known as The Great Awakening (*Y Deffroad Mawr*) not so much because of the number of its converts but rather because by the beginning of the nineteenth century the Nonconformist denominations 'were all tinged with the aftermath of the Great Revival'. As Professor R. T. Jenkins once put it 'Harris, Rowland and Pantycelyn succeeded in

Rhydfelin Chapel in the 1980s

Internal view of Rhydfelin Chapel in the 1980s showing the deacons' seat below the pulpit

Rev Thomas Morris baptizing in the River Ebbw above Pont Ebbw (Cardiff Road) at Tredegar Park, Newport, on 22 October 1843. Drawing by JF Mullock, litho by David Morris

casting the cloak of Methodism over them all'.[18] It was only after 1779, under the influence of the Revival, that Baptists began to make inroads into North Wales.

In England and Wales Methodists formed societies which provided pastoral care for their members. By the nineteenth century Baptist churches in Wales followed the Methodist practice of holding society meetings (or fellowship meetings) but while the Methodists described such a meeting as a *seiat* the Welsh Baptists used the word *cyfeilydd*. During the 1859 Revival society meetings were held after every public service.[19] Under the influence of the Evangelical Revival Dan Taylor formed in England a 'New Connexion' of the more evangelical General Baptists in 1770 and a number of New Connexion churches were formed in Cheshire but none was formed in Shropshire. Some General Baptist churches adopted Socinian beliefs[20] and became Unitarian. The Revival also had a profound influence on several eighteenth century Particular Baptist ministers.[21]

Another Calvinistic Baptist movement began in Scotland. 'Scotch or Sandemanian Baptists', as they came to be called, were founded on the principle that both the doctrine and polity of a true church must be taken in literal detail from the New Testament. Each church should have at least two ruling elders, who were responsible for the government and teaching of the church, while deacons attended to financial matters. The elders were unpaid; Scotch Baptists often had contempt for an educated ministry and were antagonistic to what came to be called 'a one man ministry.' They observed the Lord's Supper, which they called 'The Breaking of Bread' every Lord's Day and made it a central feature of their services, often holding a Love Feast (Agape) between the morning and the evening services. The Breaking of Bread could not be observed if an elder was not present. The beliefs of the Scotch Baptists spread from Scotland into England and later into Wales. A Scotch Baptist church was founded at Haggate, two miles north east of Burnley, Lancashire, in 1760[22], while a church at Shrewsbury was formed in 1800.[23] At Wrexham its minister, Robert Roberts, became a Sandemanian and by making Ramoth Jones (Rev. J. R. Jones of Ramoth, Merionethshire) acquainted with Scotch Baptist doctrines he was the means of introducing these doctrines into North Wales.[24]

At the end of the eighteenth century there were theological tensions amongst Particular Baptists as a result of the publication in 1785 of a book written by Andrew Fuller, of Kettering, entitled *The Gospel Worthy of All Acceptation*. Although he was a convinced Calvinist, he taught that it was the duty of everyone to believe the Gospel and he went as far as to define the work of Christian ministry as 'to hold up the free grace of God through Jesus Christ.' Fuller's style and theology often clashed with those of his stricter brethren but eventually his perspective overwhelmed the old order. The churches that followed Andrew Fuller retained the title Particular Baptist calling themselves 'Moderate (or Evangelical) Calvinists' and in due course most adopted open communion, welcoming to the Lord's Table all believers whether or not they had been baptized as believers. The adoption of open communion was encouraged by the St. Mary's Norwich Chapel Case in which the High Court held that a Particular Baptist church might adopt open communion if it was not barred by the church's Trust Deed.[25] William Gadsby and other high Calvinists rejected Fuller's contention that the law was 'The believer's rule of life.' Their churches, known as 'Strict and Particular Baptist'[26], practised strict (or close) communion restricting attendance at the Lord's Table to those who had been baptized as believers, some accepting only those of 'the same faith and order'. The churches that followed William Gadsby became in due course Gospel Standard churches.

Calvinistic ministers were often unwilling to baptize those converted in General Baptist Churches or to admit them to communion. For instance, those converted in the General Baptist Church at Newbridge, six miles SW of Wrexham, were not recognized by the Particular Baptists of Wrexham. So they had to walk 25 miles to Nantwich for communion. Nantwich people had to walk 32 miles to be baptized in the baptistery on the Rhual estate.[27]

Gradually the majority of Particular Baptist churches in England drew closer to the General Baptist churches and ministers were able to move freely between pastorates in Particular and General Baptist churches. For instance, in 1750 the Nantwich General Baptist Church called Henry Phillips, a Particular Baptist from Wrexham, although in 1757 he was succeeded by John Pyne, a General Baptist whose views were to cause disagreement in the Shrewsbury church. Later the re-formed Nantwich church called to the pastorate the high Calvinist Edward Evans, who had previously been pastor at Snailbeach. His predecessor, J. B. Lockwood, had left for a General Baptist Church.

Many of those who responded to Gospel preaching and became Baptists were drawn from the lower classes of society, such as farmers, farm labourers, lead miners and tradesmen. The report in *The Baptist Annual Register 1792* of the meeting of the South-West (Welsh) Baptist Association records that Brother W. Williams [Rev. William Wiliams, of Cardigan] preached in English and Welsh but adds in a footnote 'His civil title, justly and deservedly, is Esquire.' 'A gentleman of independent means' built the chapel at Plealey, Shropshire, early in the nineteenth century on the estate. He at first supported the Independents, then transferred his allegiance to the Baptists *c.* 1839, and finally to the Wesleyan Methodists *c.* 1858.[28] About 1840 James Freme of Wrentall House built a Baptist chapel at Wrentall.[29] Very few members of the gentry became Baptists and the impact on the aristocracy was minimal. A few aristocrats became Baptists including Sir Egerton Leigh, who founded the Baptist church at Rugby[30], and the Hon. George Henry Roper Curzon, who before he succeeded to the peerage as 16th Baron Teynham, served as minister of the Baptist church he founded at Ledbury, Herefordshire.[31] He was later invited to preach at Baptist churches on special occasions and no doubt helped to confer a degree of respectability on Baptists. In 1845 at Y Deml, Newport, Monmouthshire, there was great rejoicing when he visited the church and the minister, Thomas Morris, was so overcome that he forgot to address him as 'My Lord'![32] When he preached at Stafford in February 1868 he was entertained by the Mayor.[33]

The cost of building chapels and repayment of mortgages on the properties proved a heavy burden for many congregations. Country ministers used to go to London to seek help from sympathetic London merchants. It was to avoid this situation that the Baptist Building Fund was founded in 1824, whose object was 'to assist in the erection, repair or enlargement of Particular Baptist chapels throughout the kingdom'.[34] In Wales Christmas Evans was obliged to make extensive preaching tours to raise money for the churches in Anglesey.[35] In his last preaching tour when he was minister of Tabernacl, Caernarfon, he visited many places, including 'Trefnewydd' (i.e. Y Drenewydd), Caersws, Capel Newydd, Nantgwyn and Dolau.[36] There is little doubt that the need to clear chapel debts was a heavy burden for many ministers.

In 1835 *The Baptist Magazine* sought to compile statistics for 'Evangelical Baptist Churches'. While the figures published are incomplete, they do show that attendance at Baptist churches was larger than the number of members. However, by 1839 there was widespread anxiety about the state and progress of Particular Baptist Churches and a widespread longing for revival.

'Revival meetings' became a feature of the life of many churches and this continues to the present day among some Baptist churches in Mid-Wales.

Baptists also faced the challenge of others who sought to restore the purity of the New Testament church, but who came to different understandings. Especially in the seventeenth century Quakers sought converts among both General and Particular Baptists.[37] Quaker beliefs took a strong hold in Radnorshire and most of the early General Baptists in the County became Quakers.[38] Although Quaker influence in the county was eventually to decline, they built a meeting house at The Pales in the parish of Llandegley *c.* 1717 and it is the oldest Quaker meeting house in Wales in continuous use.[39] Thomas Hammersley from Berryhill, Staffordshire, became a Quaker by 1654.[40]

One of the public services of the Berks and West London Association, was devoted to prayer and addresses on the subject of Religious Revival, delivered by several ministers, instead of a single sermon. : a similar statement may be given of the Hertfordshire and South Bedfordshire Union ; while the London Association has occupied the time of several of its quarterly meetings in the same manner. The whole of the public services of the last meeting of the Shropshire Association, extending through four days, were thus occupied. The principal services of the Old Suffolk and Norfolk and of the Glamorganshire Associations were conducted in the open air. Meetings for special prayer for the revival of religion in the churches were recommended by the brethren composing the Buckinghamshire, Oxfordshire, Berks and West London, Shropshire, East Kent, Cardiganshire, Pembrokeshire, and Carmarthenshire Associations ; and held also in many of the London churches : nor is the fact unworthy of record that at a prayer meeting held during the sitting of the West Yorkshire Association at Halifax, the chapel was completely filled at 6 o'clock in the morning. ... The Bristol Association appointed deputations of their brethren to visit several of their churches in a low state with a view to promote the revival of religion among them.
(From *Account of the Proceedings of the Baptist Union, 1840*, pp.16-17)

He had been one of the Arminian Baptists who had signed a petition to Cromwell in 1651/52.[41]

In the nineteenth century Baptists faced the challenge of the Irvingite Movement and the Plymouth Brethren, both of which affected the church at Bridgnorth. The Irvingite Movement sought to restore the ministries listed in Ephesians 4: 11f – apostle, prophet, evangelist, pastor and teacher. This Movement, later known as the Catholic Apostolic Church[42] took its name from Edward Irving, a Scottish Minister, who was excommunicated by the London Presbytery of the Church of Scotland for publishing a tract declaring Christ's human nature sinful.[43] A number of Baptist ministers became associated with the Movement.[44]

The Plymouth Brethren movement also attracted a number of Baptists. At Barnstaple Robert Chapman was said by a Baptist author to have 'imbibed peculiar notions' and joined the Plymouth Brethren[45] but Chapman never held Strict Baptist views.[46] At Ledbury 13 members left the Baptist church to join the Brethren.[47] At Bridgnorth in 1844 Rev. David Payn also joined the Brethren for a short while before becoming a Baptist again.[48] The 16th Lord Teynham also became a member of the Plymouth Brethren. A report in 1844 said that 'He was first a General Baptist, then a Particular, and now he is one of the "Brethren"', although 'it is believed that, at his own expense, he built Baptist Churches in many parts of the country, even as far away as the Orkney Islands'.[49] Mr. Charles Doughty left Whitchurch Baptist Church to join the Brethren in 1884[50] but later rejoined the Baptists becoming Pastor at Donnington Wood and later at Welshpool. The seriousness with which some Baptists saw the threat of the Brethren Movement can be seen judged from the review of a tract examining the claims of the Brethren which concluded as follows:

> We must reckon the spread of the opinions and practices of the Plymouth Brethren, among the calamities of the church of Christ, and beseech our heavenly Father, to avert it, with every form of evil from us.[51]

In the 1890s the Rock Lane Chapel, Ludlow, passed into the hands of the Brethren but in the following decade it became Baptist again. In the twentieth century many Brethren joined Baptist churches, especially from the Exclusive Brethren, which experienced schisms in the 1960s and 1970s.

From the earliest days Baptist churches in England and Wales recognized a need for mutual support. There were links between the Arminian Baptists in the 1650's[52] and in March 1660 the General Baptists held an Assembly in London and issued *A Brief Confession or Declaration of Faith*[53], which became the standard Confession of the General Baptists. In 1692 the 'Brethren Meeting in or about Shrewsburry' complained to the General Baptist Assembly about a Richard Newton, who was 'teaching and maintaining Doctrines Contrary to the Articles of ffaith' and the Assembly wrote to Richard Newton. However, there was no further contact between the Shrewsbury church and the Assembly.[54] Particular Baptists did not have a national gathering until 1689 and Thomas Lowe (or Loe) of The Hurst, the pastor of the church at Hill Cliffe attended the 1689 Assembly and also the 1692 Assembly.[55]

English Particular Baptists formed the Midland Association in 1655. Likewise the Welsh Particular Baptists formed Associations, the first being formed in 1700. This Association divided into three Associations in 1790 and, as the number of churches increased, so these Associations further divided.[56] There are now thirteen Baptist Associations in Wales.

A major step in co-operation among Particular Baptists was the formation of the Baptist Missionary Society (BMS) in 1792. In an article in *The Baptist Magazine* in June 1811 Joseph Ivimey, pastor of the Eagle Street church in London, pointed out that the Society had done much to unite the Baptist denomination. However, the main obstacle to support of the Society was the lack of any 'general bond of union' between Particular Baptist churches. Ivimey proposed that there should be an annual assembly of ministers, messengers of the churches, and representatives of the associations, to be held either in London or in the provinces. Its primary purpose was to raise support for the BMS. The BMS held its first public meeting in London on Wednesday, 24 June 1812. The following day in John Rippon's vestry at Carter Lane Chapel, Southwark, John Palmer of Shrewsbury and other Particular Baptist ministers agreed to form a 'general union' of Particular Baptist churches. The proposed Union was supported by about one-seventh of the Particular Baptist ministers in England.[57] The inaugural meeting of the General Union of Baptist ministers and churches was held on the 24 June 1813. In the words of Brian Stanley, the historian of the BMS, 'The Baptist Missionary Society had given birth to the first Baptist Union'.[58]

In 1832 the Baptist Union was re-organized and its first object was:

> To extend brotherly love and union among the Baptist ministers and churches who agree in the sentiments usually designated evangelical.

The absence of a Calvinistic Declaration of Faith in the 1835 Baptist Union Constitution was to pave the way for the eventual reunion of General and Particular Baptists in 1891. The Baptist Union Constitution was revised in 1873 and for the first time it contained a Declaration of Principle. The Constitution was again revised in 1904 and 1926 and a number of changes were made later in the twentieth-century.[59]

Some churches and Associations were suspicious of the development of the Baptist Union and it is interesting that in 1879 Walter Hanson in his book on Baptist Principles was obliged to argue the case for the Union.[60] Increasingly, however, the churches came to realize the importance of belonging to the Union and the creation of the office of General Superintendent in 1917 made a significant contribution to the life of the churches.

At the beginning of the nineteenth century many Baptist ministers were poorly educated. The desire for a better educated ministry in the north of England led to the opening of Horton College in 1805 under the leadership of William Steadman and he commented in his diary,

> Most of the ministers are illiterate, their talents small, their manners dull and uninteresting, their systems of divinity contracted, their maxims of church government rigid, and their exertions scarcely any at all.[61]

The need for an educated ministry was increasingly recognised and in 1840 *The Account of the Proceedings of the Baptist Union* reported:

> Recommendations to increased efforts to provide an educated ministry were given to the churches composing (*sic.*) The Lancashire, Glamorganshire, Monmouthshire, East and North Ridings of Yorkshire, Carmarthenshire, Pembrokeshire, and Cardiganshire Associations.

The Welsh Associations, in particular, seem to have been concerned about the quality of those ministering in the churches. The Brecknockshire Association in 1837 recommended that their churches should not set apart any brother for ministry without previously consulting the quarterly meeting. A similar recommendation was made by the Old Welsh Association in 1843.

At the beginning of the nineteenth century there were four Baptist Colleges in existence at Abergavenny, Bristol, and Horton and a General Baptist College at Chilwell. Later in the nineteenth century Colleges were formed at Stepney (later Regent's Park 1810), Haverfordwest (1839) and Llangollen (later Bangor 1862). In 1856 C. H. Spurgeon founded Spurgeon's College –first known as Pastor's College and then Metropolitan College – and in 1866 at Bury (later, Manchester) a college was formed advocating close communion and Calvinist doctrine. Owing to the poor education of many of their students, in the early days the Colleges had to provide a general education in addition to theological training. In contrast to other institutions, Pastor's College took only students who had actually been preaching for two years, and even admitted some who could not read.[62]

The December Supplement to the *Baptist Magazine* from 1851 to 1860 published a List of the Baptist Ministers in England and from 1861 *The Baptist Handbook* contained an alphabetical List of Baptist ministers. From 1869 the college where a minister was trained was inserted where applicable and the date when he commenced his ministry. The beginning of a system of ministerial accreditation can, therefore, be dated from 1869, since the list carries the note: 'Names are added to this List only on the recommendation of Tutors of Colleges, Secretaries of Associations, Three accredited Baptist ministers, or Three members of the Baptist Union Committee.' In1889 the rubric in the *Handbook* went a stage further: 'A name is placed on this List by vote of the Council of the Baptist Union who require a recommendation (1) by Tutors of Colleges, or (2) by Secretaries of Associations, or Three Members of the Council'. Several ministers who served in Strict Baptist Churches were included on the Baptist Union List.

The merger of the General and Particular Baptists in 1891 meant that it would be possible to set a national scheme for ministerial accreditation. In 1896 the Baptist Union established a Ministerial Recognition Committee and the following year it decided which colleges should be recognised for training ministerial students specifically for the Baptist ministry. In 1907 the Baptist Union Assembly adopted Ministerial Recognition Rules. One important aspect of these Rules was that it made provision for the enrolment on the Probationers' List of the names of ministers who had not attended a college but who had passed an examination prescribed by the Baptist Union Council.[63] This provision enabled a number of Lay Pastors to proceed to ordination, including, for example, Frank Foxall of Madeley and Richard Pryce Jones of Montgomery. In March 2001 the name of the 'List of Accredited Baptist Ministers and Probationers' was changed to the 'The Register of Covenanted Persons Accredited for Ministry' to grant denominational recognition to Youth Specialist Ministers and Evangelists.

The numerical growth of Baptist churches in Wales resulted in the formation in 1866 of The Baptist Union of Wales (Undeb Bedyddwyr Cymru). An English section of the Union was established and its meetings became a feature of the annual conference after 1902. Today the Union has two Annual Assemblies, one for the Welsh-speaking churches and the other for the English-speaking churches.

The Baptist Union of Wales has a List of Accredited Ministers. Those who have not attended a Baptist College may enter the Baptist Union of Wales's ministry by passing the Baptist Union of Wales Examination.[64]

In 1919 the Baptist Union Council agreed to take over the responsibility for the training and settlement of deaconesses. Deaconesses in active service in 1975 were transferred to the full ministerial List. The first woman minister serving a Baptist Union church was Miss Edith Gates, who was enrolled as a Probationer Minister in 1918. Rev. Margaret Jarman, who served as a deaconess prior to her ordination, became the first woman minister to become President of the Baptist Union in 1987.

The Baptist Union also contributed to raising the standards of lay ministry by introducing schemes for the national recognition of lay pastors and lay preachers. There are, however, other lay preachers who serve the churches but have not sought national recognition.

In 1972 there was controversy in the Baptist Union caused by an address given at the Baptist Union Assembly by the Principal of Manchester Baptist College, Rev. Michael Taylor, in which he questioned the divinity of Christ. The following year the Baptist Union Assembly passed a fuller statement of belief than the Union had ever previously professed.[65] As a consequence of this address a number of Baptist churches withdrew from the Union and their Associations, while other churches delayed applying to join the Union for a number of years.

The Ecumenical Movement had a significant impact on church life during the twentieth-century. The ecumenical involvement of both the Baptist Union and West Midland Baptist Association led the church at Wem to withdraw from both the Association and the Union in 1989. That year the Baptist Assembly agreed by a large majority that the Baptist Union should belong to the ecumenical bodies that replaced the British Council of Churches. Churches that did not agree with this decision were encouraged to remain in The Baptist Union but were enabled to record their dissent by writing to the General Secretary.

Most Baptist churches have been influenced, to a greater or lesser extent, by Charismatic Renewal and some no longer calling themselves Baptist have withdrawn from the denomination.

In recent years there has been a renewed interest in seeing covenant as being the basis of Baptist life and mission.[66] No doubt pragmatic reasons led to the creation of an Accredited List of Ministers but the Baptist Union came to see it as an expression of a covenant relationship existing between ministers and the Union.

1991 Baptist Union Ministerial Recognition Rules

Baptists have always searched for ways to express the basis of the covenant relationships in which they share. Those whose names appear on the Accredited list of Ministers are a body of Christ's servants, accredited by the Churches and the Union as qualified in ability and character, and by a mutually recognised call from God. This is an expression of a covenant under which we live. These rules set out the way in which we try to submit to each other under God's rule for good order in the church and for the exaltation of our Master, Christ.

Following the Denominational Consultation held at "The Hayes" Conference Centre, Swanwick, in September 1996 the Baptist Union embarked on a process of reform. It was the concept of covenant between churches, the Associations and the Baptist Union that provided the theological undergirding of the process. Reference was made to Gainsborough Separatist covenant in which church members committed themselves 'in the fellowship of the Gospel to walk in God's ways, made known or to be made known to them'. So when the major re-organization of the Baptist Associations took place at the beginning of the twenty-first century, churches were encouraged to mark the beginning of 2001 by holding a Covenant Service. To facilitate this process the Baptist Union published the booklet *Covenant 21: Covenant for a Gospel People.*

> Creating and redeeming God,
> we give you thanks and praise for your covenant of grace
> made for our salvation in Jesus Christ our Lord.
> We come this day to covenant with you
> and with companion disciples
> to watch over each other
> and to walk together before you
> in ways known and to be made known.
> Amen.

Baptists in Shropshire and the surrounding areas

The Particular Baptist church at Hill Cliffe, Cheshire, can with some justification claim to be one of the oldest continuing Baptist churches in England as it was founded *c.* 1649. By 1661 the church had secured its burial ground and in Shropshire it seems that Stoke-upon-Tern was developing as a centre of Particular Baptist witness. There was a Baptist church at Stafford *c.* 1650 and one of its members was Col. Henry Danvers, then military governor of Stafford, who became a Baptist during his residence there. W.T. Whitley suggested that Baptist beliefs spread from Stafford to Nantwich and possibly to Shrewsbury. By 1653 people at Shrewsbury who wished to be baptized travelled to Nantwich.[67] The formation of the first Baptist church in Shrewsbury can be assigned to the period of the Commonwealth.[68] Churches, which would now be called 'General Baptist', were also formed in Bridgnorth and Ludlow in the 1650s.

During the years 1659-1686 Dissenters faced active persecution and Baptists in Shrewsbury were frequently prosecuted for their nonconformity. Following the Declaration of Indulgence in 1672 a number of Presbyterian and Independent meeting houses in Shropshire were licensed for worship. The house of Widow Zanchay in Church Stretton was licensed for use by Independents. According to some notes left by A. J. Klaiber, the house was used as a Baptist meeting house but evidence for this has not been found.[69]

William and John Price, who were Baptists, were forced to leave their home in Bucknell, Shropshire, about 1713 because of religious hostility and they moved to Garth Fawr, Montgomeryshire.[70]

Garth Fawr in 1895

Rev. John Evans, the minister of Hand Alley Presbyterian congregation in London compiled a List of Dissenting Congregations and Ministers based on information supplied to him, chiefly by Presbyterian ministers. The List, known as the 'Evans List,' was compiled for the most part in the years 1716, 1717 and the early part of 1718. In the case of the County of Salop (as Shropshire was then known) the only Baptist congregations known to Rev. John Reynolds, who supplied the information to John Evans, were at Bridgnorth (then spelt Bridgenorth), Salop (Shrewsbury) and Shifnal (then spelt Shiffnall). In Cheshire there were three 'Anabaptist' congregations, while in Radnorshire there were two Baptist groups. One of these groups was not confined to the county having meetings at Pentre in Brecknockshire and at Blaneglay in Montgomeryshire. Blaneglay should be identified as Blaenglyn on the road from Beulah to Llanidloes.[71]

The Bridgnorth church became Particular Baptist *c.*1700,[72] while most of the members of the Shrewsbury church were Particular Baptist in belief by the 1750's. During the eighteenth century the Shifnal church also became Particular Baptist. A Particular Baptist society was formed at Broseley in the Coalbrookdale coalfield in 1741. A chapel was opened on 2 February 1742. It is the oldest Baptist chapel in Shropshire still used for worship.

In 1790 Dr. John Rippon in *The Baptist Annual Register* published a list of the Particular Baptist Churches in

Broseley Baptist Chapel (painted by Ken Griffiths in 1984)

England and Wales. In Shropshire there were churches at Bridgnorth, Broseley, Shifnal, and Shrewsbury, while only the churches at Bridgnorth and Broseley had pastors.

The Shrewsbury church was without a settled pastor from 1789 to 1794 and financial problems resulted in the meeting house being shut. There was an outstanding debt and it seemed that the building would have to be sold. The outlook for the church was dramatically changed when, at the request of the remaining congregation a young man, John Palmer, began to preach to them. He was then employed by Mr. Tudor, an apothecary in the town. Palmer was asked to undertake the pastoral duties for a year and then in 1793 he was ordained as pastor. He went to London to raise money to clear the church's debt and also to attend lectures at the London Hospitals. He was able to collect £172 for this purpose, apparently a larger sum than anyone else had been able to collect. [73, 74]

Although his portrait describes him 'Dr. John Palmer', he is not so described in Baptist literature during his lifetime.

From the beginning of his ministry John Palmer was concerned with preaching the Gospel in the villages surrounding Shrewsbury. As early as 1794 he preached in Minsterley and he invited Independent ministers to join him in the work there. Arising out of their efforts an Independent church was formed there in 1805 and a Baptist church in 1817.[75] On his return to Shrewsbury from London John Palmer spent Sunday and the greater part of Monday at home so that he might attend to his patients. He then took a circuit round the country preaching wherever the opportunity offered, returning on Thursday evenings to preach the lecture at home.

When Palmer was in London in 1797 The Baptist Society in London for the Encouragement and Support of Itinerant Preaching was formed. On his return to Shrewsbury he gave himself to regular preaching throughout Shropshire and within about eight years he wrote that the church had 'upwards of 70 that do not reside within ten miles of us mostly the fruit of village preaching.' [76] In 1797-1798 he was employed by the Itinerant Society in 'preaching through some parts of Wales, where he was known as 'John the Baptist', and the adjoining English counties [including Herefordshire]'. On these visits Rev. Abraham Webster of Broseley accompanied him in 1797 and Rev. Thomas Smith of Coseley, Staffordshire, in 1798.[77] In 1800 Palmer preached at Kington, Herefordshire, where a Baptist church was formed in 1805.[78] In 1801 John Palmer spent two months in Ireland at the invitation of the Evangelical Society in Dublin. [79]

An insight into Palmer's pastoral and evangelistic activity is provided by a letter he wrote to *The Baptist Magazine* in June 1811, in which he described the effect of a storm on Monday, 27 May which had caused loss of life and considerable damage to property in the Stiperstones area. A relief fund was set up and Palmer sought gifts for the fund. He was unable to make a 'general survey' of the area until Monday, 10 June. At Snailbeach there had been no fatalities but much damage to houses and he preached in the evening in a crowded house on *Isaiah* 32: 2, *A Man shall be as a hiding place from the wind, a covert from the Storm, &c.* At Minsterley there had been fatalities and almost the whole of the Angel Inn had been swept away by the flood waters. In the afternoon Palmer preached in the village to many who had lost friends and goods on *Job* 1: 21, *The Lord gave, and the Lord has taken away; blessed be the name of the Lord.* He administered 'the supper ordinance' and 23 out of 25 partook. In the evening he visited 'Abberley' (the spelling reflecting the Shropshire pronunciation of 'Habberley'). There

Dr. John Palmer – portrait in Claremont Baptist Chapel

the flood waters were very high but there had been little damage. He preached there on *Isaiah* 59: 19, *When the enemy shall come in like a flood, &c.* Palmer was 'strongly requested' to visit 'a considerable village called Worthier (i.e. Worthen)'. The village had not been much affected by the flood and on Wednesday afternoon he 'addressed more than 100 very attentive persons in the street'. He was not interrupted on what was 'the first attempt to introduce the Gospel.' On Thursday he went to Pontesford, where nine people had been swept to death by the flood waters. Three had been saved from the part of the bridge that remained standing. In the afternoon Palmer stood on the remains of the bridge and 'addressed a large and very attentive company from *James* 4: 14, *Whereas ye know not what shall be on the morrow, &c.*'

To aid the work of village preaching Palmer formed an Itinerant Society for Shropshire and this enabled payments to be made to preachers for supplying preaching stations. At least five of these preachers became ordained pastors, Joseph Ashford at Welshpool, David Crumpton at Llandrinio and Sweeney Mountain, W. Mayberry at Minsterley, William Owen at Madley, Herefordshire, while Edward Evans, an assistant preacher of the Newtown church, became the pastor at Snailbeach.

In addition to registering his cottage 'Enon' for nonconformist worship in 1803,[80] John Palmer registered meeting houses at Bishop's Castle[81] and Ellesmere[82] in 1798, a meeting house at Hookagate in the parish at St. Chad's, Shrewsbury in 1807.[83] By 1814 he had formed churches at Oswestry (1806), Wellington (1807) Whitchurch (1808), and Wem (1814). He had a significant role in the formation of a church at Ludlow in 1812 but the church had closed by 1823 and may have closed as early as 1815. Palmer co-operated with the (Calvinistic) Independents commencing a work at Minsterley, which led to the formation of an Independent church there in 1805 and a Baptist church in 1817.

Palmer's influence was not confined to Shropshire. In Wales Palmer reformed the church at Wrexham, Denbighshire (1805), formed a church at Welshpool, Montgomeryshire (1820) and commenced the work at Llandrinio, Montgomeryshire. On a visit to Aberystwyth he baptized converts in the River Rheidol. He made frequent visits to Liverpool and he was one of the first to have a ministry among seamen. He was one of the group of ministers who took part, in 1812, in the discussions which led to the formation of the Baptist Union the following year.[84] He was a supporter of the Baptist Missionary Society: in 1815 he was elected to the Society's Committee and he also became Treasurer of The Shropshire Auxiliary Society in aid of Baptist Missions and Translations when it was formed that year.[85] He preached at the quarterly meeting of the (Welsh) South-east Baptist Association in 1808[86] and the annual meetings in 1818 and 1819.[87]

A contemporary assessment of Palmer's influence was given in Hulbert's *History and Antiquities of Shrewsbury*:

> The benefits arising from his ministry were not confined to the town and county of Salop. Wales and various other parts of the Kingdom were the scenes of his successful labours. He was a man of no common talents. He possessed great versatility and genius. He spoke with fluency, and would versify with utmost quickness. Mr. Palmer's sermons were generally of colloquial character. He would, however, sometimes attain the sublime. His sermon on the death of Princess Charlotte was popular at the period, and passed through two editions. He died May 15th, 1823, having just entered his 56th year. Mr. Palmer was not only a laborious and faithful Pastor, but he had the character of being a sincere friend. His charities were numerous considering his property, and in all his endeavours to relieve the wretched or to assist those whom he believed had claims on his protection and care, his relatives or otherwise, he experienced the unwearied assistance of the lady to whom in the year 1808 he had the happiness to be united.

His wife, Susannah [neé Tovey] came from Wallingford, Berkshire, and on her husband's death, she returned to Wallingford. However, Palmer's ministry was not without its critics. Thomas Brocas, a member of the Methodist society at Shrewsbury, wrote to him in 1815 strongly criticizing his views of predestination and saying 'it is well for the character of God that there is no such thing in the bible.'[88]

No information is available for the work of the Baptist Itinerant Society from 1798 to 1813 but the report of the Society published in 1814 states that help had been given to 'worthy, laborious ministers' in various counties, including Shropshire. As the work grew, auxiliary societies were formed to support the work similar to those established to support the work of the Baptist Missionary Society. The name of the Society was changed to The Baptist Itinerant and Home Mission Society and abbreviated in 1822 to The Baptist Home Mission Society. In 1846 the aim of the Society was changed from the encouragement of itinerant preaching to the formation of Baptist churches where there had been none.[89]

Edward Goff, who was a native of Huntingdon in west Herefordshire, moved to London where he became a wealthy coal merchant. He left money for the promoting or establishing of schools for poor children in Herefordshire and surrounding counties. Under the usual arrangements made by his trustees, it was customary for the schoolmaster also to be the village pastor.[90] John Palmer had preached at Tenbury, Worcestershire, his birthplace, but it had not resulted in the formation of a church. However, in 1819 Goff's Trustees opened a school there and it served as the Baptist chapel on Sundays.[91] At Pontesbury a Baptist chapel was opened in 1828 and it was used during the week as a Goff's School.[92]

A Baptist congregation was established in Shropshire *c.* 1817 at Dawley Bank by a Baptist evangelist who regularly travelled from Birmingham. However, the church at Dawley was listed in the *Baptist Manual* until 1849. Other Baptist churches in Shropshire were formed at Oldbury (1815), Market Drayton (1818), Donnington Wood (1820), and Welshampton (1820), but the Market Drayton church closed in 1843. There was a Baptist congregation in Hadley from 1816 and a small Baptist chapel was built there in 1831.[93]

Table 1 shows that the number of Baptist congregations in Shropshire grew from 11 in 1811 to 21 in 1831.

Table 1
Baptist Churches in Shropshire in 1811 and 1831

1811		1831	
Church	*Minister*	*Church*	*Minister*
Bridgnorth	T. Edmonds	Bridgnorth	R. Clarke
Broseley, 1st church	J. Thomas	Broseley, 1st church	J. Thomas
Broseley, 2nd church		Broseley, 2nd church	T. Jones
		Chirbury	Supplies
		Donnington Wood	T. E. Wycherley
		Hadley	
		Market Drayton	T. Littleton
		Minsterley and Snailbeach	J. Lakelin
		Oldbury	
Oswestry	W. Paine	Oswestry	T. Cooke
		Pontesbury,	J. Francis
		Quatford	
Rollaw		Rollaw	
Shifnal		Shifnal	J. Tunnicliffe
Shrewsbury	J. Palmer	Shrewsbury, 1st church	M. Kent
		Shrewsbury, 2nd church	A. Sangster
Shrewsbury, Sandemanian	J. Hinmers	Shewsbury, Sandemanian	
Wellington	R. Pryce	Wellington	W. Keay
		Welshampton	J. Fenn
Wem		Wem	W. Gough
Whitchurch	J. Yeats	Whitchurch	J. Phillips

Notes:

Broseley, 1st church, was known as either Broseley (Old Meeting House) or Broseley (Old Chapel), while Broseley, 2nd church, was at Birch Meadow. Shrewsbury, 2nd church, was at Castle Foregate.

It is not known whether the congregation at Hadley was a branch of Wellington or a separate church.

In 1812 David Bogue and James Bennett in their *History of Dissenters* reported that in Shropshire there were 3 Presbyterian churches, 20 Independent churches and 11 Baptist churches.

In the 1835 List of the Evangelical Baptist Churches, published in *The Baptist Magazine,* only three of the seventeen Shropshire churches reported their statistics. They show that, as elsewhere in England, attendance was significantly greater than the church membership, no doubt because admission to church membership required baptism as a believer.

Table 2
Shropshire Baptist Churches and their Adherent Strength in 1835

Church	*Pastor*	*No of Members*	*Average No of Hearers*	*Children in Sunday School*	*Population*
Broseley, 1st church	J. Thomas	15	100	100	
Wem	J. G. Stephens	52	150	35	1932
Whitchurch	J. Philips	65	140	100	

Table 3 lists the twenty five Baptist churches in Shropshire in 1839. Eleven churches had Sunday Schools. Oswestry was the largest church, although the two churches in Shrewsbury had together a greater membership. The Wem church had the greatest number of preaching stations.

Table 3
Baptist Churches in Shropshire in 1839

Church	*Pastor*	*No. of Members*	*Sunday School Children*	*Village or other Stations*
*Aston Clunsland	- Humphreys	19	50	1
*Bridgnorth	D. Payne			
*Broseley, 1st church (Old Chapel)	J. Thomas	27	50	1
*Broseley, 2nd church (Birch Meadow)	T. Jones			
*Chirbury	T. Bird	15		
*Donnington Wood				
Hadley				
Maesbrook				
*Market Drayton	T. Littleton			
*Minsterley				
*Oldbury		24		
*Oswestry	R. Clarke	101	110	
Plealey				
*Pontesbury	J. Francis	89	180	7
Quatford				
*Shifnal (Aston Street)		21	20	
*Shrewsbury, 1st church (Claremont Street)	M. Kent	95	150	
*Shrewsbury, 2nd church (Castle Foregate)	W. Hawkins	88	65	3
*Shrewsbury, 3rd church**				
*Snailbeach (Lord's Hill)	E. Evans	64	120	3
*Sweeney Mountain	D. Crumpton	24		1
*Wellington	W. Keay	78	129	3
*Welshampton		16	50	3
*Wem		52		13
*Whitchurch	J. Phillips	68	100	3

Notes:
* The church was listed in *Baptist Union Proceedings* 1840, from which the membership figures are taken.
** Nothing further is known of this church founded in 1834.

By 1839 there was anxiety in Shropshire churches about the state and progress of their churches and the need for Revival. At the Claremont Street Church in Shrewsbury a series of revival meetings was held in 1839 and this led to a large accession of members. In two years 107 were added by baptism alone.[94] The Association Annual Meeting was held at Oswestry 28-30 June 1840 and the programme consisted of 'a series of revival services'. On the final evening of the Association Meeting one man and two women were baptized and they were received into membership at Oswestry on 11 July.[95]

According to the *Baptist Union Proceedings* 1843 a second Baptist church was formed at Bridgnorth in 1841, presumably as a result of a disagreement at the Castle Street church, but this church did not survive and nothing further is known about its history.

The Religious Census in 1851 showed that Baptists were relatively weak in Shropshire, Staffordshire and Cheshire.[96] In Table 4 we list the Shropshire congregations which made a Census return,[97] together with statistical information about Baptist churches taken from *The Baptist Manual* 1852.

Table 4
Baptist Congregations in Shropshire in 1851

Church	*Pastor*	*No. of Members*	*Sunday Scholars*	*Stations*
*Aston [a]		8		
Bettws-y- Crwyn (branch of Maesyrhelem)	T. Harvard			
*Bridgnorth	A. Tilley	103	110	
*Broseley, 1st church (Old Chapel)			54 [b]	
*Broseley, 2nd church (Birch Meadow)			86 [b]	
*Dawley Bank	A. Cox	31	150	3
*Donnington Wood	J. Morgan	27	150	1
Hadley [c]	H. G. Grainger		62 [d]	
*Ightfield		21	25 [b]	
*Market Drayton				
Maesbrook				
Much Wenlock			12 [b]	
Ollerton			15 [b]	
*Oswestry		30	60	1
*Pontesbury, 1st church (Chapel Lane)	E. Roberts	52	72	2
*Pontesbury, 2nd church				
Quatford				
*Shifnal, 1st church (Aston Street)				
*Shifnal, 2nd church (Zion, Salop Road)		23	95	1
*Shrewsbury, 1st church (Claremont Street)		66	60	1
*Shrewsbury, 2nd church (St. Austin Street)	J. Arnesby	40		
*Shrewsbury, 3rd church				
*Snailbeach (Lord's Hill & Perkin's Beach)	E. Evans	70	100	3
Stoney Stretton	G. Darrall			
*Wellington	H. G. Grainger	70	50	1
*Welshampton		19	15 [b]	
*Wem	W. Jones	20		2
*Whitchurch, Green End	W. Bontems	56	88	
Whitcott Keysett				
Wrentnall [e]	E. Roberts			

Notes:
* The church was listed in *The Baptist Manual* 1852.
[a] Known as 'Aston in Clun' or 'Aston Clunsland'.
[b] Average for 12 months (Census return)
[c] Probably a preaching station of Wellington.
[d] Attendance on Census Sunday, 30 March 1851
[e] Probably a preaching station of Pontesbury, Chapel Lane

The Market Drayton church was reopened in 1857 and churches were formed at Madeley in 1858 and in Shrewsbury at Coleham in 1859, while in the border town of Oswestry (*Croesoswallt* in Welsh) the Welsh Baptists opened a church in 1860. The Rev. Thomas Howe in his address to the Shropshire Association in 1862 drew attention to the lack of growth of the number of Baptist churches in Shropshire compared to the progress made by Independent churches. He pointed out that in 1790 there were 4 Baptist churches while in 1861 there were 24. The Independents had about 6 chapels in 1790 but by 1862 they had about 60. He attributed the slower growth of Baptist churches to 'the almost entire lack of suitable machinery for Home Missionary purposes'. However, new churches were formed at Oakengates (1862) and Coxall on the Welsh border (1870).

A further attempt was made to form a Baptist church at Ludlow in 1874 but the chapel had passed into the hands of the Brethren by 1893. However, by 1901 the cause had become Baptist again. In the twentieth century churches were formed at Newport (1992) and on the Crowmoor Estate at Shrewsbury (1992), while Chorley became independent of the mother church at Bridgnorth in 1948.

The years 1858-1860 marked what became known as the Second Evangelical Revival and J. Edwin Orr has traced its course and influence in Great Britain. He assumed that it was an unvarying movement that began in the south-west of Scotland before it was diffused as an unbroken movement across the rest of Britain.[98] However, more recent studies have shown that the revival in both North-East Scotland and also in America was more diverse than hitherto supposed.[99] In Shropshire Baptists and Congregationalists at Wellington in the Revival period increased membership by 66 per cent and Methodists by 75 per cent.[100] Dr. J. Edward Cranage, who has been described as 'an unconventional Anglican',[101] became a deacon of the Baptist church at Wellington in 1860. Inspired by a visit to Ireland to see the Revival there, he left the Baptist church to set up an undenominational mission among the poorer people of Wellington.[102] However, until the end of his life, he remained a Trustee of the Baptist Church.[103]

During the nineteenth century there was a renewal of Baptist life in Montgomeryshire and Radnorshire. In Montgomeryshire John Jones 'of Newtown', who preached in both English and Welsh, enjoyed much success as a preacher, evangelist and church planter until his untimely death, aged 49, in 1831. Through his zeal and hard work daughter congregations were formed at various places, including Caersws (1824), Sarn (1826), and Mochdre (1830). He also preached at Hen Castell (Old Castle) [104] and this led to the formation of a church at New Wells in 1838.[105] Thomas Thomas from Bristol College settled at Nantgwyn, where he was ordained in 1802. He planted churches at Staylittle, Llanidloes and Cwmbelan.[106] In 1808 the great Welsh Baptist preacher Christmas Evans registered a building for worship in Trefeglwys, near Caersws.[107] In the 1840s Baptists formed churches using buildings formerly used by the Independents in the village of Kerry and at Cwm in the parish of Mainstone.

In Radnorshire a Baptist church was formed in 1801 at Maesyrhelem on the side of the Ithon valley, near the turnpike road that led from Builth and Llandrindod to Newtown. Maesyrhelem Chapel was erected in 1805 and took its name from the nearby farm where meetings were first held. Baptisms took place in the River Ithon. The first pastor was Rev. Joseph Jones, from New Wells, near Newtown, who was the proprietor of Maesyrhelem Farm and formerly co-pastor with James Evans at Rhydfelin.[108] As a result of his preaching, together with that of his co-pastor at Maesyrhelem, Abraham Evans, branch churches were formed at Bettws-y-Crwyn in Shropshire and at Gravel in the parish of Llangynllo in Radnorshire.[109]

The growth of Baptist churches in Wales was undoubtedly facilitated by churches appointing assistant preachers, who would preach in the mother church and so release their pastors to engage in evangelistic activity in other places. Assistant preachers might have oversight of branch churches and might in due course be ordained. For instance, Edward Evans, assistant preacher at Caersws became the pastor at Snailbeach in 1832, while Joseph Drew, the assistant at Welshpool in 1843, became pastor there in 1845.

Signature of John Jones
Minister, Newtown 1810-31

Signature of Benjamin Price,
Cymro Bach, Minister, Rhydfelin 1828-40 & Newtown 1831-40

Table 5
Select Group of Churches, Ministers and Assistant Preachers in Montgomeryshire and Radnorshire in 1831 and 1843
Names of Branch Churches and their dates of formation and the names of Assistant Preachers are in italics

		1831		1843	
Church	*Date Formed*	*Minister*	*Assistant Preacher*	*Minister*	*Assistant Preacher*
Rhydfelin *Caersws* *Mochdre*	1792 *1824* *1830*	Benjamin Price	 *Edward Evans*		
Newtown *Sarn*	 *1826*	Benjamin Price	*Joseph Davies* *Edward Trow*	John Williams -	- -
Maesyrhelem *Bettws-y-Crwyn*	1801 *1803*	Joseph Jones Abraham Evans	- *Will. Breeze* *David Evans* *Charles Lloyd* *Edward Rees*	Thos. Harvard	*W. Breeze* *D. Evans* *D. Mantle* *W. Davies*
Welshpool *Lodge*	1823	Henry Morgan	 *William Lewis*	-	*J. Drew*
Sarn	1826	-	-	John Jones	-

Because congregations were small, churches in both England and Wales found it difficult to support their ministers and many pastors found it necessary to support themselves by secular employment. For instance, Joseph Ashford at Welshpool received no stipend and worked as a tradesman[110], William Bird at Chirbury as a tailor[111] and John Williams of Coleham, Shrewsbury, as a mercer.[112] John Jones of Newtown[113] and James Gay of Coxall[114] ran schools. David Crumpton worked briefly as a teacher in a free school for poor children[115], possibly in the short-lived Goff School at Sweeney Mountain[116], while at a later date Thomas Rowson was a schoolmaster.[117] George Thorne, who founded the Baptist church at Peterhead, Aberdeenshire, in 1859[118] and subsequently reopened the Baptist church at Welshpool, worked for the Inland Revenue.[119]

In some cases the call to ministry enabled men to leave situations of abject poverty and improve their circumstances. For instance, D. L. Pughe of Newtown whose work as a weaver 'could hardly procure him the bare necessities of life' was encouraged to train at Pontypool Academy and subsequently served in a number of Baptist pastorates.[120] Thomas Brocas, who criticised John Palmer for preaching Calvinism, observed that Baptist lay preachers like Everal and Frances, earned as much in one week preaching Calvinism as they used to earn in a month or six weeks weaving flannel.[121] John Harrison from The Bog in West Shropshire came to Sarn in 1864 and for the first time he was able to send his children to school.[122]

There were several Baptist ministers who received no stipend as they were of independent means, such as Rev. Joseph Jones at Maesyrhelem.[123] In Wales many of the ministers were farmers and so they had horses which enabled them to move around the countryside. Sometimes churches would pay the wage of a farm labourer to work on a farm while the farmer was engaged in his ministerial duties.

Churches were at first unable to provide accommodation for ministers and their families. Dawley Baptist Church provided a house for its minister when the chapel was erected in 1846, while Sarn Baptist Church did not provide a manse until 1866. Little is recorded about the willingness of ministers' wives to accept privation for themselves and their families. However, the Memoir of Mrs. Elizabeth Wycherley, the wife of Thomas E. Wycherley who had served at Donnington Wood, mentions that her husband 'was enabled to labour there for about six years, notwithstanding the trifling aid he received from the people, through her self-denying labours'[124] Later on in the nineteenth century Rev. John Jones (known as 'John the Rock') wrote,

> Many ministers' wives were sorely tried by straightened circumstances. The care of a young family, a pantry and a wardrobe but scantily furnished often prove too much for the temper and the strength of women, who would be amiable and gentle were they in more easy circumstances.[125]

Although he was commenting on the situation in Radnorshire similar remarks could no doubt have been made about the situation of ministers' wives in rural areas of England.

In England some Anglican landlords did not want Baptist chapels on their estates and it was probably the inability of the Baptists at Chirbury to obtain a site for a chapel which led to the closure of the work there. At Snailbeach Baptists had identified a suitable site for the erection of a chapel but the 4th Marquis of Bath refused to allow them to build on his land. However, they approached another local landowner, the 6th Earl of Tankerville, in the hope that a recent dispute with Lord Bath over shooting rights would make him more sympathetic. Sure enough he provided them with land for the building of Lord's Hill Chapel in 1876 – just across the stream which formed the boundary between his land and that of the Lord Bath.[126] Lord Tankerville was probably sympathetic as he was an evangelical Christian and he served as Vice President of the Trinitarian Bible Society from 1884 until 1899, the year of his death. Baptists at Brockton also had difficulty in obtaining a site as a consequence of opposition by local Anglicans.

Even when Baptists were able to obtain suitable sites for the erection of chapels the cost involved was often a heavy drain on their resources. Sometimes wealthy Baptists built chapels at their own expense as at Broseley in 1742 and again in 1803 at Birch Meadow, at Sarn in 1827, at Ightfield in 1844, and at Craven Arms in 1872.

Debts caused the closure of the churches at Market Drayton and Welshpool in the 1840's and the chapels passed out of Baptist hands, although in both cases the properties were later recovered for use by the denomination.

Baptists because of their rejection of infant baptism faced much criticism from Anglicans, Independents and Wesleyan Methodists. In 1776 Rev. Samuel Medley of Liverpool visited the Baptist society meeting in High Street, Shrewsbury, and baptized some believers. Controversy began when Rev. Richard De Courcy, Vicar of the nearby St. Alkmund's church, wrote and published in 1776 a tract entitled 'Letter to a Baptist minister relating to his conduct in the Baptisation of Certain Adults at S --- y'. Mr. Phillips, a deacon of the Baptist church then published an Address he had given at the church under the pseudonym 'Parmenas'. This resulted in two rejoinders from the Vicar. Mr. Medley was then drawn into the controversy, as was Rev. Benjamin Francis, of Horsley, who wrote under the pseudonym 'John the Dipper from Enon, near Salim' a satirical poem entitled *The Salopian Zealot; or the Good Vicar in a Bad Mood*. Other publications followed, including one by Rev. Joseph Jenkins of Wrexham, who was one of the few Baptist ministers with a university education. R. F. Skinner, who has summarized the controversy concluded,

> In spite of angry expressions, common to both sides, the Baptist case is generally well argued from the scriptures, and their writers were not disposed to lay much weight on the Vicar's claims from Church History, Tradition and the Articles.[127]

In 1693 James Owen of Oswestry, an Independent minister, published a tract in defence of infant baptism. As the Welsh Baptists had no one ready to cross swords with him, his tract, in translation, was sent to Benjamin Keach and his reply, translated into Welsh, appeared in 1696.[128] A hundred years later in 1795 Peter Edwards, the Independent minister in Wem, wrote *Candid Reasons for Renouncing the Principles of Antipædobaptism*, in which he explained his reasons for changing his views on baptism. It was a formidable attack on the Baptist position, since Edwards had been a Baptist minister at Portsmouth for ten to eleven years before going to Wem. This came to the notice of James Dore, of London, who in 1795 published Abraham Booth's *The Principles of Antipædobaptism.* Edwards renewed his criticism in 1822 in *The Baptists System, its own condemnation. Wherein is shown the delusive cast of the Baptist scheme* and in 1829 Abraham's Booth's reply was republished.[129]

In a sermon a Wesleyan minister in Shrewsbury attacked Particular Baptist theology. This led William Hawkins of Castle Foregate, Shrewsbury, to deliver a deliver a series of Lectures replying to his criticisms and also those of Thomas Brocas.[130]

Some Anglican incumbents refused to allow the burial of Baptists in parish churchyards. This caused particular hurt when children were refused burial on the grounds that they were 'unbaptized'. So many chapels were obliged to have their own burial grounds. It was not until 1880 that the Burial Act provided that any Nonconformist minister might bury people in any parochial churchyard and so there was no need for chapels to have their own burial grounds.

Two brothers, Thomas and William Butler, established a small congregation calling itself the 'New Testament Church' in Shrewsbury by late 1837. They had very similar views to the Sandemanian Baptists. They subsequently joined with other similar congregations to form the Association of Churches of Christ, which held its first national general meeting in 1842. The Shrewsbury congregation suddenly disintegrated in the 1870s. It is likely that the death in 1871 of Thomas Butler, the founder and elder of the church for more than 30 years precipitated its demise.[131] The formation of the Shrewsbury church appears to have had little effect on the Baptist churches in Shrewsbury, although in 1842 Catharine Richards withdrew from the Claremont church to 'join the disciples'.[132] However, in Wrexham in 1837 a few members of the Baptist Church in Chester Street separated themselves to form a Church of Christ congregation in Bank Street.[133] In 1854 Rev. J. B. Rotherham resigned his pastorate at Wem to join the Disciples of Christ.

The formation of several Particular Baptist Churches in Shropshire and the Welsh Borders in the early eighteen hundreds led to the formation of a Shropshire Association of Particular Baptist churches in 1808. The Broseley (Old Meeting House), Shifnal and Shrewsbury churches left the Midland Association to become founder members of the new Association. The churches at Oswestry, Wellington and Whitchurch joined the newly formed Shropshire Association. In 1809 these six churches together had 304 members.[134] Other churches in Shropshire subsequently joined the Shropshire Association. Churches at Burslem, Chester, Welshpool and Wrexham also joined, while the church at Oldbury (then in Shropshire) joined the Midland Association in 1812.[135]

As early as 1813 the Shropshire Association was concerned with overseas mission and at the Annual Assembly a resolution was passed:

> That it is incumbent on the churches to do all they can to aid the Baptist Mission.

Two years later The Shropshire Auxiliary Society in aid of Baptist Missions and Translations was formed. The 1815 Association Circular Letter listed the 21 stations of the 'Baptist Eastern Missionary Society [i.e. the Baptist Missionary Society] as well as the translations of Scripture by the Serampore missionaries and translations printed for the Calcutta Bible Society. However, the Shropshire Auxiliary Society was short-lived and in 1826 the Association resolved at its Annual Meeting:

> That it is very desirable to form an Auxiliary Missionary Society in the County of Salop, and such a meeting to be formed, at the second half-yearly meeting to be held in Shrewsbury.

The Shropshire Association had a Calvinistic Declaration of Faith, which was printed in the Association's Circular Letters. The report of the 1816 Annual Meeting of the Association in *The Baptist Magazine* gave the name of the Association as 'Shropshire and Cheshire'[136] but the name was never formally changed to 'Shropshire and Cheshire'. At the 1818 Annual Meeting at Wrexham Rev. John Hinmers was appointed Association Secretary and it was agreed that he should keep a book for the minutes of the 'association and quarterly meetings.'

Objects of the Association

The first object of this Association is to devise means for the spreading of the Gospel in the County by obtaining from their respective Churches pecuniary aid for this purpose and seeing that the same is properly applied by enabling suitable Persons to preach the Gospel in the dark Villages of the County and neighbourhood and at all our publick meetings; to encourage each other by conversation and prayer in the good work of the Lord.

2^{ndly} that while we disclaim all interference with the government of the Churches we are ready at any time to assist with our advice when solicited in any matter of difficulty which may occur having only in view the advancement of the Kingdom and Glory of our blessed Redeemer by the conversion of sinners to God and the establishment of Saints in their most holy faith.

At this time Welsh was understood and spoken by many in Shropshire (and in agricultural parts of the county the language was retained until the mid-nineteenth century). So at the Annual Assembly of the Midland Association held at Shrewsbury (Amwythig in Welsh) in May 1801 when John Palmer was the Moderator, Thomas Jones, minister of the church at Glynceiriog, Denbighshire, preached in Welsh.[137] Likewise in 1810 at the Annual Assembly of the Shropshire Association in Oswestry Thomas Jones by then minister of Rhydwilym, Carmarthenshire, prayed in Welsh and Thomas Davies of New Bridge, Denbighshire, preached in Welsh.[138] In 1815 the Quarterly Meeting was held at Oswestry and Samuel Edwards of Glynceiriog preached in Welsh.[139] In Radnorshire there was a gradual decline in the use of Welsh, although Welsh services at Nantgwyn Chapel continued until about 1860.[140] However, the Radnorshire and Montgomeryshire Association continued to publish its Circular Letters in both English and Welsh until the early years of the twentieth century and at its Association meetings to hold some services in Welsh until 1930. Some of the ministers who served the Shropshire churches were Welsh speakers such as Richard Richards, who served at Wem (1876-80) and was subsequently pastor of the Welsh church at Birmingham.

The theological divisions among Particular Baptists surfaced in Shropshire during the ministry of Rev. Abraham Webster at Broseley. The church members anxious to 'keep the unity of the Spirit in the bond of peace' agreed to dissolve their 'Society (as the church was then called).' A new Society was then formed on 27 December 1801 with a set of articles of faith that did not differ in material points from those already held. Those who did not join the new Society withdrew to form the Strict and Particular Baptist Church at the top of Birch Meadow.[141]

Those who founded the Baptist churches which belonged to the first Shropshire Association were Calvinistic in theology but it is not known how many of them followed Andrew Fuller in their thinking. Richard Pryce, who served at Wrexham, came from Newtown Baptist Church and studied under Dr. George Lewis at the Independent Academy at Wrexham.[142] Lewis was a staunch Calvinist who taught that the universal invitation of the gospel was consistent with the doctrine of personal election and limited atonement.[143] There were also tensions at the Shrewsbury Church during the ministry of John Palmer's successor, Manoah Kent (1823-1844), and this led to the formation of a second church in the town at Castle Foregate in 1828. Another church was also formed at Shrewsbury in 1834 but it closed in 1842. The church at Welshpool was dissolved because of internal dissent in 1833 as was the church at Pontesbury in 1841, and the churches were then reformed but in Pontesbury a second church was also formed in the village. It met in a private house. The original Shifnal church in Aston Street left the Shropshire Association in 1828 and a second Baptist church was formed in 1842. In 1840 the churches at Broseley, Birch Meadow, Market Drayton, Oldbury, Shrewsbury, Castle Foregate, Pontesbury, 2nd church, together with churches at Bilston and Wolverhampton, formed the Strict Baptist West Midland Baptist Association. This Association was short-lived and only the church at Broseley, Birch Meadow, survived into the twentieth century.

Although the Strict Baptists came to regard themselves as another denomination, in the early years of the nineteenth century the division among Particular Baptists was not as marked as it was to be later in the century. So in October 1808 Mr. Price, the pastor of the Birch Meadow Chapel, preached at the Quarterly Meeting of the Shropshire Association[144] and in 1824 when Mr. Thomas Jones was ordained pastor of Birch Meadow Chapel the ministers of Broseley (Old Meeting House), of Oswestry and Donnington Wood took part in the service. [145] The second Baptist church at Shrewsbury joined the Shropshire Association in 1830. In 1871 on the Sunday following the opening of the new chapel at Wem, 'two eloquent and impressive sermons were preached by the Rev. W. Stokes',[146] who was a strict communionist. The Wem church adopted open communion one month later but it seems that they wished to express their agreement on the essentials of the Gospel by extending an invitation to him.

At the beginning of the nineteenth century all the Baptist churches in Shropshire practised closed communion but gradually the churches adopted open communion. The church at Market Drayton, which was formed as result of the initiative of the Association, was formed as an open communion church in 1857. Shrewsbury, St. John's Hill, remained a Strict Baptist cause until about 1870, while Bridgnorth called John Boyd Warren, a Strict Baptist, in 1870. The 1862 Trust Deed of the church at Wyle Cop, Shrewsbury,[147] gave the church the right, if it so desired, to admit to the Lord's Supper 'any person or persons professing repentance towards God and faith in our Lord Jesus Christ'. Claremont Street, Shrewsbury, did not adopt open communion until 1903 and it restricted church membership to those baptized as believers until March 2005. By the beginning of the twentieth-first century only the Lord's Hill and Snailbeach church still observed closed communion.

The theological disagreements and the decline of some churches meant that by 1844 the Shropshire Association had ceased to exist. An attempt was made to reorganize the Association at the end of 1848 but without success and for several years no Association of Baptist churches existed in the County. In the absence of an Association it was support for the Baptist Missionary Society that provided the focus for the co-operation of Baptist churches in the County.

In September 1853 the church at Claremont Street, Shrewsbury wrote to other churches inviting them to meet there to consider reviving the Association. This resulted in thirteen churches forming the second Shropshire Baptist Association in October that year. One significant difference with the earlier Association of Particular Baptists was the absence of a Calvinistic Declaration of Faith, although the Secretary of the

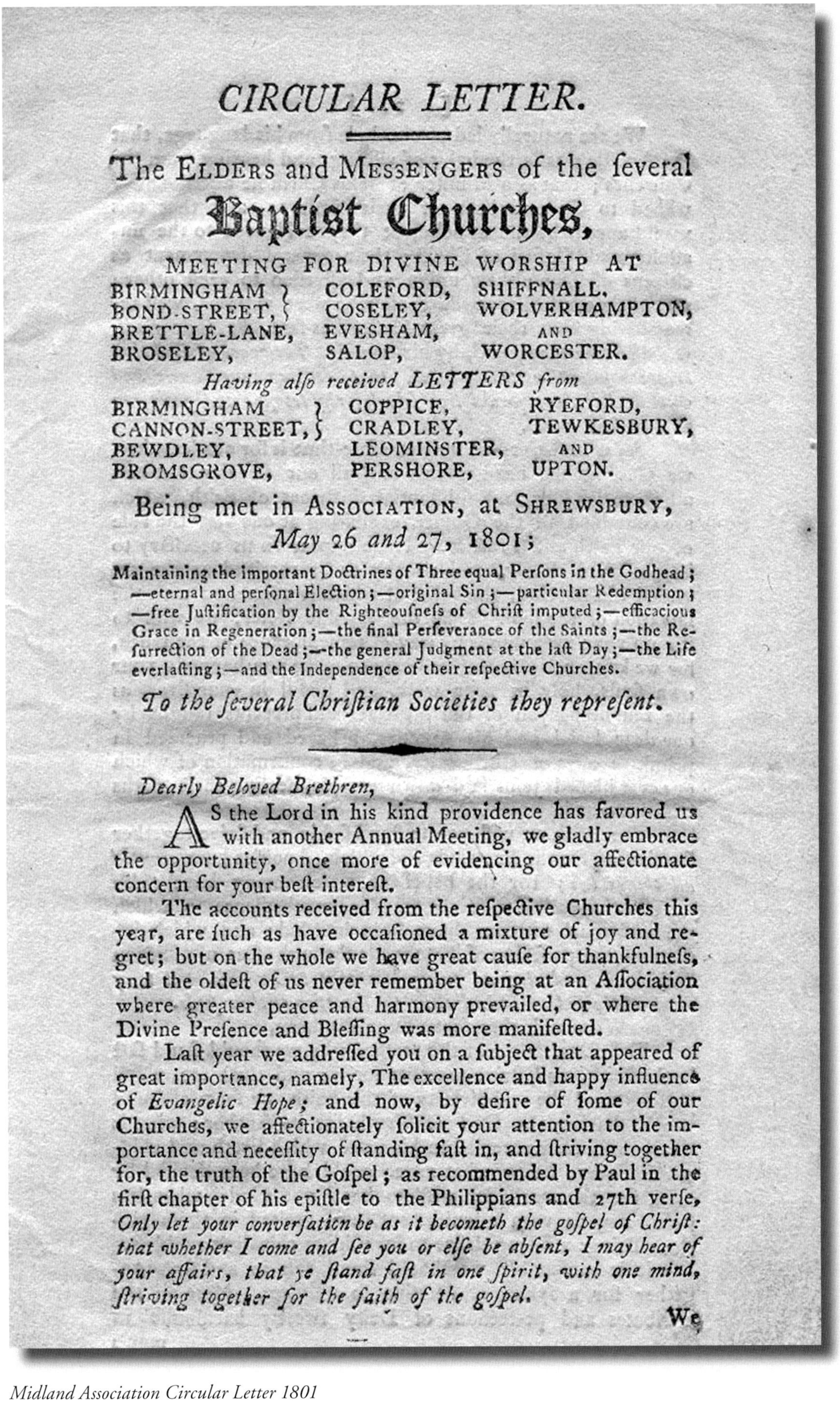

CIRCULAR LETTER.

The ELDERS and MESSENGERS of the ſeveral

Baptist Churches,

MEETING FOR DIVINE WORSHIP AT

BIRMINGHAM BOND-STREET,	COLEFORD,	SHIFFNALL,
BRETTLE-LANE,	COSELEY,	WOLVERHAMPTON,
BROSELEY,	EVESHAM,	AND
	SALOP,	WORCESTER.

Having alſo received LETTERS *from*

BIRMINGHAM CANNON-STREET,	COPPICE,	RYEFORD,
BEWDLEY,	CRADLEY,	TEWKESBURY,
BROMSGROVE,	LEOMINSTER,	AND
	PERSHORE,	UPTON.

Being met in ASSOCIATION, at SHREWSBURY,

May 26 *and* 27, 1801;

Maintaining the important Doctrines of Three equal Perſons in the Godhead; —eternal and perſonal Election;—original Sin;—particular Redemption; —free Juſtification by the Righteouſneſs of Chriſt imputed;—efficacious Grace in Regeneration;—the final Perſeverance of the Saints;—the Reſurrection of the Dead;—the general Judgment at the laſt Day;—the Life everlaſting;—and the Independence of their reſpective Churches.

To the ſeveral Chriſtian Societies they repreſent.

Dearly Beloved Brethren,

AS the Lord in his kind providence has favored us with another Annual Meeting, we gladly embrace the opportunity, once more of evidencing our affectionate concern for your beſt intereſt.

The accounts received from the reſpective Churches this year, are ſuch as have occaſioned a mixture of joy and regret; but on the whole we have great cauſe for thankfulneſs, and the oldeſt of us never remember being at an Aſſociation where greater peace and harmony prevailed, or where the Divine Preſence and Bleſſing was more manifeſted.

Laſt year we addreſſed you on a ſubject that appeared of great importance, namely, The excellence and happy influence of *Evangelic Hope;* and now, by deſire of ſome of our Churches, we affectionately ſolicit your attention to the importance and neceſſity of ſtanding faſt in, and ſtriving together for, the truth of the Goſpel; as recommended by Paul in the firſt chapter of his epiſtle to the Philippians and 27th verſe, *Only let your converſation be as it becometh the goſpel of Chriſt: that whether I come and ſee you or elſe be abſent, I may hear of your affairs, that ye ſtand faſt in one ſpirit, with one mind, ſtriving together for the faith of the goſpel.*

We

Midland Association Circular Letter 1801

MEETINGS IN SHROPSHIRE

On Lord's day, February 25th, sermons were preached on behalf of the mission, at Wellington by Mr. Carey, and at Shrewsbury by Mr. Saffery. Public meetings were held during the week at the following places: Monday evening, the 26th, at Wellington; Tuesday, the 27th, at Shrewsbury; Wednesday, the 28th at Pontesbury; and Thursday, the 29th at Wem. On Lord's day, March 3rd, three sermons were preached by Mr. Saffery. The weather during the week was extremely unfavourable, yet the various meetings were well attended, and although, owing to the very depressed state of trade in the county, the collections were not all of them equal to those of some former years, there was increased interest manifested in the missionary cause.

From *The Missionary Herald* in *The Primitive Church Magazine*, April 1844

Association, Rev. David Crumpton of Oswestry, was a staunch Calvinist. Each church contributed to an Association Fund, one object of which was 'To encourage the preaching of the gospel in new stations, under the direction of any of the churches of the Association'. The Association established preaching stations in Madeley and Market Drayton and this led to the formation of Particular Baptist churches in these towns.

The Association ceased to meet after June 1865. So the three Baptist ministers in Shrewsbury issued an invitation to churches to attend a Conference in Shrewsbury on 16 May 1867 to discuss the possibility of reviving the Association. As a result the following month eighteen churches joined the new Shropshire Association. The Rules of the new Association set out its purpose as follows

> That its objects be the cultivation of fraternal intercourse, the consolidation and extension of Baptist Churches within its sphere, the aiding of our Home and Foreign Missions, and the promotion of Baptist interests generally.

As the interests of the Association included Foreign Missions, a Secretary for the Baptist Missionary Society for the County was appointed.

Table 6 below lists the churches in membership with the Shropshire Association in 1839 and those that joined the reorganized Associations in 1853 and 1867. It will be seen that only eight churches belonged to all three Associations at these dates, namely the chapels at Broseley (Old Chapel), Oswestry, Pontesbury, Shrewsbury (Claremont Street), Snailbeach, Wellington, Wem and Wrexham. However, the Snailbeach church did not provide the Association with a Statistical Return in 1878 and seems to have taken no part in Association life. In 1869 the church, then known as the Lord's Hill church, called to the pastorate Rev. William Jenkins and the church joined the Old Welsh Association. It remained a member of this Association until 1887 when it rejoined the Shropshire Association.

The only Shropshire church to join the Baptist Union in 1832 was Whitchurch, which did not belong to the Association. The first church belonging to the Association to join the Baptist Union was the church at Llandrinio, Montgomeryshire, which had joined by 1839. By 1840 the church at Burslem, by then in the Lancashire and Cheshire Association, had joined the Baptist Union and by 1843 the church at Wrexham had also joined the Union and it was the first Baptist church in Denbighshire to do so. There seems to have been considerable resistance by most churches in Shropshire to joining the Baptist Union and they did not become members until 1870 when the Shropshire Association itself joined the Union.

In view of the responsibility given to Association Secretaries of recommending the names of ministers for inclusion on the Baptist Union's Accredited List (see p. 18), it is not surprising that Associations felt that they had responsibility, together with the churches, of encouraging and giving guidance to prospective ministers. The Minutes of the Shropshire Association record, for example, how the Association sought to give guidance to Mr. Amos Alfred Blacklidge, who had become a member of Donnington Wood Baptist Church following his baptism by Rev. Josephus Judson in June 1904. (see page 34)

A. A. Blacklidge entered Pastors' College in 1909 and left in 1912. Although originally a member of Donnington Wood, he was a member of Oakengates Church by the time he entered College. He made a notable contribution to Baptist life in the East Midlands.

In addition to A. A. Blacklidge at least nine other men

Table 6
Churches belonging to the Shropshire Baptist Associations in 1839, 1853 and 1867

1839*	1853**	1867**
Aston Clunsland		Aston-on-Clun
	[Bridgnorth, joined 1854]	Bridgnorth
Broseley, 1st church	Broseley, 1st church	Broseley 1st church
Chirbury		
	Dawley-Bank	Dawley Bank
Donnington Wood	Donnington-Wood	
Llandrinio	Maesbrook & Llandrinio	Maesbrook and Llandrinio
		Madeley
		Market Drayton
		Oakengates
Oswestry	Oswestry	Oswestry
Pontesbury	Pontesbury	Pontesbury
Shiffnall	Shiffnal, 2nd church#	[Shifnal, 2nd church, joined 1868]
Shrewsbury, 1st church	Shrewsbury, 1st church	Shrewsbury, Claremont Street
Shrewsbury, 2nd church		Shrewsbury, St. John's Hill
		Shrewsbury, Wyle Cop
Snailbeach	Snailbeach	Snailbeach
Sweeney Mountain		
Wellington	Wellington	Wellington
Welshampton		
		Welshpool
Wem	Wem	Wem
	Whitchurch & Ightfield	Whitchurch & Ightfield
Wrexham	Wrexham	Wrexham

Notes:
* Information taken from *The Proceedings of the Baptist Union* 1840.

** Information taken from *Shropshire Baptist Association Minute Book.*

The Rules of the Association refer to the 1st church but it seems that they should have referred to the 2nd church.

The contemporary spellings for Shifnal have been retained in 1839 and 1853.

from Shropshire churches known to have trained at Baptist Colleges, prior to entering the Baptist ministry:

Bristol:	Ivor Reginald Waddelow from Oswestry
Cardiff:	John Alan Lewis Edwards from Claremont, Shrewsbury
Horton:	John Jackson from Oswestry
Manchester:	Dennis Edgar Weller from Donnington Wood and Charles Leslie Evans from Coxall
Rawdon:	John Harper from Claremont, Shrewsbury, and William Ernest Moore from Madeley
Pastors':	John Swancott Adams from Welshpool and Samuel Jones from Wellington

Mr. Alfred Edward Walley, who served as Lay Pastor at Wem for thirty years, trained at Manchester with a view to training for service with the Baptist Missionary Society but was unable to proceed to the mission field for health reasons. Andrew Grice from Claremont, Shrewsbury, began a course at Bristol Baptist College as a ministerial student in 2004. In the twentieth-century many Baptist ministers were trained at the London Bible College (now London School of Theology), including Joseph Brian Edwards, a member of Claremont, Shrewsbury.

During the nineteenth-century distances between the Baptist colleges and the Shropshire churches meant that it was difficult for tutors or students to supply the churches, although in the summer vacation students might have a 'summer pastorate' at a church. However,

Annual Meeting held at Birmingham on May 30th 1905

A letter was received from Mr. L. M. Stevens (Donnington Wood), commending Mr. A. Blacklidge as a local Preacher, and it be resolved that Mr. Blacklidge be recommended to the Churches in that neighbourhood as willing to give his services for six months.

Executive Committee Meeting held at Shrewsbury November 13th 1905

The Secretary mentioned the case of Mr. A. A. Blacklidge, of Donnington Wood, a Local Preacher, anxious to devote himself to, and qualify for, the work of the Ministry. It was agreed that he be recommended to apply to the Colleges to ascertain their terms of admission, to continue his preaching as opportunities offer, and to endeavour to obtain preparatory training for entering College, and that the Churches be asked to avail themselves of his service and render him any assistance in their power

Executive Committee Meeting held at Shrewsbury September 19th 1907

The Secretary reported on correspondence relative to Broseley Old Chapel Trust. It was resolved ... that the Secretary write to Mr. Blacklidge, not advising him to accept the invitation, but encouraging him to continue preaching there and elsewhere as heretofore.

Rev. Gethin Davies, Classical Tutor at Llangollen, was able to serve as the pastor of the Welsh church at Oswestry 1870-1874, while Benjamin Lewis from the College was apparently 'student pastor' there 1888-1889. Improved transport in the twentieth-century made it possible for students at Manchester Baptist College to supply some Shropshire churches on a regular basis.

It was not until 1956 that the first deaconesses were appointed to churches in Shropshire, namely Sister Constance Nash at Donnington Wood, and Sister Margaret Jarman with the Pontesbury Group. Sister Heather Hunt assumed responsibility for Crowmoor Mission in 1962, while Sister Margaret Popham was called to Ludlow in 1961, Sister Joan Magill to Ludlow in 1964, and Sister Winifred Russell to Madeley and Broseley in 1965. In 2000 a Shropshire church had for the first time a woman minister, when Wellington, Union Free Church, called Rev. Mary Stringer.

The Baptist Union also contributed to the raising of standards of lay ministry by introducing schemes for the national recognition of lay pastors and lay preachers. Ministers like Rev. Eric Hayden, who served at Shrewsbury from 1952 to 1956, arranged classes for lay preachers.[148] Mr. George Roberts served as a lay preacher for over fifty years and became a recognised lay preacher in 1962 but by June 2001 Mr. Clifford Challinor was the only recognised lay preacher in active service in Shropshire. There are, however, other lay preachers who serve the churches but have not sought national recognition.

Baptist Churches in Wales were slower to adopt open communion than the churches in England. By the 1890's there were some churches in the Radnorshire and Montgomeryshire Baptist Association which were admitting to the Lord's Table those who had not been baptised as believers. In 1899 the Association Annual Meeting passed by a large majority a Rule restricting admission to communion to those who had been baptized on profession of faith. This Rule was not acceptable to the church at Sarn, which withdrew from the Welsh Association and joined the Shropshire Association. Its sister church at Cwm also joined the Shropshire Association while retaining its membership of the Welsh Association. In 1918 the Montgomery church transferred its membership from the Radnorshire and Montgomeryshire Baptist Association to the West Midland Baptist Association.

During the last twenty years of the nineteenth century the membership of English churches began to decline.[149] Over the period 1880-1900 the churches at Bridgnorth, Dawley, Oswestry and Wellington grew but by 1900 there was only one Baptist church at Shrewsbury as the church at St. John's Hill had amalgamated with the Claremont Street church in 1872 and the Wyle Cop church had closed in 1885. In 1899 during the ministry of Rev. David Morgan Davies an effort was made by the Baptist Union to inaugurate a 'Forward Movement', apparently with the object of forming a second Baptist church at Wyle Cop, but after many meetings and much correspondence the scheme was abandoned.[150] The Baptist Union had supported the work of the ministry in the Madeley Group of Baptist churches but the membership at Madeley had declined from 24 in 1880 to 10 in 1900. The churches at Oakengates, Pontesbury, Wem, and Whitchurch had also declined in size.

In 1900 Rev. D. M. Davies caused controversy at the Shropshire Baptist Association by his Presidential address on the subject 'The position of Baptists in the forthcoming century.'

THE SALOP BAPTIST ASSOCIATION

STRONG DISAPPOVAL OF THE PRESIDENT'S VIEWS

The President gave his address, the subject of which was "The position of Baptists in the forthcoming century." In years gone by, he said, Baptists had laid stress on baptism by water, but that was only of secondary importance. He thought that in the coming century, Baptists would have to lay more stress on baptism by the Holy Ghost. Baptism in water was human, and they should remember that John the Baptist laid stress on the baptism by Fire. The baptism of the Holy Ghost could not be administered by John the Baptist, but Jesus Christ could administer the baptism of the Holy Ghost. Jesus Christ never immersed anyone. He ordered his disciples to do that, but never did so himself. The reason was because he administered the baptism of the Holy Ghost. There were many who told us that baptism was only a question of "much water" or "little water". It was nothing of the kind. If we went to the Law and the Testimony, there was on the human side undoubtedly immersion of believers, on the other side, there was the baptism of the Holy Spirit. Without baptism of the Holy Ghost there was no hope of salvation. He believed that the minute they, as Baptists, began to emphasize the baptism of the Holy Ghost, the other denominations would accept the human baptism of immersion. As Baptists, they had raised what was secondary – water baptism – to the primary place, and had placed what was primary – baptism by the Holy Ghost – in the background. ("No, no"). Another thing he wanted to point out was that where baptism of the Holy Ghost had been administered, it was as a result of prayer. And now the question came, how many of their brethren who were members of Baptist Churches, and had been immersed in water, were baptized by the Holy Ghost? It was not their province to judge one another, but let each judge himself. The man who was clothed with the spirit of God was clothed with power. It did not matter how a man worked in connection with a church or chapel, unless he had the power of the Spirit, he could do nothing. They as Baptists belonged to the vanguard of the Christian Army, but it was strange that they were blind and had lost sight of the power which came from the Holy Spirit of God.

The constant interruptions and cries of "No, no" by the delegates, showed that they did not agree with sentiments expressed by the President.

Mr. T. Roberts, Minsterley, said that the President had referred repeatedly to Acts ii, and he would like to know what was his view of the words in that chapter. We all believed that Peter was inspired, and we knew that Peter said, "Repent and be baptized everyone of you, and ye will receive the gift of the Holy Spirit." Mr. Davies said it was perfectly clear that in the second chapter it was said, "Repent, Baptize, Receive the Holy Ghost," but in the tenth chapter it said, "Receive the Holy Spirit" and then be baptized.

(From a newspaper cutting in the Shropshire Baptist Association Minute Book).

Mr. Davies' views were not acceptable to most of those present. He was thanked for his address but the Assembly took the unprecedented step of declining to include his address in the Annual Report, which said that it was 'an able address, but bristling with points not in harmony with the views of most of the brethren present.'

Davies, who was 'gifted in Welsh, Greek and Hebrew'[151], was probably aware of the interest in theological circles in Wales in the doctrine of the Holy Spirit.[152] In 1896 *Y Greal* contained both a review of the book by Dr. A. J. Gordon, of Boston, called *The Ministry of the Spirit*, [153] and an article about Dr. Gordon, of Boston, who was described as one of the truly great men of the century.[154] The significance of Gordon's book was that he viewed the church as a body designed for the Holy Spirit. This was an aspect of the doctrine that Western theologians had shown little interest in, preferring to concentrate on the relationship of the Spirit to the other persons of the Trinity and the nature of his work in the life of the individual. Gordon held that 'it seems clear from the Scriptures that it is still the duty and privilege of believers to receive the Holy Spirit by a conscious, definite act of appropriating faith, just as they received Jesus Christ'.[155] There seems little doubt that D. M. Davies also held that the Baptism of the Holy Ghost was a post-conversion experience.

In Wales at the beginning of the twentieth-century there was a widespread feeling that there was need for revival in the churches. At the quarterly meeting of the Radnorshire and Montgomeryshire Baptist Association in April that year Mr E. P. Morris, Llandrindod, presented a paper entitled 'Is there a dearth of conversions?' [156] The title of the paper suggests that there was such a dearth.

Shortly before his death in January 1903 David Howell, the evangelical Dean of St. David's Cathedral, who was better known in Wales under his bardic name Llawdden, wrote an article entitled 'The great need of Wales', in which he declared:

> The chief need of my country and my nation at present is a spiritual revival through the outpouring of the Holy Spirit. [157]

Similar views were expressed in June 1903 by Mr. C. E. Pryce in his Presidential Address to the Radnorshire and Montgomeryshire Baptist Association.[158] The 1904-06 Revival began in the Calvinistic Methodist Church at New Quay, Carmarthenshire in February 1904.[159] However, prior to this date there had been localized revivals in other places. For instance at Mochdre, Montgomeryshire, there was a revival following a mission conducted by Rev. David Davies, Maesyrhelem. Rev. George Phillips, Newtown and Rev. Ben Withers, New Wells. Over 50 people were baptized. Subsequently, in the Welsh Revival nearly a hundred were added to the church at Maesyrhelem and over 50 to Pound Aloes. At Rhydfelin Rev. J. L. Bowen, of Mochdre, baptized 15 young people in Fachen Pool.[160] However, the churches at Bettws-y-Crwyn and Coxall seem to have been the only Baptist churches in Shropshire affected by the Revival.

Fachen Pool in 2004

By the end of the nineteenth century it was apparent to some that the Shropshire Baptist Association would need to merge with another Association. In 1899 there were informal discussions with the Secretary of the North Wales English Union about a possible amalgamation but the Association Committee was against this proposal and the matter was dropped. However in 1905 Rev. Josephus Judson and Rev. Edwin Hardin from Wellington Baptist Church proposed that the Shropshire Baptist Association should merge with the West Midland Baptist Association, which had been formed in 1892 by the merger of the General and Particular Baptist Associations in the West Midlands. Although the proposal was not accepted at the time, the merger did take place in 1916. The final Annual Meeting of the Shropshire Association was held at Wrexham in May 1916 and Rev. Isaac Brook delivered the last Shropshire President's Address choosing as his subject 'The Relation of the Church to the Life of the Nation'. The churches in the Wrexham area joined the North Wales English Union, which since 1913 had been part of the Lancashire and Cheshire Baptist Association. The remaining churches of the former Shropshire Association, including the church at Victoria Road, Knighton, formed a District of the West Midland Association and Mr. Brook became Chairman of the District.[161]

As a consequence of Rev. Michael Taylor's address to the 1971 Baptist Union Assembly the churches at Grosvenor Road, Chester, and Bradley Road, Wrexham, withdrew from the Baptist Union and also the Lancashire and Cheshire Baptist Association, while the new Baptist church at Crowmoor, Shrewsbury, delayed joining the Union for a number of years.

Claremont, Shrewsbury, was one of the churches that took no action about the Inter-Church Process, choosing rather to ignore it. Some churches, like that at Donnington Wood, chose to have their names published in *The Spirit of '88 Directory* that lists churches and organizations that had opted out of the Inter-Church Process.

The West Midland Baptist Association sought to encourage mission in the churches by the appointment of Rev. Andy Bruce as Association Missioner in 1989. The nineties were designated by most Christian communions as 'A Decade of Evangelism (or Evangelisation)'. Mr. Bruce encouraged individual churches to develop their own strategies for mission. At the Autumn Assembly held at Queens Road Baptist Church, Coventry, on Saturday 23 November 1991 churches met together with other churches in their District to discuss their strategies and to see where they might work together. Nine churches were represented but the churches of Bridgnorth, Chorley, Lord's Hill, Sarn and Crowmoor, Shrewsbury, were not. The small church at Ludlow reported that there was the exciting prospect of a partnership between the church and the South Shropshire District Council, which led to the erection of The Rockspring Centre in 1995.

Table 7 lists the churches that belonged to the

Shropshire Association in 1900 and those that belonged to the Shropshire District / Cluster of the West Midland Baptist Association in 1917 and 2000.

In Shropshire in 1900 there were 16 Baptist churches together with 9 branch churches, plus the churches at Bettws-y-Crwyn and Coxall which were in membership with the Radnorshire and Montgomeryshire Association. During the twentieth century new churches were formed at Crowmere Road, Shrewsbury and Newport, while the branch churches at Chorley and Donnington Wood became independent. The church at Wellington merged with Wellington Congregational Church to form Wellington, Union Free Church. The churches at Aston-on-Clun, Bettws-y-Crwyn, Market Drayton, Oakengates, Shifnal and Whitchurch closed, together with nine branch churches. The churches at Brockton and Wem left the denomination. Amongst the Welsh churches the church at Cwm closed, while that at Bradley Road, Wrexham, left the denomination. Chester Street, Wrexham, left the Shropshire Association and is now in membership with the (English) North Western Baptist Association.

On 1 January 2001 the West Midland Association merged with the Worcestershire Association to form the Heart of England Baptist Association. All but two of the Baptist churches of the Shropshire District (then known as the Shropshire Cluster) joined the new Regional Association. The name of the Shropshire Cluster was then changed to the 'Shropshire Group of Baptist Churches'. The church at Lord's Hill and Snailbeach, which had played little part in Association life in recent years, decided that it would not belong to any Association, while the church at Sarn re-joined the Radnorshire and Montgomeryshire Association.

One consequence of the formation of the new Regional Associations was that the office of Area Superintendent was abolished on 31 December 2001 and Regional Ministers now carry out their work. The former Area Superintendent, Rev. Brian Nicholls, was appointed Regional Minister for Mission Development and Team Leader, while the former Association Secretary, Rev. Barrie Smith, was appointed Regional Minister for Pastoral Care. During his time as Area Superintendent Mr. Nicholls developed the concept of Pastoral Ministers, who would help him in his work of caring for Ministers and other Church Leaders. They were appointed after consultation with the Ministers and other Pastoral Leaders of the churches in the area. Rev. Alan Edwards was appointed the Pastoral Minister for Shropshire. Rev. Brian Nicholls returned to the pastorate in 2005 and the Association was reorganized with regional ministers being appointed to geographical areas rather than to specialist tasks with Rev. Keith Judson as the Regional Minister Team Leader.

Table 7

Churches which Belonged to the Shropshire Baptist Association in 1900 and the Shropshire District / Cluster of the West Midland Baptist Association in 1917 and in 2000

Branch churches are shown in italics

1900	1917	2000
Aston-on-Clun	Aston-on-Clun	
Bridgnorth *Chorley*	Bridgnorth *Chorley*	Bridgnorth
Brockton and Rowley *Bromlow*	Brockton and Rowley	
	Bromlow	
Broseley, Old Chapel	Broseley, Old Chapel	Broseley, Old Chapel
		Chorley
	Craven Arms	
Dawley	Dawley	Dawley
	Donnington Wood	Donnington Wood
Lord's Hill & Snailbeach *Tankerville*	Lord's Hill & Snailbeach *Tankerville*	Lord's Hill & Snailbeach
	Ludlow	Ludlow
Madeley	Madeley	Madeley
Market Drayton	Market Drayton	
		Newport
Oakengates	Oakengates	
Oswestry, Salop-road *Llandrinio* *Maesbrook* *Sweeney*	Oswestry, Salop-road *Llandrinio* *Maesbrook* *Sweeney*	Oswestry, Weston Avenue
Pontesbury	Pontesbury	Pontesbury
Sarn & Cwm	Sarn & Cwm	Sarn
Shifnal, Zion	Shifnal, Zion	
Shrewsbury, Claremont-street	Shrewsbury, Claremont-street	Shrewsbury, Claremont
		Shrewsbury, Crowmoor
Wellington *Donnington Wood`*	Wellington	Wellington, Union Free
Wem	Wem	
Whitchurch *Ightfield* *Prees Heath*	Whitchurch *Ightfield* *Prees Heath*	
Wrexham, Chester-street *Bradley-road* *Holt*		

Aston-on-Clun

Aston-on-Clun was a township and village about ½ mile south of Hopesay (in the ecclesiastical parish of Hopesay) and is now 2 miles WSW of the town of Craven Arms. In Thomas Conder's map of Shropshire it was called Clunton, while in other early documents it was called Aston on Clunsland. In 1830 a Mission Room was built in this village to meet the needs of a small group of Nonconformists who were residing in the area.[162] The mission station was supplied by the Shropshire Itinerant Society. The Shropshire Association Minute Book records the payment in 1832 of £1 0s 0d to Mr. Price of Newtown (i.e. Rev. Benjamin Price) for Mr. (Edward) Evans for his supply at Aston and also at Clunton Clun. Later the same year further payments were made directly to Mr. Evans for supplying at Aston.

The church at Aston Clunsland was formed in 1836 and its first pastor was a Mr. Humphreys. By 1839 the church was in membership with the Association. In 1843 the church called a Mr. Howard as its pastor and a new chapel was opened on 22 June 1844. The pulpit, which was opposite the entrance, had two turned wood-candlesticks on the front corners.[163] Baptisms took place in a nearby brook. The congregation included those who came from Clun and also from Newton (now Craven Arms), which did not then have a Baptist church. There were 27 present on Census Sunday, 30 March 1851. The church did not have a Sunday school. [164]

The Shropshire Association was reorganized in 1854 but the church, then known as Aston in Clun, did not join until 1862. When the Association was reorganized again in 1867 the Aston-on-Clun church became one of the founder members. In 1862 Matthew Matthews, a member of the Baptist Church at Tredegar, was ordained as pastor at Aston-on-Clun[165] and he served there until 1867. In 1868 Mr. John Henry Wait accepted an invitation to the pastorate.[166] He was a draper and one of those who signed the Indenture for the land in Wyle Cop, Shrewsbury, required for the erection of a chapel there.[167] He had pastoral oversight of the Aston church again between 1881 and 1884.

The Association sought to find ways for providing oversight for the church. In 1887 the Association appointed Rev. William Jenkins of Lord's Hill and the Secretary (Rev. W. J. Dyer of Bridgnorth) to visit the church. In 1888 the church agreed to give half of their collections towards the expenses incurred by the Association in providing pulpit supplies. Mr. Jenkins appears to have had pastoral oversight of the church until 1891 when he wrote to the Association Secretary saying that he could not carry on the work at Aston-on-Clun any longer. The Old Welsh Association had been approached about assuming responsibility but decided not to do so. They were in favour of putting a Mission Pastor or a Colporteur in the District supported by the two Associations and the Baptist Union. However, nothing came of this suggestion.

Former Aston-on-Clun Chapel

Tablet above chapel entrance

In 1900 it was suggested that the Shrewsbury church should approach the Aston-on-Clun Church with a view to assuming responsibility for the work but it became clear that difficulties of travelling did not make this a viable proposition. In 1902 Mr. Jenkins, by now of Sarn and Cwm, reported to the Executive Committee that he had visited Aston and some of the friends from Knighton had also helped. Links between Victoria Street, Knighton, Radnorshire, continued for a number of years and the West Midland Association General Secretary reported in 1917:

> The Churches at Craven Arms and at Aston-on-Clun have received the special attention of the Rev. T. Rhys Broad and the Deacons of Victoria Street, Knighton, much to the benefit of these churches.

In May 1929 the church requested that Rev. E. G. Cole of Shrewsbury should undertake the oversight of the church and the Shrewsbury church readily agreed. Rev. J. D. Hamer, who on his retirement from South-street, Brierley Hill had come to live in Craven Arms, was asked in 1930 to undertake the oversight of the church for an initial period of one year. He was to be responsible for 36 Sundays a year and to receive a remuneration of 20 guineas. In 1932 he moved to Knighton, Radnorshire, but continued as pastor until his death at the age of 80 in 1943. The church then met with the Area Superintendent, Rev. J. Ivory Cripps to discuss future oversight. In 1944 Rev. John Brown, minister of Knighton, Victoria Street, was appointed pastor of the church for one year. It was agreed to pay him 25 shillings for a Sunday evening service and to pay his railway fares when he visited in the area. The arrangements with Mr. Brown were reviewed each year and in 1951 his remuneration was raised by 5 shillings per Sunday. He continued as pastor at Aston-on-Clun after his retirement from the Knighton church until his death in February 1957 at the age of 81 years. During his pastorate baptisms took place at Knighton, Victoria Road. In the 1960's the church was under the oversight of another retired Baptist minister, Rev. Alexander Leitch, who was a member of Norton Street, Knighton, and also had oversight of Felindre, Radnorshire. During the pastorate of Rev. Matthew Francis at Shrewsbury, Claremont (1957-63) once a month a preacher from the Shrewsbury church conducted the service at Aston. One of these preachers was Alan Edwards who subsequently entered the Baptist ministry.[168]

A declining membership and the state of the chapel resulted in closure of the work in the village by 1972. However, the sale of the building and site for the sum of £250 was not completed until the early 1980s. The building is now used as a store and sadly the pulpit and other fittings have been removed.

Ministers

Humphreys	1837-42(?)
Howard	1843-48(?)
Matthews, Matthew	1862-67
Wait, John Henry	1868-76
Joint Pastorate with Newton, Craven Arms	*1881-84*
Under the oversight of Claremont, Shrewsbury	*1929-30*
Hamer, John David	01.07.1930-30.10.43
Brown, John	1944-17.02.57
Leitch, Alexander *(oversight)*	1963-70(?)

Barrow

At Barrow, a village 2 miles E of Much Wenlock, Rev. John Thomas of Broseley registered a dwelling house for worship in 1811,[169] but a church was not subsequently formed there.

Bettws-y-Crwyn

Bettws-y-Crwyn, which was on a Drovers' Route from Carmarthenshire and Cardiganshire to Ludlow,[170] was called Bettws on Thomas Conder's map of Shropshire. Joseph Jones of Maesyrhelem in Radnorshire and his co-pastor Abraham Evans began Baptist work in the parish. They did not confine their evangelistic activities to the neighbourhood of Maesyrhelem but 'went forth as evangelists into other neighbourhoods that needed the Gospel of Christ'.[171] These included Velindre (Felindre)[172] in Radnorshire and Bettws-y-Crwyn in Shropshire. A rough road separated Felindre from Maesyrhelem, about seven or eight miles distant. Bettws-y-Crwyn is about 4 miles distant from Felindre. The countryside is rough and hilly and so it must have been hard work to travel along rough mountainous roads in the winter season in order to preach the Gospel.

Black Mountain Chapel

In 1809 Joseph Jones licensed 'Tyn-y-vron', the house of William Lucas for Baptist worship and again in 1810 he licensed 'Cwm Micon' the home of William Mapp.[173] In 1826 two Baptists began to hold prayer-meetings at Old Gravel and Pentre in Radnorshire. Shortly afterwards they held 'a society meeting[174] or what is called by some an inquirers' meeting'. Two women sought membership with the Baptists and were afterwards baptized at Bettws.[175]

In the list of the Particular Baptist Churches of Wales in *The Baptist Magazine* in 1831 Bettws is listed as a branch of Maesyrhelem and it was served by four unordained preachers - Edward Rees, David Evans, Charles Lloyd and William Breeze.

Rev. Joseph Jones died in 1834 at the age of 78. He was succeeded in 1836 by Rev. Thomas Harvard. He was responsible for Maesyrhelem and its branch churches, including that at Bettws-y-Crwyn.[176]

At the time of the 1851 Religious Census there was a congregation at Bettws but it did not have its own building. On Census Sunday a congregation of 75 met at a farm. George Lloyd, a deacon and a farmer, of Cwm House, Bettws, completed the Census form.[177]

Bettws remained a branch of Maesyrhelem until it called as its own minister, Rev. Thomas Jones from New Wells, Montgomeryshire.

It is now believed that Black Mountain Chapel was erected by Baptists and not by the Primitive Methodists as had been thought at one time.[178] Baptisms probably took place in a brook on a local farm.

Thomas Jones continued as minister until his death in 1873. He was buried near the entrance to the chapel and his tomb has the following inscription:

> Sacred
>
> TO THE MEMORY OF
> THE REV. THOMAS JONES OF WHITCOTT
> *Who died May 6th 1873*
> AGED 59 YEARS
>
> THE BELOVED PASTOR OF THIS CHURCH
> FOR UPWARD 22 YEARS
>
> *They that be wise shall shine as the brightness of the firmament, and they that turn many to righteousness as the stars for ever and ever*

The Baptist church at Bettws-y-Crwyn was not listed in *The Baptist Handbook* until 1874 when it was called Bettws (Clun). The date of formation of the church was given as 1803, presumably the date at which Baptist work began in the parish. In 1873 the church called to the pastorate Rev. Thomas Rowson, who throughout his ministry was both a minister and a schoolmaster.[179]

From 1876 onwards the church was only able to have a pastor by being grouped with other churches and in 1876 Rowson assumed responsibility also for the church at Felindre, a church in membership with the Old Welsh Baptist Association. He served as pastor of these two churches until 1891 when he moved to Welshpool. He took a prominent part in the musical activities of Radnorshire and conducted choirs at the eisteddfodau. A short time before his death in 1934 he composed a tune which was printed in the festival programme for that year.

Rowson lived at Bettws-y-Crwyn until 1875 when he moved to Felindre, a small village in the parish of Beguildy, midway between Knighton and Newtown. The Felindre site was large enough to build a cottage that was divided into two dwelling houses. The house nearer the chapel was let for use as a shop, while the other house was used as the manse.[180] The church also provided stabling for those who rode to the services on horseback.

W. G. Mansfield was sent to Cwmgwyn to open a Wesleyan chapel there, but he changed his views on baptism was baptized by Rev. David Davies of Maesyrhelem. Bettws-y-Crwyn and Felindre were without a minister and he was called to the pastorate in 1891.[181] The Bettws church joined the Old Welsh Association in 1892. In 1893 it received a grant from the Association's Home Mission Fund along with the churches at Craven Arms, Llangullan and Rhydfelin.

Rev. Thomas Rowson

During Mansfield's pastorate the Felindre church formed a branch at Cwmgwyn, a hamlet on a road from Felindre to Newtown.[182] In 1877 Rev. Hubert Vavasour Griffiths, who owned the Ddol (originally a small homestead, *tŷ unnos*[183]) gave land for a Wesleyan chapel at Cwmgwyn. The Wesleyan cause was never strong and the last record of any activity while it was still a Wesleyan chapel was its Sunday School Anniversary on 30 August 1891. Amongst the local preachers were J. D. Hamer, Cwmgwyn, and W. G. Mansfield, Felindre, who were to become Baptist ministers. Two staunch Baptists from South Wales moved into the area: Edward Davies lived at The Waen and Abraham Jones at Windy Hill. They set up a Committee with the aim of purchasing the Wesleyan chapel. They first rented the chapel and then after three years purchased it from the Methodists for use as a Particular or Calvinistic Baptist Church.[184] The work at Cwmgwyn became an independent church in 1906 when it was received into the Radnorshire and Montgomeryshire Association.[185] About 1903 the size of the chapel was doubled, land having been given for this purpose by the farmer of the adjoining Ddol Farm.

Felindre Chapel

At Bettws and many Baptist churches in Radnorshire there were converts during the Welsh Revival and reports in local newspapers describe baptismal services at Felindre both in the river and in the new baptistery in the chapel.[186]

The records of the Felindre church show that in 1912 the Bettws church made a financial contribution of £12 to Felindre church. This amount was increased to £26 from 1924-1927. It fell to £20 in 1928 and £15 in 1929 and 1930. From 1931-1933 a £10 contribution was made, falling to £7 in 1935 after which financial contributions ceased.[187]

In 1950 the Executive Committee of the Radnor and Montgomery Baptist Association was concerned about the situation of the weaker churches in the Association. They recommended to the Association's Half-Yearly Meeting *inter alia* that Ministers should conduct Harvest Services and three nights of mission at Bettws. Rev. W. H. Jones, Llandrindod, offered to take the Harvest Services and Revs. D. J. Richards, Knighton, A. Williams, Maesyrhelem, and T. Dacey, Rock, offered to take the mission. Mr. Richards also offered to take a service once a month. The Executive Committee suggested that Bettws, Cwmgwyn and Felindre should be linked together again and three members were deputed to consult with the churches. However, by the Annual Meeting in June 1951 it was reported that the churches at Bettws and Felindre had not replied to letters, while the church at Cwmgwyn 'was content to continue as at present but was prepared to receive a deputation from the Association to discuss the matter'. However, the Bettws chapel closed because of its poor state of repair. Through the efforts of Mr. R. Hudson, who had been Church Treasurer at Bettws, the chapel was re-opened on 10 October 1956. Mr. Hudson paid for the repair of the chapel roof, while Rev. D. J. Richards used his skill as a carpenter to carry out repairs. Mr. Richards then held monthly services until he retired in 1966. [188]

From 1977 to 1983 the Bettws church belonged to the Kerry Group of Baptist Churches and there was a monthly service at which the Kerry minister preached. The churches received a Grant towards the minister's stipend from the Baptist Union of Wales Sustentation Fund. In 1987 the church at Kerry, which was then without a minister, approached the church at Sarn about the possibility of forming a new Group of Churches comprising Sarn, Kerry, New Wells, Cwmgwyn and Bettws-y-Crwyn. There is no record of any discussion on this proposal by the deacons or church members at Sarn. However, it is likely that the Sarn minister, Rev. Penry Davies, who was disabled and approaching retirement, felt that he could not undertake the travelling involved in caring for another four churches.

The ending of cattle droving meant that many of those who had been involved moved away from the area and many of their small 'one-night houses' (*tai unnos*) in the hills with their small pieces of land were sold to neighbouring farmers. Some of these houses became shelters for animals. The decrease in the population inevitably led to a decline of churches in the area. The church at Cwmgwyn has only 2 members, although services are held twice a month, while the church at Felindre has only 1 member and services are held in the chapel only occasionally. The New Wells church closed in 1988 and the Bettws-y-Crwyn church in September 1996.

Ministers

Branch of Maesyrhelem, Radnorshire	*1806–c. 51*
Jones, Joseph	1806-19.05.34
Havard, Thomas	1836–51
Jones, Thomas	1851- 06.05.73
Rowson, Thomas	1873 -91 (and Felindre 1876-91)
Joint pastorate with Felindre	1892-1910
Mansfield, William George	22.01.1892-1910
Joint pastorate with Felindre and Cwmgwyn	*1923-29*
Pugh, Hugh Thomas	1923–29
Joint Pastorate with Ackhill and Bleddfa, Radnorshire	*1929-30*
Griffiths, William T.	1929-30
Felindre, Cwmgwyn and Bettws-y-Crwyn Group	*1930-46*
Williams, T. Rhys	1930-46
Joint Pastorate with Felindre	*1947-50*
Thomas, David John	1947-50
Joint Pastorate with Knighton, Coxall and Knucklas	*1956-66*
Richards, David John	1956-66
Kerry, New Mills, Cwmgwyn and Bettws-y-Crwyn Group	*1977 until at least 1987*
Bridge, John Richard	1977-29.09.83

Bishop's Castle

In September 1798 John Palmer of Shrewsbury, together with three others registered 'An Edifice or Building known by the name of Meeting House' for worship by Independent Baptists.[189] The cause, however, did not prosper and no more information is available.

Bridgnorth

Bridgnorth is situated on the ridge of the sandstone cliff on the west bank of the River Severn and it was called Bridgnorth to distinguish it from Quatford, 2 miles SSE, where there was once another bridge over the Severn. Members of the Parliamentary Army probably founded the church in the town. The first reference to Baptists in Bridgnorth is on 1 February 1651 (or 1652) when thirteen General Baptist fellowships, including Bridgnorth, sent a letter of congratulation to Oliver Cromwell. James Browne and Thomas Jeffreyes signed it on behalf of the Bridgnorth Baptists.[190] By 1699 the Baptists were using the old St Sythes chapel on the river bridge.[191]

The opposition faced by Baptists at the time is made clear by an entry in the journal of Mr. John Sing on 27 August 1699 when he recorded how an old man, who attended the Baptist meeting, was denied relief by the parish:

> The next day being the last Sunday in the month, there was a sort of vestry, or parish meeting at the parish church, which I was obliged (though of very uneasy mind) to attend upon. Amongst other cases, there was a very poor man that applied for relief, to whom the bailiff entered fourpence per week, with a penny loaf, to be given every other day at church. It was answered by some present, "He does not come to the church." "Where does he go then?" replied the bailiff. "To the church at Bridge end," said the overseers (meaning the baptist meeting there). "Nay, then," replied the bailiff, "let the church at Bridge end maintain its own poor, for we will have nothing to do with them." And, accordingly, the poor old man was dismissed without allowance. My heart ached for the complainant.[192]

John Sing is probably to be identified with the John Synge who leased two messuages lying on the bridge in 1659.[193] At first John Sing appears to have been in the General Baptist network, since even as late as 1711 he advised the General Baptist Church at Netherton, Worcestershire about its choice of a pastor.[194] However, the Bridgnorth church was reformed as a Particular Baptist church c.1700[195] and a meeting-house was opened in West Castle Street.

An application was made for a licence to worship in the house of Elizabeth Wilkes in 1707.[196] It is believed the house was in the Low Town to the east of the River Severn but no further information is available. It is not known whether this meeting was for those who were not happy with the new Particular Baptist stance of the church at West Castle Street or whether it was a 'cottage meeting' for those who were unable to attend the meetings there.

The first date in the Church Book is 1705, where it mentions, as it does also in 1706, the payment of expenses to a messenger to the (Midland) Association. Mr. John Sing became the pastor about 1712. The John Evans List of Dissenting Ministers and Congregations (1716-1718) records that the congregation was drawn from farmers and tradesmen. There were 40 hearers, 3 voters for the County and 11 Burgesses.

The Church Book records the death of John Sing as follows:

> Our honoured minister, Mr. John Sing, who was a faithful minister of our Lord Jesus Christ, and preached the gospel freely for upwards of 40 years, sweetly slept in our Lord Jesus Christ, July 12, 1753 N.S. [197]

After John Sing's death the church appears to have had no minister until John Macgowan came to the town from Warrington in 1759. He had served as pastor of Hill Cliffe from 1748 to 1759 and had carried on business as a bread-baker during his pastorate there.[198] He left Bridgnorth and settled at Devonshire-square, London, in 1766. The Strict Baptist historian Ralph Chambers said of him,

> He was a character, quaint and original to a degree, yet withal a well-grounded minister. One of his books has the title 'Dialogues of Devils', and is a highly imaginative work somewhat in the style of Bunyan.[199]

Macgowan was succeeded in 1788 by Henry Butterworth, who remained at Bridgnorth until June 1813 when he moved to Leominster to take charge of the church there. The next pastor was William Pain from Oswestry. When he arrived at Bridgnorth the church had been reduced to three members. By 1821 the membership had risen to eight.[200] However, there then followed a period of rapid growth in the congregation, especially on Sunday evenings, and a gallery was added to the chapel in 1824.

Members of the Sing family occupied various positions in the Church under different Ministers for some 200 years. John Sing's son, John Sing (II), was for many years a deacon of the church, while his grandson, John Sing (III), was 'a warm friend of the cause of Christ,' although he never joined the church. A great grandson of the first John Sing, called Joseph, was baptised with his wife on 5 August 1821. He became the first Mayor of the town after the passing of the Municipal Reform Act of 1835. Joseph was a very enthusiastic Christian and encouraged families and especially young people to become church members.[201]

A Catholic Apostolic Church was erected in the town in 1835[202] and in 1838 dissension arose in the Baptist church through the propagation of Irvingite teachings and these 'wolves in sheep's clothing found their way into the fold and were corrupted from the simplicity which is in Christ.' This led to a stricter measure being taken in respect of applications for membership.

Rev. David Payn, who had become pastor in 1839, joined the Brethren. In his letter of resignation in April 1844 he spoke of the 'painful necessity of separation' and he wished the church 'the enjoyment of peace and love'. The church, in return, passed unanimously a resolution of 'deep regret that circumstances should have occurred to separate the connection that had so happily existed between Mr. Payn and the church as pastor and people.' He only remained with the Brethren for six months and later confessed that they were the most unhappy months he had ever experienced. In 1860 he became minister of Leamington Spa Baptist Church.[203]

During the first year of David Payn's pastorate it was decided to rebuild the chapel. The building, which now had 400 seats[204], was opened for worship on 7 July 1842. At the opening services the Teachers presented a New Testament to every Sunday School scholar. The cost of the building was £1,400.

Bridgnorth Chapel

On Census Sunday 1851 the church had a morning congregation of 107 and 65 Sunday scholars, while the evening attendance was 130.
The minister, Rev. Alfred Tilley, who completed the Census Return, observed 'The congregations on this Sabbath were unusually small in consequence of great affliction and its being Mid-Lent Sunday.' [205]

In 1870 the church called to the pastorate James Boyd Warren, a Strict Baptist, who had been baptized by Rev. C. H. Spurgeon. He trained at Pastors' College but it was said of him that 'it is doubtful whether his scholastic attainments ever exceeded mediocrity'.[206] On the list of pastors in the church building he is called 'Mr. Warren,' since like other Strict Baptist ministers at the time he did not use the title 'Reverend'.

Rev. John Dyer served as Pastor from 1880 to 1883 and again from 1899 until he retired from the Ministry in 1913. An important part of his work was to train young men to "Speak and Preach", whilst he had a great Christian influence on the affairs of the town.

The church had only 27 members when Bernard Thompson came to Bridgnorth in 1972 from a joint Congregational and Railway Mission Church at Stoke-on-Trent. There were frequent baptisms and the membership reached 127 in 1984. He left in 1987 to become pastor of the Ridgeway Christian Fellowship. Wallingford.

Alterations were made to the interior of the church building in the 1980's without the need for planning permission but Listed Building Consent is now required for any further alterations. Major alterations including the removal of pews were carried out in 2006. Ray Gill retired in April 2007.

The church had joined the Midland Association by 1705 and Association meetings were held there in 1706, 1714 and 1745, but there is no mention of the church in Association records after 1777.[207] Thereafter the church did not belong to an Association until it joined the reorganized Shropshire Baptist Association in 1854.

Minisiters

Sing, John	*c.* 1712-12.07.53
Macgowan, John	25.03.1759-3.10.1766
Butterworth, Henry	01.04.1768–13.05.06 (ordained 19.06.80)
Edmonds, Thomas	10.1806 -06.13
Pain, William	05.1816-22
Shoveller, John	1823-26
Clarke, Robert	1827-38
Payn, David	1839- 04.44
Tilley, Alfred	01.1846- 01.56
Keen, Charles Thomas, Junior	1857-58
Jennings, David	1.3.1859-63
Keen, Charles Thomas, Junior	1864-68
Warren, James Boyd	1870-73
Vasey, Thomas	1874-80
Dyer, William John	1880-93.
Griffiths, John Josiah	1894-99
Dyer, William John	1899-1913
Brook, Isaac	1915-20
Campbell, Archibald Spence	1924-28
Watts, Frederick Charles	1929-35

Bridgnorth Ministers *continued*

Benfield, George Ernest, MA, BA	1941-44
Smith, Archibald William	1946-49
Pressler, W. C. (Lay)	1959-62
Jones, William Kenneth, BD	1965-72
Thompson. Bernard	1972-87
Smith, T. (Lay)	1987-91
Gill, Raymond, MSc	1993 - 04.07

Brockton

Brockton is situated on the Shrewsbury to Montgomery road and is adjacent to the village of Worthen. At Worthen lived Mr. Thomas and Mrs. Sarah Jones and their daughter Maggi, members of Sarn Baptist Church, Montgomeryshire, and Mr. Richard Hughes, a member of New Wells Baptist Church, near Newtown, Montgomeryshire. They assembled for a special meeting on Friday, 28 January, 1876, held at the home of Mr. Thomas Jones, to form themselves into a church of the Baptist Denomination, in the presence of Rev. T. T. Phillips of Lord's Hill, Shropshire, and the Rev. John Harrison of Sarn. Mr. Thomas Jones was appointed to act as Deacon and Mr. Richard Hughes to act as Secretary.

Brockton Chapel

On Sunday afternoon, 30 January 1876 services were held in the afternoon at the home of Mr. Richard Hughes (Cause Farm) and in the evening at the home of Mr. Thomas Jones, the preacher being the Rev. J. Harrison. The Lord's Supper was celebrated at the close of the evening service.[208]

The number of church members at 1 January 1882 had risen to eight. Much difficulty was faced in an endeavour to obtain land on which to build a place of worship due to opposition from the Anglican Church. A portion of land owned by a doctor in Brockton was duly purchased on which to build a chapel and have room for a burial ground. In 1959 a hall was added at the rear of the Chapel and the graveyard extended.

The fellowship flourished and the records for 1907 show a membership of 10 with 36 Sunday School scholars and 4 teachers.

The Members at Brockton were responsible for a Mission Room founded in the hamlet of Rowley. The Mission was founded about 1887 and closed about 1926. Rev. Thomas Evans, pastor at Pontesbury from 1886, usually took the services on the second Sunday of each month and administered the Lord's Supper at the close of the evening service. This continued until he retired in March 1904.

Arthur Burton was born in Bridgnorth, where he worked as a draper's assistant. Sensing a call to ministry he passed the Baptist Union Examination and became the first pastor of Brockton and Bromlow in 1916.[209] In 1931 the fellowships at Brockton and Bromlow were grouped with Montgomery under the Rev. John Leslie Baines, who lived in Montgomery but then the Bromlow Mission closed.

Steps were taken to set up a tripartite grouping of the Brockton, Lord's Hill and Pontesbury Baptist Churches under one minister and this was adopted on 22 March 1949. In 1966 the grouping was dissolved.

Under the influence of Charismatic Renewal the church at Brockton ceased to be Baptist and it is now known as Brockton Christian Centre. Thomas and Sarah Jones were the great grandparents of Mrs. Ann Andrews, whose husband, Gordon, is an elder of the Church today

Ministers

Burton, Arthur	1916-23
McKay, David William	1923- 2.11.30
Joint Pastorate with Montgomery	*1931-39*
Joint Pastorate with Lord's Hill and Pontesbury	*1949–66*

Bromlow

Bromlow is situated 6 miles SW of Pontesbury. The work was begun in 1889 by Rev. W. Jenkins of Lord's Hill and at the Annual Meeting of the Shropshire Association that year he was given a grant of £2 'towards the expenses of his new Mission at Bromlow'. However, in 1900 the mission became a branch of Brockton and Rowley. A 'Mission Room' was erected in 1902.

The minutes of the Shropshire Association's Annual Assembly in June 1903 record:

> Bromlow: Mr. Richard Roberts reported on the work here, stating that there were four members; that they were acting independently; and that he had undertaken to arrange for the pulpit. Rev. W. Jenkins [of Sarn] added a few words on the subject and it was resolved Revs. W. Jenkins, A. Parker [Lord's Hill], and the Secretary [Rev. Isaac Watts (Wem)] visit Bromlow, Institute the Church, administer the Lord's Supper & give instructions in the privileges and duties of Membership.

The new Church was welcomed into the Association. Mr. Richard Roberts, the grandfather of George Roberts, became Church Secretary and Lay Pastor.

In 1905 the Mission Room, a one storey building, was moved to a more convenient site, the total cost of the work involved being thirty-seven pounds ten shillings and the Church asked for assistance from the Association in meeting this cost. It was not until 1912 that the debt was cleared. By then the Sunday evening services were well attended and Membership had reached double figures.

When Richard Roberts died in September 1913, the Church at Pontesbury became responsible for the oversight and supply of speakers. Then, due to the outbreak of the First World War, there was a decline in membership. In 1916 the Bromlow Church was grouped with Brockton under Rev. Arthur Burton and then in 1923 it became a branch of Brockton under the pastorate of Rev. D. W. McKay. Attendance declined and the work at Bromlow closed in 1932

Ministers

Branch of Lord's Hill	1889-1900
Branch of Brockton	1900-1903
Roberts, Richard (Lay)	1903-09.13
Joint Pastorate with Brockton	*1916-23 and a branch of Brockton 1923-32*

Broseley (Old Chapel or Old Meeting House)

The Broseley Church Book[210] records the beginning of Baptist witness as follows:

> The preaching of the Gospel at Broseley was begun att y^e^ house of Jacob Wyke y^e^ sixteenth day of September 1741 by Mr John Oulton Pastor of y^e^ Baptist Church at Leominster and by him Mr Robert Morris of Wellington. There were preached ab^t^ ten Sermons before the new Chapel was opened which was y^e^ second day of February 1741=42 from wch time about the space of 2 years but we had no constant supply but what by the providence of God ministers of other congregations were sometimes sent to assist and some from vs distant places from us in which time several persons received the Gospel and were baptized afterwards. Mr. John Waine who had been one of our helpers came and resided with us and ye number of converts increased to ab^t^ fifteen whereof there were four me viz. Jacob Wyke John Jones George Cartwright who on or about ye first of December 1749 (according to ye Gospel rule) Incorporated themselves together & became a church.

Robert Morris of Wellington was the minister of the Baptist church at Shrewsbury in 1725.[211] and one the ministers who came from 'distant places' was Evan Jenkins of Wrexham, who was said by the Baptist historian Joshua Thomas to be 'the chief means to raise and put in order the Baptist church at Broseley'. [212]

Shortly after the Broseley church was formed John Waine and his sister Hannah obtained their dismission from Brassey Green, Cheshire, and Isaac Wyke and three others their dismission from Leominster. John Waine was ordained as pastor on 9 October 1751 by Rev. Philip Jones of Upton-on-Severn, Rev. John Johnson of Liverpool, and Rev. Evan Jenkins. At the same service Isaac Wyke was ordained as ruling Elder and George Cartwright as Deacon. Although John Waine preached in English at the Welsh Association in 1753 the Broseley church did become a member of an Association until about 1796 when it joined the Midland Association.[213]

Broseley Old Chapel
(Photograph taken on 16 September 1941 to mark the Bicentenary)

Broseley Chapel, which was erected by Isaac Wyke, is the oldest place of worship in the town[214] and predates the parish church of All Saints, which was built in 1745.[215] The original chapel had three bays with an entrance in the middle bay on the N side but it was extended to the W in mid nineteenth century and a new entrance was constructed at the E end. It is said that worshippers came from as far afield as Ludlow, Wellington and Shifnal. [216]

Isaac Wyke left property to the church when he died in 1755. There were several other bequests to the chapel in the remaining years of the century. Some of the original property of Broseley Baptists was sold over the years but a Charity Commission Confirmation Order of 1908 expressly mentions not only the chapel but also the minister's house, garden and pigsty, a cowshed, meadow, and Corporation stock. These are still in the ownership of the chapel, although the house has not been occupied by a minister for many years. The field and cowshed were acquired by Deed of Gift on 24 January 1854 made by a descendant of Isaac Wyke, and contains a highly interesting and unusual bequest of 'all mines and seams of coal lying under the messuage and premises and land adjoining (i.e. the meadow).' This is surely one of the rare instances of mining rights belonging to a Nonconformist place of worship. [217]

Dr. J (or I) Perrott, who had given a silver communion cup to Cannon Street Baptist Church, Birmingham, in 1760, also gave a silver communion cup of 1704 to Broseley Chapel in 1763.

The founders of the Broseley church affirmed their belief in one God, Father, Son and Holy Ghost and 'also in the doctrine of personal Election, particular redemption, Effectual calling and y^e^ final perseverance

Broseley Communion Cup given in 1763.

of Saints.' 'The Articles of Faith professed and to be believed by everyone who is baptized before they are admitted to the Lord's Supper' went on say 'for a more particular account of our faith and order we now refer ourselves first to the written word of God & and then to the confession of our faith put forth by the elders & messengers of ye baptized Churches & licensed by authority in Aug. 1688 [i.e. The Particular Baptist Second London Confession]'.

Abraham Webster came to Broseley about 1792 but several members of the church became dissatisfied with his ministry. An account published in 1854 to mark the Jubilee of Birch Meadow Chapel records that someone stood up from his seat and said,

> "Friends, we have been served out with milk and water plentifully, with scarcely enough of the one to colour the other, but our minister effects no disguise now; he gives us water, out and out water, and that not of the purest kind. The Holy Ghost is not in his creed. Jehovah is only candidate, and man's will is the supreme arbiter in this world and the world to come. Can you follow such a leader? I cannot, and God helping me I will have no more of his trash".[218]

It is not surprising that Abraham Webster resigned the pastorate on 13 December 1801. The members then agreed that 'in order to maintain Peace and Unity among ourselves, to dissolve, break up, and annihilate our present Church State or Society.' A new Society was formed on 27 December 1801 with articles of faith that did not differ in any material point from those previously held. This Society met in the original chapel and Abraham Webster became a member. However, on 24 January 1802 he was dismissed to the Baptist church at Liverpool meeting at Matthew Street, where he became the pastor. Those who did not join the new Society withdrew to form a new Particular Baptist Church at the top of Birch Meadow.[219]

On 26 April 1802 John Thomas came from Bewdley and he served as pastor until 25 March 1841. The Midland Association held its Annual Meeting at Broseley on 22 & 23 May 1804 and John Thomas wrote the Circular Letter on the subject "A due attendance and proper behaviour in the House of God". In 1811 he was one of the applicants for the registration of dwelling houses for worship at Morville, Much Wenlock, Ironbridge, Barrow and Donnington, Wellington.[220] He died at the age of 89 on 1 November 1849.[221]

John Thomas' son, James, entered Bradford Baptist College in 1821 and in 1823 he was accepted by the Baptist Missionary Society for service in India. He was ordained as a missionary at Shrewsbury on 7 June 1826. He died in Calcutta on 20 July 1858.[222] To mark his departure to India a tree, known as 'the missionary tree', was planted beside the Broseley chapel. James Thomas's son, Herbert James, after training at Bristol College served with the Baptist Missionary Society in India from 1881 until his retirement in 1920.[223] He came to Broseley in 1941 as a Deputation Speaker, so renewing the family link with the Old Chapel.

During the nineteenth century the membership at Old Chapel declined, from 66 members in 1803 to 6 members in 1890.[224] On Census Sunday 1851 the church claimed an average attendance of 150 (including 54 Sunday scholars).[225]

By 1870 both the Chapel and the School Room had fallen into such a state of decay that they were hardly fit to be used. The Trustees decided to repair the buildings at a cost of about £200. To meet this cost they were obliged to appeal for public help and to raise money a bazaar was held in the Town Hall.
The buildings were re-opened on Sunday, 10 September 1871, when the preacher was the 16th Lord Teynham.[226]

By 1876 it seemed that the Broseley Church could no longer function as an independent cause. The Minutes of the Annual Meeting of the Shropshire Association that year record:

> A Committee was appointed to deal with the case of the Broseley Church. On their recommendation the following resolution was adopted: - That the Revs Messrs Wotton, Jenkins & Vasey be deputed to go over to Broseley to re-organise the church; & that for the present it be attached to, & under the care of the churches at Dawley, Madeley, & Bridgnorth; and that ultimately the church be reorganised by the Association as a branch of one of the above-named churches. The deputation from Broseley agreed to this resolution.

However, the following year the Broseley church called Charles H. Doughty as its pastor. From 1893 until 1963 the Madeley church had pastoral oversight of Broseley, apart from 1901 when Broseley called its own minister. Thereafter ministers of the churches at Dawley or Wellington would conduct weddings and funerals as necessary.

In 1935 further renovations were made to the buildings and electric light was installed, the chapel being reopened on 9 March. Just after the 1939-45 War a new Sunday School room was added because the old room, converted from the vestry, was too small. It was intended that both the Church and the Community could also use this room for social functions.

The Bicentenary of the Church was celebrated in

1941. On Sunday, 21 September the services were conducted by Rev. A. S. Langley, the Secretary of the West Midland Baptist Association, and on Wednesday 24 September there was a Special Thanksgiving Service when the preacher was Rev. H. Ingli James of Coventry. Extensive renovations of the buildings were undertaken in preparation for the Church's 250th Anniversary, which was held on Saturday 14 and Sunday 15 September, 1991, the Shropshire District holding its Assembly at the Church on the Saturday.

Ministers

Waine, John	12.1749-05.68 (ordained 9.10.51)
Marston, John	07.1770- *c.* 06.78 (ordained 23.04.72)
Faulkner, -	16.10.1783-
Dawson, -	1788
Crowther, William	1789
Webster, Abraham	*c.* 1792-13.12.01
Thomas, John	26.04.1802-25.03.41
Wilshere, J. *(Co-pastor)*	*c* 1841
Jones, William	09.02.1845-50
Yale, William	05.08.1856-
Jones, E.	23.10.1859– 62
Carter, J. W.	1863
Hemus, Frederick.	1870-75
Doughty, Charles Henry	1877–78
Walker, B. G.	1880
Baugh, Timothy	1881-84
Under the Pastoral Oversight of Madeley	*1893–1901*
Wilson, Reuben	1901
Under the Pastoral Oversight of Madeley	*1901-1963*

Broseley (Birch Meadow)

In 1803 the house of George Crompton in Broseley was registered for worship by 'Independent Baptists'. Shortly afterwards a meeting house at the top of Birch Meadow was registered.[227] This new Chapel was opened on 31 August 1803. An ironmaster John Guest and a local draper George Crompton paid for the building. The design of the building, like that of the Old Chapel, reflected Strict Baptist theology, for the baptistry was in the middle of the chapel, showing 'that this must first be passed before the table further on'.[228]

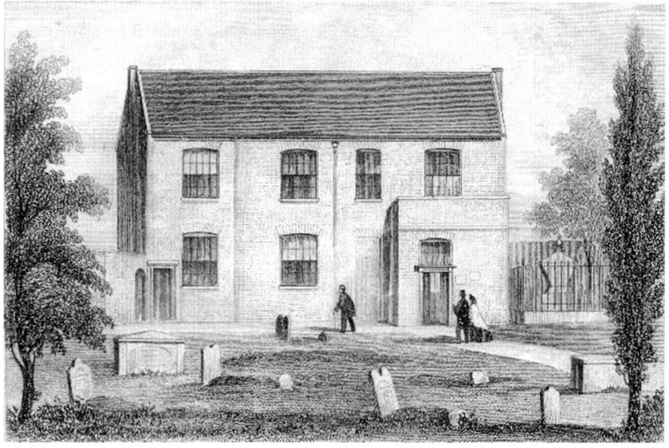

Birch Meadow Chapel in 1864

Thomas Jones was the best-known pastor of the church and he ministered from 1821 until 1840 and again from 1874 until 1883. He was baptized in 1815 and joined the church. He supplied the pulpit in 1821, without any intention of becoming its pastor. At first he worked as a clerk in Bridgnorth and walked over eight miles to Broseley to preach.[229] Notwithstanding the division in the original Baptist cause at Broseley, when he was ordained to the pastorate various Baptist ministers took part in the service including the pastor of the first church at Broseley (Old Chapel). The report of the service in *The Baptist Magazine* is as follows:

> On the 20th May, 1824, Mr. Thomas Jones was ordained to the pastoral office over the second Baptist church in Broseley. Mr. Cook, of Oswestry, described the nature of a gospel church; Mr. Jones of Newtown, asked the usual questions, and delivered the charge from Exodus iv. 10, 11, 12. Mr. Thomas, pastor of the first Baptist church offered up the ordination prayer, which was accompanied by the laying on of hands. In the evening, Mr. Cook preached to the people. The newly ordained pastor concluded the service with prayer. Messrs. Snow, of Donnington Wood; [Benjamin] Evans, of Bradford Academy; and Smith, of Bilstone [*sic*]; took part in the services of the day.[230]

In 1840 Thomas Jones moved to Blackheath (then in Kent) and preached in various churches, principally at Enon, Chatham, Kent. He returned to Broseley in 1874 and served as pastor until his death in 1883. He left instruction that no tombstone or tablet should be erected to his memory. His friends, however, decided to renovate and improve the chapel in his memory. This cost £400 and the chapel was re-opened on Sunday, 23 November 1884 when the preacher was Mr. S. K. Bland of Ipswich.[231]

Thomas Jones was succeeded by Arthur Shinn, whom he had baptized.[232] Although he was a Strict Baptist his name was on the Baptist Union Accredited List. During his pastorate it became necessary to renovate the pulpit and one of his sermons was printed and sold to help towards the cost. It was also freely distributed at Open-air Meetings at Willey Park.[233]

Thomas Jones published in 1839 a satirical letter entitled 'New Light, or the Particular Baptists not particular', in which he reproved the departure from the truth of professedly Baptist churches in the Midland counties. So it is not surprising that Birchmeadow Chapel joined the West Midland Baptist Association when it was formed in 1840. This Strict Baptist Association protested against what they conceived to be the 'damnable heresies' and 'profane babblings which will increase unto more ungodliness' of the Midland Association.[234] The West Midland Association appears to have been short-lived and to have ceased to exist by 1844.

A Sunday School was opened in 1814 and its Jubilee was duly celebrated in 1864, both by a tea and a meeting at which a number of former scholars took part[235] and by the publication of a history of the Sunday School.[236] On Census Sunday 1851the morning congregation was 90 together with 69 Sunday scholars while the evening congregation was 120. The Sunday School Superintendent, who completed the Census Return, reported that 'Generally there is no public service in the afternoon. The Sabbath Scholars are taught however from 2 p.m. to 4 p.m.'[237] During the nineteenth century Birch Meadow Chapel was more prosperous than Old Chapel, although it closed by *c.* 1927. On its closure the rail which had stood in front of the communion table and also some of the pews were acquired by Old Chapel, Broseley, where they may be seen today.

Ministers

Price, -	1808
Gosney, -	*c.* 1812-18
Muckley, William*	
Jones, Thomas	1821-40 (ordained 20.05.24)
Field, -	1850
Veale, Henry (*Supply*)	*c.* 1854- at least 57
Baugh, Timothy,	1861–63
Bodenham, J.	1870
Jones, Thomas	1874 - 04.07.83
Shinn, Arthur	1886-1900
Hall, W.S.	1908-10
Gilpin, James	1910

*William Muckley was pastor at Broseley after 1819[238] and it has been assumed that he was pastor at Birch Meadow Chapel rather than at Old Chapel.

Buildwas

At Buildwas, 2½ miles WNW of Ironbridge, a dwelling house was registered for worship by Baptists in 1804[239] but a church was not subsequently formed there.

Burslem

The town of Burslem, Staffordshire, was described in 1841 as 'finely situated on a gentle eminence to the north of Newcastle under Lyme and the largest and most populous town of any in the district'.[240] Baptist work in Burslem can be traced to the beginning of the nineteenth century.[241] In 1797 Richard Thompson opened a cotton mill at Cross Heath, Wolstanton, Newcastle-under-Lyme. His son Thomas, who settled in Newcastle-under-Lyme in 1798 preached on supply there 'to our Independent brethren' later extending his missionary activities to Burslem and Hanley, finding support at Burslem. He and an inhabitant of Burslem erected a chapel in High Street (later Greenhead Street) in 1806, and shortly afterwards they with other Baptists, who had come into the area, formed a Particular Baptist church. Thompson was invited to be its first minister and he was ordained in the church in 1809. The work clearly progressed and by 1828 the chapel needed to be repaired and a gallery built.[242]

Former Burslem Chapel built in 1806 (Demolished in 2002)

Thompson became Moderator of the Lancashire and Cheshire Association in 1811. He was one of the signatories at the foundation of the Baptist Union, but in 1816 ill health forced him to resign the Burslem pastorate. The Association accepted an invitation to hold its meeting at Burslem in 1816 and printed the following rather quaint note:

> As Burslem lies at a distance from most of the churches in the Association, and the friends there precluded by that circumstance from having much

intercourse with their Brethren on these occasions, it is particularly requested that as many from the other churches will attend there as possibly can. N.B. The road turns to the left at the Red Bull, Six miles south of Congleton. Put up at Mr. Cotton's, Leg of Man Inn.[243]

In 1826 the church joined the Shropshire Baptist Association and the Association's Annual Meeting was held at Burslem in 1828. However, by 1835 during the pastorate of William Muckley the church had ceased to be in membership with any Association. By 1838 there was a Sunday school attached to the church with *c.* 115 pupils.

In 1839 the Burslem church rejoined the Lancashire and Cheshire Baptist Association. The church became a station of the Lancashire and Cheshire County Mission, which gave it a grant of £10 in 1844 when the pastor was John Pulsford. In 1845 there were 30 baptisms; more than in any other church in the Association. However, the Report of the County Home Mission about Burslem was as follows:

> The information furnished to your Committee respecting this station is very scanty. From the letter sent to the Association it will be seen that, it has assumed a more pleasing aspect than it had previously presented. The labours of its present pastor have been much blessed. As the object of this society, however, is not to sustain weak interests, but to establish new Churches that promise to become self-supporting, your Committee cannot recommend to their supporters to grant aid, for any considerable time, to communities circumstanced as the one at this place.

Nevertheless the Annual Meeting of the County Mission did give a grant of £5 but there was no Grant in the following year.[244] In 1848 Pulsford became pastor of Salem, Burton-on-Trent, Staffordshire. In 1851 the attendance at the chapel averaged 80 and at the Sunday School 50.

From 1855-58 the minister was Rev. John William Kirton. After he resigned the pastorate he went to live in Stafford to work for the United Kingdom Alliance. The Midland Association was seeking to plant a Particular Baptist church there and he was one of those asked by the Association to preach there[245] and in the *Baptist Manual* 1859 he is listed as the pastor of the Stafford Church. However, after the Stafford church was duly constituted it called Rev. C. T. Keen, Junior, from Bridgnorth as its pastor. Mr. Kirton subsequently wrote a number of books of which his *Buy your own Cherries* (1863) was the most famous.[246]

To help the struggling churches of the district in 1868 several ministers and others established the North Staffordshire Baptist Union (known as the Staffordshire Baptist Association after 1874). One of the fruits of this co-operation was the employment of a colporteur, with the assistance of the Metropolitan Tabernacle Colportage Association. Then help from the Baptist Union enabled Rev. Clarence Chambers to serve as District Evangelist from 1878 to 1882.[247]

The original chapel, which seated 120, was sold *c.* 1873 to Burslem Ragged School and a new chapel seating 370, was built on Liverpool Road (now renamed Westport Road) in 1876/7. There was a joint pastorate with Newcastle-under Lyme from 1873 to 1876 and, after another pastorate, Rev. William Bonser served as minister from 1882-83. He, together with Rev. Clarence Chambers, was responsible for the formation of the church at Fenton.

The membership had increased to 97 by 1900 and the Sunday school attendance then averaged 200. The church left the Lancashire and Cheshire Baptist Association in 1904 to join with its neighbouring churches in membership of the West Midland Baptist Association[248] and in 1905 a joint pastorate was formed with the church at Newcastle-under-Lyme. Thereafter, apart from the pastorate of Rev. Harry Brinley (1918-20), the minister of the Burslem church had pastoral oversight of at least one other church.

The chapel was burnt down in 1944, but the church continued until 1949, its members, who in that year numbered 46, worshipping either at Hanley or Newcastle. The site of the chapel was then sold. The funds went in 1949 towards the cost of a new manse at Newcastle, the building of Hanley Baptist Church in Meigh Street, and in 1952 to the cost of the new Sunday school at Newcastle.

Ministers

Thompson, Thomas	1808-16 (ordained 09)
Mann, Isaac	1811
Beetham, John	1817
Hinmers, John	1820-21
Lakelin, Joseph	1824 -26
Hodgkins, Benjamin	27.09.1825
Snow, -	1830
Muckley, William	1831-at least 1837
Jones, W.	1838
Archer, William Elisha	03.01.1841-43
Pulsford, John	1844–48

Burslem Ministers *(continued)*

Barker, William	1848–52
Kirton, John William	04.1855-58
Phillips, T.	1863
Sargent, Joseph E.	1866-68
Joint pastorate with Newcastle-under-Lyme	*1873-76*
Field, Henry Cowles	1873–79
Cooke, W. G.	1880-81
Bonser, William	1882-83
Ross, William	1885-90
Taylor, John Cameron, ATS	1892–97
Burrows, Robert Alanson	1897-1902
Joint Pastorate with Newcastle-under-Lyme and Longton, Stoke-on-Trent	*1905-08*
Langley. Arthur Swainson	1905-08
Bach, Albert Ernest	1905
Joint Pastorate with Newcastle-under-Lyme	*1908*
Bach, Albert Ernest	1908 -12
Brinley, Harry	1918-20
Joint Pastorate with Newcastle-under-Lyme	*1922-23*
Rogerson, James Paten	1922–23
Joint Pastorate with Longton, Stoke-on-Trent	1932-
Davies, Zechariah	1932-34
Joint Pastorate with Newcastle-under-Lyme and Butt lane, Stoke-on-Trent	*1935-42*
Wilson, William Bernard, BA, BD	1935–41

Chester (Commonhall Street, later Hamilton Place)

Baptist work in Chester has had a somewhat chequered history and some of its detail is obscure. Chester was a garrison town and so there were probably Baptists there during the Commonwealth period. After the passing of the Conventicle Act in 1664 the Governor of the Chester garrison reported the presence of an "Anabaptistical crew',[249] although it has to be recognized that sometimes the term 'Anabaptist' was used as a derisory description for all Dissenters.

Records dating from 1862 found in the old Ebenezer chapel in Milton Street state:

> It appears that the first Baptist church in Chester was formed in 1686, meeting in a room in Bridge Street. In 1706 they moved to Trinity Street until 1786, when they moved to a room in Foregate Street. They again moved, this time to Commonhall Street until the year 1806, when they began worshipping in their new chapel in Hamilton Place.[250]

Notwithstanding this statement it seems unlikely that a Baptist church existed in Chester *without a break* from 1686 until 1908 when the church in Hamilton Place closed.[251] However, a Baptist church may have indeed been formed in 1686, since when Hannah Amery of Chester died in 1709 she was buried at Hill Cliffe, there being no Baptist burial ground in Chester.[252] At the ordination of John Sedgfield [Sedgefield] at the Liverpool Church in 1718 Samuel Simson of Chester, a merchant, was one of those who took part in the service but after Simson's death the following year, little is known of the Chester church. Although John Taylor heard of it in the middle of the century[253], the cause was so obscure that Josiah Thompson of London was unaware of it when he collected information about Dissenting congregations in the period 1772-1774.[254] John Fawcett preached there in August 1774 and again two years later.[255] This, the first Baptist church in Chester, seems to have closed shortly afterwards

Another Baptist church arose following a split in the Presbyterian chapel in Crook Street (now Trinity Street), which had been built during the ministry of Rev. Matthew Henry and had become known as 'Matthew Henry's Chapel'. The congregation included some who believed in the Independent form of church government. So when Rev. John Chidlaw became the sole pastor of the church in 1765 and he made clear his Socinian[256] views, some withdrew from the church. They met for prayer and the reading of Matthew Henry's *Commentary on the Bible* in a room on the south side of Commonhall Street. From time to time various Nonconformist ministers gave help.

As a result of this secession two societies were formed. The first was an Independent society, which was formally constituted as a church in 1772, a chapel in Queen Street being erected in 1777. The second was a Baptist society that continued to meet in a room in Commonhall Street.[257]

Joseph Jenkins, whose father had been pastor of Wrexham, Chester Street (1740-52), returned to Wrexham in 1769. He exercised for a while some pastoral oversight of the Independents at Chester who had withdrawn from Matthew Henry's Chapel. He preached a sermon at Chester following a terrible explosion of gunpowder there on 5 November 1772. His sermon was printed and subsequently a Welsh translation by Rev. Benjamin Evans, of Llanuwchllyn, Merioneth, was also published.[258]

Joseph Jenkins, who was ordained at Wrexham in 1773, baptized seven people in Chester and they presumably became members of his church at Wrexham.[259] The minutes of the church meeting there indicate steps taken to form a Particular Baptist Church at Chester in 1779:

> At a Church Meeting, January 1st, 1779,
> Our Brother and Sister, John[260] and Mary Mellor, having intimated by our Pastor their desire of being dismissed in order that with others they might be formed into a Baptist Church in Common Hall Lane, Chester, the Independent Church which lately met there having built another Meeting House, It was unanimously Agreed, That they be dismissed for the above purpose; and that we consider that Church, when settled agreeably to the Order of the Gospel, as a Church of Jesus Christ, and take pleasure in being helpful to its comfort and advancement.[261]

However, a later minute of the Wrexham church indicates that the new church at Chester was not formally constituted until 1792:

> At a Church-Meeting, April 29, 1792,
> Application having been made to us by our Brethren and Sisters, John and Mary Mellor, Thomas Crane, Mary Whalley, and Jane Price for a letter of dismission from this Church for the purpose of joining together with others to form a Particular Baptist Church in Common Hall Lane, Chester, the same was agreed to, and that a letter be drawn up for this purpose.[262]

In 1793 Samuel Hatch who was taking emigrants from Liverpool to America, gave the church temporary help. In February 1796 James Aston came to Chester and the following year he baptized thirty people. A chapel was opened in 1800 in Hamilton Place, near Watergate.[263]

In 1805 Aston moved to Lockwood, near Huddersfield, where he remained until his death in 1830.[264]

Controversy was caused in Chester by the arrival of Samuel Stennett. While pastor of Dublin Baptist Church, he had adopted Sandemanian views in 1805. This led to conflict with Andrew Fuller and his departure from Dublin. At Chester he did not join the existing Scotch Baptist Church but made an unsuccessful attempt to introduce his Sandemanian views into the church at Hamilton Place.[265]

Possibly as a result of controversy about Sandemanian doctrines the church was re-formed in 1806. The church, which had 25 members, joined the Shropshire Association in 1815.[267] The following year the Association met at Chester and its minister, Mr. Inglis, was chosen as Moderator. Membership statistics were last reported to the Association in 1822 when the church reported 13 baptisms and there were 34 members. In 1825 the church ordered 12 copies of the Circular Letter. The church then ceased to belong to the Shropshire Association and from then on it did not belong to any Baptist Association.

Thomas Littleton, who had been pastor of Market Drayton, became pastor of Hamilton Place, in 1833. Walter Giles, Senior, became pastor about 1850 but the church, in the words of the Baptist historian W. T. Whitley, 'hovered between life and death'.[267] Then from 1857 until his death in 1895 the honorary pastor of the church was a local watchmaker, Paul Price, who was a high Calvinist.[268] However, it was during his pastorate that Ebenezer Strict Baptist Mission was formed at Milton Street.[269] The church at Hamilton Place closed in 1908 and the building was demolished in 1913.[270]

Ministers of Commonhall Road, later Hamilton Place

ASTON, James	1797-1805
Church was re-formed in 1806	
SHEPHERD, John	1811-14
INGLIS, -	1815
BOTTOMLEY, W. C. (Minister)	1826 -28
LITTLETON, Thomas	1833 -
GILES, Walter, Senior	*c.* 1850
PRICE, Paul (*Honorary*)	1857-11.10.95
EMERSON, John	

Chester (Scotch Baptist) [271]

The Scotch Baptist church in Chester was formed in 1793 and J. Simm served there as pastor for thirty years. Scotch Baptist beliefs spread from Chester to Wrexham and to North Wales. A chapel seating about 220 was erected in Pepper Street in 1828 by J. Simm, who purchased the materials of an old church in Bridge Street that was pulled down. The cause ran down and the church sold the building for use by English Presbyterians, while retaining for their own use an upstairs vestry at the back of the chapel. The Presbyterian Church flourished under the ministry of Rev. William Hunter and a new building had to be erected in Bridge Street. The Presbyterians then sold the Pepper Street building to the Welsh Independents and this sale seems to have extinguished the little Scotch Baptist church. Interestingly, Mr. Hunter became a Baptist and he preached a powerful sermon in the Music Hall explaining his change of views on baptism.

Chester (Ebenezer)

In March 1877 two men from the Hamilton Place church, together with their wives and others, formed Ebenezer Strict Baptist Mission in Milton Street 'with the object of carrying the good news of the Gospel to the poor in the neighbourhood'. This work continues as Ebenezer Baptist Church, which now meets in Francis Street.

Chester (Grosvenor Park, later Upton)

As the Hamilton Place church was high Calvinist, it is not surprising that attempts were made to form another Baptist church in the city. *The Baptist Manual* in 1855 lists a second Baptist church in Chester, although no further details are given. This church was probably short-lived. In 1871 an attempt was made to open another English Baptist church, for the Pepper Street chapel had become available again. After the English Presbyterians vacated the premises, it had been acquired by the Welsh Independents who used the chapel until they erected a new chapel in Albion Park. The Lancashire and Cheshire Baptist Association purchased the property in 1871 in order to plant a church. The work prospered and in 1880 a new chapel was erected in Grosvenor Park.

The Grosvenor Park Church thrived for several decades but in the late 1950s a road building and demolition programme meant that large numbers left the area and at one time the membership declined to single figures. However, with the arrival of a lay pastor, R. Hulme, in 1970 and emphasis on evangelism the situation changed. In the late 1970's it was decided to move to the suburbs and in September 1980 the church moved to Upton, where a new building was erected, and the church changed its name to Upton Baptist Church.[272] The church left the Baptist Union following the 1971 controversy caused by Rev. Michael Taylor.

The Grosvenor Park building was acquired by a group of Baptists 'upholding the doctrines of Grace' and the building is now known as Zion Tabernacle.[273]

Chester (Hoole)

In 1881 local people worshipping at Ebenezer Baptist Chapel decided to open a mission in a Reading Room / Lecture Room in New Peploe Street in the Bishopsfield area of Hoole. Following the death of the Reading Room's owner and his wife, the property was put up for sale in 1911. Ebenezer Baptist Church was unable to raise the funds to purchase the property. A member of Grosvenor Park Baptist Church intended at first to acquire the building as a business proposition but he offered it to his church. The members were invited to join Grosvenor Park Church and this arrangement continued until 1952 when Hoole Baptist Church was formed as an independent cause. The church is in membership with the North Western Baptist Association and the Baptist Union and with a membership in 2004 of 96 has the largest membership of the Baptist churches of Chester.[274]

Chirbury

The village of Chirbury is 3 miles from Montgomery. John Hall, a founder member of Pontesbury Baptist Church, began the work in the village in 1829 and during the eighteenth months he was there was instrumental in raising a school of eighteen members. He was then asked to go to Gorsley, where there was a Goff's School, and he served with great distinction as the pastor of the Baptist church.[275]

The Chirbury church was received into the Shropshire Association in June 1831.[276] On Friday, 19 September 1834 Mr. William Bird of Churchstoke, Montgomeryshire was 'set apart to the pastoral office over the church'.[277] By trade he was a shoemaker. At the same service Mr. Evans, probably Samuel Evans, tailor of Chirbury[278], was 'set apart by prayer for the office of deacon.' The church was still in existence in 1841, since on 15 July that year Elizabeth Breeze was received into membership of the church at Welshpool

IN
MEMORY OF
JOHN HALL.
50 YEARS PASTOR
OF THE CHURCH
WORSHIPPING IN THIS PLACE.
A MAN OF GOD.
A GOOD MINISTER OF JESUS CHRIST.
A FRIEND OF ALL IN NEED.
HIS FAITHFUL PREACHING OF THE GOSPEL
HIS DEVOTED CARE OF HIS FLOCK.
AND THE ABUNDANT SUCCESS OF HIS LABOURS
HAVE EMBALMED HIS MEMORY.
IN THE GRATEFUL HEARTS OF HIS PEOPLE.
HE ENTERED INTO REST
MAY 11TH 1885. AGED 79 YEARS.
THIS TABLET WAS ERECTED AND CHAPEL RESTORED AS A TRIBUTE OF
AFFECTION BY THE MEMBERS OF THE CHURCH AND MANY FRIENDS.

John Hall's Memorial Tablet in Gorsley Baptist Chapel

by transfer from the church at Chirbury. As far as is known, the church never erected its own building. The church was last listed in *Account of the Proceedings of the Baptist Union* in 1843 and presumably closed soon afterwards.

Minister

Bird, William	1834-40

Chorley

Baptist work at Chorley began when some members of the Bridgnorth Baptist Church, who resided in the area of Chorley, held meetings in the village at Pear Tree Cottage above the cellar of the Duck Inn. Chorley is first listed as a branch of Bridgnorth in *The Baptist Handbook* in 1857. 1867. Largely through the efforts of Mr. Richard Price, it was decided to build a chapel at High Green in 1878. Lady Crompton of Chorley Hall gave the land for the chapel. Apparently she became disaffected with the Church of England when the vicar of Stottesdon refused to bury her baby in consecrated ground on the grounds that it had not been 'baptized'.[279] She laid one of the foundation stones of the chapel on 23 September 1878. The chapel was registered for the solemnization of marriages in 1884. A baptistry was built in 1887 and the first baptisms took place in 1892.

For some time the pulpit was supplied by preachers from Bridgnorth and the Pastor undertook to conduct services on alternate Sundays. In the days of limited transport this meant that on occasions the journeys had to be made on foot.

About 1970 the church was given land on the other side of the road opposite the chapel and this is used as a car park and burial ground.

The church at Chorley was first listed as a branch of Bridgnorth in *The Baptist Handbook* 1867. The Trusteeship of the premises was transferred to the West Midland Baptist Trust in 1934. The church became independent of the mother church of Bridgnorth in 1948 and joined the West Midland Baptist Association in 1950, although it did not join The Baptist Union.

Ministers

Whitney, Geoffrey H. (Lay)	1978-83
Stirrup, Eric (Lay)	1983-03.01
Vincent, Alan (Joint Lay Leader)	12.2000 (inducted 06.01)-
Vincent, Sue (Joint Lay Leader)	12.2000 (inducted 06.01)-

Church Stretton

A dwelling house was registered for use by Baptists in 1808[280] but a church was not subsequently formed in this town.

Coxall

Coxall is in the parish of Bucknell. William and John Price, who were Baptists, were forced to leave their home in Bucknell about 1713 because of religious hostility and they moved to Garth Fawr, Montgomeryshire.[281] We know of no further Baptist work in Bucknell parish until 1865. The church book of Coxall Baptist Church, which dates from 1871, records:

Mr. Thomas Rogers, having with his wife settled at

Coxall Baptist Chapel

> Coxall Farm opened their doors for the preaching of the Gospel 29th September 1865 when a sermon was preached by Rev. J. Smith, Pontesbury.

Rev. Joseph Smith served as pastor of Pontesbury Baptist Church from 1850 to 1852 and thereafter worked as an evangelist in Shropshire and the adjacent counties, dying at the early age of 41 in 1869.[282]

Soon after 1865 a granary was converted into a Meeting Room where a few friends met together for public worship, having a sermon, sometimes two, preached every Sabbath by supplies from Knighton. This continued until April 1870 with pretty good attendance and then Rev. J. H. Wait supplied the pulpit and the church agreed to pay him £10 for his services. The church was formed in 1870.

Mr. William Smith, farmer of The Oak, gave land for building a chapel by the road between Bucknell and Bedstone. The land was transferred to Mr. Rogers on 26 May 1871. A Mr. or a Mrs. Evans of Knighton laid the foundation stone of the chapel on 6 June 1871. The building, which has been described as 'Welsh in appearance'[283], was opened for worship 2 January 1872. Later a Sunday School was opened 'with very pleasing signs of success'.

When Mr. Wait was unable to be at Coxall, Mr. James Gay, a local schoolmaster, preached at the chapel. As he was not able to devote a whole Sunday to the ministry at Coxall, Mr. Wait resigned and James Gay was appointed in his place. In 1873 Gay became minister of the church at Knighton.

In 1876 Rev. J. H. Wait became pastor at Coxall and the following year the church joined the Old Welsh Baptist Association.[284] By 1880 Mr. Wait was also responsible for the branch church at Whitcott. From 1879-1891 he was listed in the *Baptist Handbook* as an Accredited Minister and his address was given as Bucknell (sometimes Bucknall), Shropshire.

In August 1878 Rev. William Williams became pastor of the Knighton church and the Coxall church requested that he should become their pastor as well. The Knighton church agreed and the joint pastoral arrangement has continued until the present.

The church was blessed by the Welsh Revival and in February 1905 fifteen candidates were baptized by Rev. William Williams.[285] A newspaper cutting said to date from 1906 describes mission meetings held at Coxall conducted by Miss Richards, one of Evan Roberts' missioners:

> Miss Richards from Jan. 31st to Feb. 7th inclusive conducted a week's mission. The Chapel was crowded every night and splendid results have followed, 36 have decided to follow Christ.

A further newspaper cutting of 1906 relates,

> A Baptismal service was held on Sunday April 1st, when the pastor Rev. Williams, baptized seventeen candidates in the presence of a very large congregation, many not being able to gain admittance. The service was a very impressive one and several more candidates are waiting to be baptized on May 6th.[286]

The chapel was renovated in 1928 at a cost of £28, which was principally raised by means of a sale of work. The graveyard was extended in 1930, the land being given by Capt. J. R. H. Harley.[287]

In 1947 a member of the church C. Leslie Evans, son of the then Church Secretary and brother of the present Church Secretary, entered Manchester Baptist College to train for the ministry. As far as is known he is the only former member of the church to have entered the Baptist ministry.

Ministers

Wait, John Henry (*Supply*)	1870
Gay, James	- 1873
Wait, John Henry	1876-8
Joint pastorate with Norton Street, Knighton	*1878-present*

Craven Arms

At the junction of the turnpike roads, north-south from Shrewsbury to Ludlow, and west-east from Clun to Bridgnorth, in the ecclesiastical parish of Stokesay stood an inn catering for the needs of travellers. Thomas Conder's 1784 Map of Shropshire shows New Inn. This inn was replaced by the present inn built *c.* 1830,[288] and called The Craven Arms in honour of the local landowner, the Earl of Craven. With the coming of the Shrewsbury and Hereford Railway, about 1852 the first steps were taken towards the building of the 'new town' of Craven Arms. Buildings were erected in the vicinity of the railway station *c.* 1852. Following the completion of the Central Wales Line to Swansea in 1891, the owners of the meadows between Newton and Coverdale realized their obvious potential. Land was soon marked out in building plots and roads were built and by 1890 most of the buildings for the new town were in place. William, 2nd Earl of Craven (1809-66), and George, 3rd Earl (1841-83), were presumably responsible for the development.[289]

Rev. Matthew Matthews, who had been pastor at Aston-on-Clun, began holding services in a cottage and this continued until in 1872 when Mr. H. T. Alcroft built a chapel for him in the township of Newton.[290] The church was first listed in *The Baptist Handbook* in 1873, where it is called 'Newton, Craven Arms' while the following year it was called simply 'Newton'. By 1876 a branch was opened at Vernot's Common and then by 1882 the church at Aston-on-Clun had become a branch cause. It was not until 1886 that the church was called 'Craven Arms' in *The Baptist Handbook.*

In 1879 the Newton church left the Shropshire Association but it was not until 1883 that it joined the Old Welsh Association. At its 1884 Conference the Association gave 'a hearty vote of thanks to J.D. Alcroft Esq., of London, for his great kindness and generous liberality in supporting the Baptist cause at Newton, Stokesay, Salop, and his great kindness towards our esteemed brother, M. Matthews'. In 1887 the Association also recorded its 'heartiest thanks for his liberality to the church in restoring their chapel'.

In 1888 the Old Welsh Association created a Home Mission Fund and in its first year churches and individuals contributed £13 15s 5½d and to this amount the Craven Arms church gave 13s 6d. The only church to benefit from this Fund during its first year was the Craven Arms church which received £4 9s 10½d. The church received further grants in subsequent years.

In 1917 the church left the Welsh Association to join the Shropshire District of the West Midland Baptist Association but the church's days were numbered. In 1919 the General Secretary of the Association reported:

> For many months only occasional services have been held in the Chapel at Craven Arms and at last these could not be continued. Various plans were suggested and tried but none proved successful, and ultimately it was decided that there was no need for a Baptist Church, that the requirements for Free Church worship were met by other denominations and the building has been closed.

In the 1990's a number of members of Crowmoor Baptist Church, Shrewsbury, began work in Craven Arms, which resulted in the formation of an Evangelical Church there.

Minister

MATTHEWS, Matthew	1872-05.11.1906

Cwm

The remote hamlet of Cwm is 5 miles W of Bishop's Castle and 4 miles E of Sarn, near Offa's Dyke (Clawydd Offa), in Cartwright Township in the parish of Mainstone. On local road signs, but not on Ordnance Survey maps, it is called 'The Cwm'. It was in Montgomeryshire until 1974 when the county was incorporated into the new county of Powys.

In 1833 James Morrish of Bishop's Castle registered a meeting house in the occupation of George Weaver at the Mainstone in the parish of Mainstone as a Place of Religious Worship by an Assembly or Congregation of Protestants. A building erected in 1837 for the Independents was used by them until 'there was scarcely *any* congregation and *no* preacher'. The building was then taken over by the Baptists at Sarn. The earliest account of a baptism there [1845] is as follows:

> On the Lord's day, May 18, our pastor, Mr. W. Jones, baptized two candidates in the open air. The first went down with him into the water was an aged man nearly ninety. The almond tree flourished, the grasshopper was almost a burden, and yet he went through the service. The other had been an Independent.[291]

At the time of the 1851 Religious Census the chapel was known as Philadelphia Chapel (a name that was subsequently dropped). The average attendance over the year was 20 scholars in the morning and 40 in the afternoon.[292] In 1873 the cause at Cwm became a separate church in membership with the Old Welsh Association. However, the minister of Sarn continued to serve as pastor of Cwm.

Former Cwm Chapel (now a private house)

The work at Cwm progressed and there was need for a larger building. It is believed that the building which was opened in 1897 was originally two cottages. A grass island in the road in front of the present building is thought to be the site of the first building. The new building, which had 130 seats, as well as a stable for two horses, was built by Messrs. E. Davies and Son of Newtown and was opened on 29 October.[293] As the Chapel did not have a baptistry, baptisms took place in the brook in front of the Chapel.

Rev. William Jenkins

The Sarn Church organized a rota to take their minister to Cwm, first by pony and trap and later by car. Rev. William Jenkins, who served from 1899 to 1916, was a keen cyclist and the Sarn church provided him with a bicycle to make his journeys to Cwm and for his pastoral work. In the 1930s the church purchased a car for its minister. Rev. Penry Davies (1948-56 & 1975-80) found driving a car difficult and he either cycled to Cwm or caught a bus from Llywn Cowrid Corner to the Bluebell Inn and then walked to the Cwm Chapel. Services at Cwm were on Sunday afternoons except on the third Sunday of the month when there was an evening service.

When the Sarn Church left the Welsh Association in 1899 and joined the Shropshire Association, the Cwm Church also joined the Shropshire Association but retained its membership of the Radnorshire and Montgomeryshire Association. So the Cwm church continued to practise close communion. Rev. William Jenkins served as President of the Shropshire Association from 1904 to 1905 and the Radnorshire and Montgomeryshire Association from 1914 to 1916. At the close of his ministry in 1916 the Cwm Church left the Welsh Association.

The services at Cwm were suspended in 1973 at the end of the ministry of Rev. Robert Davies. It was hoped to re-open the church on the arrival of the next minister, Rev. Harold Nicklin. He commenced his ministry at Sarn on 7 April 1974, and was inducted to the joint pastorate of the Sarn and Cwm churches on 20 April that year. Sadly his health deteriorated rapidly and he died on 20 May 1975. As there now seemed no prospect of re-opening the work at Cwm, the building was sold. For a while it was used as an art gallery, known as the Dyke Gallery, but the venture was not successful and it was converted into a private house.

Minister

Branch of Sarn	*c. 1845-73*
Joint Pastorate with Sarn	*1873- 1973*

Dawley[294]

A congregation of Particular Baptists was formed at Dawley Bank in 1817 and an evangelist, Mr. Meabury (or Meabry), travelled regularly from Birmingham to conduct services. He became a member of the Shropshire Itinerant Society and is to be identified with Mr. Maybery, the Shropshire Itinerant, who became pastor at Minsterley in 1817.[295] However, a new start was needed in 1829. At first services were held in cottages and baptisms were conducted in the open air in a stretch of water known as Morgan's Pool. The pioneers of the work were two men both named James Jones. One had been baptized by John Palmer of Shrewsbury and was a deacon at Wellington Baptist Church and the other was a deacon at Old Chapel, Broseley. Dawley was not listed among the Shropshire churches in the *Baptist Manual* until 1849. In *The Baptist Handbook* from 1861 onwards 1846 was given as the date of founding of the church.

James Jones (Mossey Green)

Land, which had previously been used as a bullring, was purchased for the erection of a chapel on 1 December 1840 for £29. The first building with a seating capacity of 200, together with a house for a minister, was erected in 1846 at a cost of £400. The following year additional ground was bought at the back of the building on which to build a schoolroom at a total cost of £136. In May 1851, in an effort to provide further accommodation, galleries were added on three sides of the sanctuary of the chapel. On Census Sunday 1851 the chapel was attended by 60 adults in the morning and 180 in the evening. There were 90 Sunday scholars in the morning and 110 in the afternoon. Rev. Alfred Cox, who completed the Census Form, commented that 'We are now erecting galleries which seat 140 more persons'. At the time the chapel served worshippers from Hadley, Ketley Bank, and Newdale as well as from the various settlements in Dawley.[296]

Notwithstanding the erection of galleries by 1859 the building was totally inadequate to meet the demands of all who wished to worship at Dawley Bank. So although there was still an outstanding debt of £140, it was resolved to pull down the chapel, the schoolroom and minister's house, and erect a new building on the site.[297] The foundation stone of the new chapel was laid on 14 May 1860, the opening services being held on 30 September 1860. These services were continued on 14 October when the preacher at both the morning and evening services was the 16th Lord Teynham. A vestibule was added to the front of the church in 1896, whilst in 1906 the walls of the vestibule were raised to include stairs to a new gallery and an organ loft. During the building operations meetings took place in other Churches and schoolrooms. The congregation returned to the church building in January 1907.

A pipe organ was installed in the front of the Gallery in 1863 but in 1936 was made redundant when another organ purchased at a cost of £620 was placed next to the pulpit, as a memorial to a previous organist and choirmaster, and oak panelling was also installed.

In 1862 a Burial Club was formed in connection with the Sunday School, the sum of one penny per member per month, entitling a bereaved family to a bonus of £2. Then in 1871, it was decided to purchase ground to be used as a cemetery across the parish boundary at Lawley Bank.[298]The Club itself continued until March 1911.

A house, which had been the residence for the minister since around 1881, became the property of the Church when the Coalbrookdale Company Estate was sold.

Congregations remained large until slum clearance and rebuilding in the 1960s scattered the community around Dawley Bank. In the 1990's it was decided to demolish the church building and replace it with a building more suitable for present day use. Prior to the demolition of the old building a Thanksgiving Service was held on Saturday, 9 October 1999. It was led by the lay pastor, Mr. John Wye, and two former ministers took part in the service, Rev. Douglas Monkley (1970-75) and Rev. Peter Hayes (1990-96). The new building was opened on Saturday, 13 January 2001, and the address was given by the President of The Baptist Union, Professor Graham Ashworth, CBE.

Dawley Chapel (1860)

Dawley Chapel (1946)

Dawley Chapel (2001)

Ministers

Wrigley, W.	5.10.1848-49 (ordained 01.01.49)
Cox, Alfred	24.11.1850-52
Lawrence, Henry	30.05.1854- 55
Skemp, Thomas	01.08.1857- 08.11.63
Thorne, John Wright	24.07.1864–67
Deavin, Charles	24.01.1868-14.05.70
Wootton, William	1870–76
Wilson, George	1876–79
Spanton, Emery	1881–89
Cook, James E. W.	1890–92
Lester, Arthur	1892-1920
Williams, William	1920-31
Jones, Henry Mostyn	1931-48
Evans, David Morgan	1950-58
James, Geraint Llewellyn	1959-21.06.64
Williams, Morgan Watcyn	1965–69
Monkley, Douglas Reginald	1970-75
Price-Stephens, Edward	1977-87
Hayes. Peter John	1990 -96
Wye, John (Lay)	1997-02
Allcock, Andrew John, BA, BSc	14.09.2002 -

Donnington Wood

It is evident that a number of Baptist families were residing in the Donnington area at the beginning of the nineteenth century. At Donnington William Snow and four others registered his house for worship in 1811.[299] Among those who signed the application were Thomas Wycherley, who was to become pastor at Donnington Wood, and Richard Pickering, who registered his own house for worship in 1813.[300] Pickering, who was described as an engineer in 1813, became a manager of a brickworks according to the 1841 Census. The house of John Barnett, labourer, at Donnington Wood was similarly licensed in 1814.[301]

In 1820 a Baptist church was formed at Donnington Wood. The minutes of Claremont Baptist Church for June 25 record the dismissal of Sister Mary Cartwright to unite with 11 others to form a 'Church of the same Faith and Order at Donnington Wood'. A chapel with a vestry was erected in 1830.[302] This building, which is in Queens Road, is at a bend in the road known locally as 'The Bell Corner', named after The Bell Public House. The building has been altered somewhat and is now for commercial purposes. A plaque on the front of the building had the somewhat unusual wording, 'Baptist Chapel - Established 1820 - Restored 1906.'[303] There was a burial ground beside the chapel.

By the time St. Matthew's Church was erected in 1843[304] Nonconformity was well established in Donnington Wood. When the 2nd Duke of Sutherland, who was the local landowner, was standing near the site where the Church was being erected, he said to a poor miner that it would be a great asset for the area to have a church. The miner replied, 'Yes, zur, if thur is a godly mon in it, what prach-is th' gos-pull; thank the Lord! foaks here know what's the gos-pull, 'fore the church walls are up.' A fascinating glimpse of life at the time was published in a book *Sights in the Pit and Peeps in Glory* recounting the religious experience of Mary Rider, who attended the Baptist Sunday School. She died from consumption in 1862. She was laid to rest in the parish church's burial ground but the funeral service was preached by the Baptist minister, Rev. Frederick Hemus, presumably in the Baptist chapel.[305]

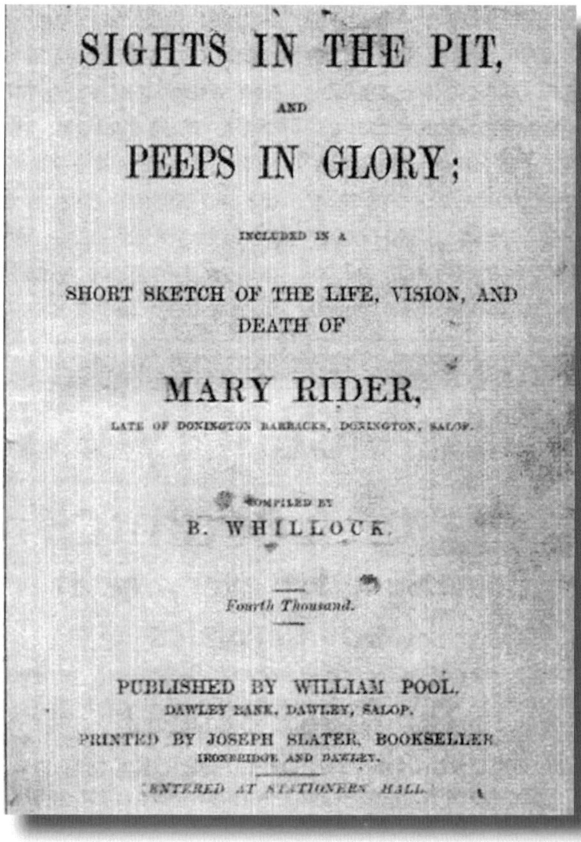
SIGHTS IN THE PIT,

AND

PEEPS IN GLORY;

INCLUDED IN A

SHORT SKETCH OF THE LIFE, VISION, AND DEATH OF

MARY RIDER,

LATE OF DONINGTON BARRACKS, DONINGTON, SALOP.

COMPILED BY

B. WHILLOCK.

Fourth Thousand.

PUBLISHED BY WILLIAM POOL,
DAWLEY BANK, DAWLEY, SALOP.
PRINTED BY JOSEPH SLATER, BOOKSELLER
IRONBRIDGE AND DAWLEY.
ENTERED AT STATIONERS' HALL.

From 1822 until 1880 the church had its own minister. On Census Sunday 1851 50 people attended the service in the morning, 100 people in the afternoon, and 200 in the evening. The average congregation was given as 100 adults and 170 Sunday scholars.[306] In the 1850's Donnington Wood was thought to be a place where a minister might regain his strength after an exhausting pastorate elsewhere! So Rev. Cornelius Morell, who had been forced to resign the pastorate at Netherton, near Dudley, because of ill-heath, came to the village about 1857. He intended to remain at Donnington Wood for about twelve months. However, he did not stay long as he was pressed to give assistance at the church at Brettel Lane, Staffordshire.[307] The church then called to the pastorate a shoe-maker, Frederick Hemus. Timothy Baugh, who had previously been a pastor at Aston Street, Shifnal, came to the church in 1878 but only stayed for a year. In the 1881 Census he is described as an Iron and Brass founder employing 3 men and a boy.

From 1885 until 1905 for varying periods Wellington, Madeley, and Oakengates Baptist Churches had oversight of the church at Donnington Wood. In 1902 the Wellington church gave notice that it intended to discontinue its oversight, although the Wellington minister, Rev. E. Hardin continued to preside at church meetings until May 1903. In 1905 the Donnington Wood church invited Charles Doughty, a retired railway signalman, of Church Aston to become the Pastor at the princely sum of 7/- per week. He remained for four years until he moved to Welshpool. The report of the General Secretary of the West Midland Association in 1917 stated that 'The Pastor of the Wellington Church, when appointed will have oversight at Donnington Wood' but this does not appear to have happened.

From 1909 until 1956 lay preachers filled the pulpit and it must have been sometime in this period when the church adopted open communion. In 1952 and again in 1953 the church had student pastors from Manchester Baptist College. Although the church had wished to have a fulltime minister from the end of World War 2 and it had extended an invitation to Rev. Frederick Baker of Sarn in 1946, it did not have pastoral oversight until 1956 when the church called a deaconess, Sister Constance Nash. During her ministry the membership rose from 20 to 52.

After 1905 the baptistry in the chapel was not used and baptisms took place at Wellington Free Church. However, four people who were baptized there in 1939 made a pledge to be responsible for putting the Donnington Wood baptistry in order. Rev. Glyndwr Morgan, of Wellington, dedicated the new baptistry on 18 February 1940. A major post-war refurbishment of the building was undertaken and this culminated in a week of special meetings in April 1951 for the Baptist Advance Campaign. Ministers from the West Midland Baptist Association were visiting speakers and four students from Manchester Baptist College helped in the visitation of the neighbourhood.

Donnington Wood Chapel erected in the 1820s

Donnington Wood Chapel erected in 1968-69

Owing to the deteriorating condition of the church building, it was decided to erect a new building in the same area, and land was purchased from the then H. Brown Bus Company in Queen's Road in the Spring of 1966.

The estimated cost of the new Church building was £10,000. Sacrificial giving raised £2,000 but it was necessary for the church to have a loan of £8,000 from the Baptist Union Corporation.

The stone laying ceremony on Saturday 30 November 1968 was performed by Mr. George H. Dean, BEM, JP, who had previously served as Church secretary for 38 years. On Saturday 20 September 1969 members and friends walked from the old chapel to the new one, which was officially opened by Mrs. Isabella Poppitt of Canada. Originally she had planned to bequeath her bungalow opposite the new church to Mr. Dean but he persuaded her to give it instead to the church for use as a Manse, as the minister had to live in a house provided by the local Council. Rev. Stephen Winward, President of the West Midland Baptist Association, dedicated the new church building and the preacher was Rev. Constance Nash. The preacher at the evening service was Rev. Dennis Weller, who had been brought up in the church and baptized there before entering Manchester Baptist College to train for the ministry. Also taking part in the service was Mrs. Rhoda Weller (neé Dean), a former member representing the fifth generation of her family to be in membership with the church. On 13 March 2004 a service was held at the church to mark 60 years of service in the Gospel by Rev. Dennis Weller, when the preacher was Rev. Michael Collis of Sarn.

Ministers

Snow, -	1822–30
Ashford, Joseph	1830-31(?)
Wycherley, Thomas E.	1831-37
Bonner, William Harding	*c.* 1838
Jones, W.	1839-49
Morgan, Joseph	1849-55
Brindley, -	1856
Morell, Cornelius	1857
Hemus, Frederick	1858–70
Bristow, Thomas Smith	1871-72
Rigby, B. W.	1873
Ruscoe (or Roscoe?), J.	1873-78
Baugh, Timothy	1878
Roscoe, J.	1880
Branch of Wellington	*1884*
Joint Pastorate with Madeley and Shifnal, Zion	*1885-88*
Joint Pastorate with Oakengates	*1889-98*
Joint Pastorate with Wellington	*1899-1905*
Doughty, Charles Henry,	1905-09
Drake, Ralph (*Student Pastor)*	1952
Williams, David Tryweryn (*Student Pastor)*	1953
Nash. Sister Constance (Mary)	1956- 66
Francis, David John Francis, BA, DipTh	1967-72
Hayden, Eric William, MA	21.07.1973-18.07.76
Message, Hugh	09.09.1978-31.12.81
Rous, Derek, MBE, BA (Lay)	1996-12.2006

Ellesmere

Elllesmere is 16 miles NW of Shrewsbury and in 1659 there was a General Baptist Church there.[308] It had ceased by *c.* 1700, since Richard Gough wrote in *The History of Myddle*, which he began that year:

> Thomas Wolp was a shoemaker in Ellesmere. Hee was a good religiouse man, of sober and discreet discourse, but hee was somewhat tormented with a crew of Phanaticall persons in that towne, which were termed Anabaptists or Dippers. The ring-leader of them was John Caper, a glover, butt I believe they are now extinct in that place.[309]

In September 1798 John Palmer of Shrewsbury, together with three others registered 'An Edifice or Building known by the name of Meeting House' for worship by 'Independent Baptists' in Ellesmere.[310] The cause, however, did not prosper.

Fitz

The hamlet of Fitz lies 5 miles NW of Shrewsbury between the River Perry and the River Severn. The house of George Bean called Albion House was registered for Baptist worship in 1799[311] but a church was not formed there.

Frodesley

Frodesley is a village 7m SSE of Shrewsbury and in 1711 an Anabaptist meeting was registered at the house of John Wilcox. [312] The cause seems to have been short-lived.

Hadley[313]

Hadley is 1¼ miles ENE of Wellington and in 1816 the house of George Dean, a Particular Baptist, was licensed for worship. In 1841 his house lay on the south side of High Street and meetings were probably still being held there. It was afterwards greatly enlarged at the rear, probably soon after 1840, and in 1851 the Baptist meeting room, presumably, an extension to Dean's house, was building used exclusively for worship. In 1851 it had 139 sittings and on Census Sunday: there were 25 adults and 62 Sunday scholars in the afternoon and 45 in the evening. [314] The Census return was signed by H. G. Grainger, the minister of Wellington Baptist Church. On March 6 1859 Mr. Jones of Hadley baptized two people at Donnington Wood but it is not known whether they had any connection with the chapel at Hadley.[315] The subsequent history of this cause is unknown.

Highley

The village of Highley is on a ridge on the steep West bank of the River Severn, 5½ miles SSE of Bridgnorth and coal was mined in Highley until 1969. Following an evangelistic campaign by Miss Bythaway from Walsall *c.* 1939 a group of believers met in the village. After several years Mr. Rogers, who owned the local fish and chip shop, gave land in the High Street for building a chapel and the foundations were laid in the 1940s. A local builder, Mr. Reg. Hughes, with the help of his father-in-law, Mr. Rogers, built the chapel in the 1950s. It was known at first as 'The Mission'.

Highley Chapel in April 2003

The church had lay leadership until Rev. Stanley Woods was appointed in 1959 and the church's name was changed to The People's Church *c.* 1960. He built the baptistery and during his ministry the church grew. After 6½ years he left to work in Guyana and, after his return to England, he became Pastor of The People's Chapel, Partington, and an Accredited Baptist Union Minister.

After an interregnum of about 18 months the church called an Assemblies of God minister, Tom Chapman, but he died after only 3 years. It was during his pastorate that the name of the church was changed to Calvary Free Church. He was succeeded by Rev. Jonathan Booth, who came to the church after 3 years study at Birmingham Bible Institute. He served as pastor for 6½ years before he moved to Wales to become British Director of World Horizons. Kevin Banks, a member of Bridgnorth Baptist Church, then became Lay Pastor and ministered there until 1983 when he went to London to train at a Bible College. Several members then left and the cause closed, although two of the Trustees continued to meet in the building for prayer.

By the end of 1982 Bridgnorth Baptist Church and its minister, Rev. Bernard Thompson, were involved in discussions about the future of the work at Highley. A minute of the Bridgnorth church meeting held on 4 July 1983 recorded that 'A few people are still needed to commit themselves to go to Highley every Sunday morning for a time'. Members were asked to pray about whether they should be involved there and it was reported that two members of the church, Geoff Wilkinson and Steve Ward, were overseeing the work but another six were needed to commit themselves to the work for the next six months. A minute of 3 October 1983 referred to money spent on repairs and decoration. A minute of 29 April 1985 recorded that 'Steve and Geoff are finding it difficult' and then on 9 December that year it was reported that the work had been terminated.

A fresh start was then made at Highley and the church was re-opened on 11 December 1986 and the Trustees appointed Mr. Eddie Gormiak as its Pastor. Initially, Cannon Street Baptist Church, Birmingham, and The People's Church, Partington, gave financial help to the church. Then at a service on Sunday 13 September 1987 Rev. Peter Egginton, the Secretary of the West Midland Baptist Association, formally constituted the church of 10 members as Highley Baptist Church. In February 1988 Rising Brook Baptist Church, Stafford, pledged £20 a month to support the cause and the following month the church was accepted into membership of the Association. The West Midland Baptist (Trust) Association (Incorporated) became the Trustees of the property in 1988.

The Pastor was encouraged to become an Accredited Minister of the Baptist Union and he began part-time study. Unfortunately, the church was unable to support him adequately and he was forced to leave Highley in June 1991. There was then some discussion with The People's Church, Bridgnorth, to see if its pastor could provide oversight.

The church was in an unsettled state and there were those who wished to take the church out of the Association. In July 1991 the church changed its name to Highley Independent Baptist Church and the following year the church now called Highley Evangelical Church withdrew from the Association.

The church once again closed but it was re-opened by Anthony Hyams, who was described as a 'Pentecostalist', but he left the pastorate for personal reasons. Tim Howells came from an 'independent church' at Walsall to help the church and in due course he became its Pastor. The Trusteeship of the building was transferred in 1998 to the Evangelical Fellowship of

Congregational Churches Trust Ltd. The church, then known as Highley Evangelical Church, continued until 2003.

For a number of years the building has suffered from damage to its foundations caused by the roots of trees on the adjoining property. The chapel is in poor state of repair and its future is uncertain.

Ministers

Originally known as The Mission the name was changed to The People's Church	*c.* 1960
Woods, Stanley	1959-66
Chapman, Thomas	1969-72
Church renamed Calvary Free Church	*c.* 1970
Booth, Jonathan	1974 -1980
Under the oversight of Bridgnorth Baptist Church	*1981-c. 1985*
Banks, Kevin (Lay)	1981-1983
Wilkinson, Geoff (*Lay*)	1985(?)
Highley Baptist Church formed 13.09.1987 in membership with the West Midland Baptist Association	*1987-92*
Gormiak, Edward	1986- 06.91
The church, then known as Highley Evangelical Church, left the Association in 1992.	
Hyams, Anthony	1994
Howells, Tim	1995-2002
Highley Evangelical Church in fellowship with the Fellowship of Evangelical Congregational Churches	*1988-2003*

Holt

The Church at Holt, Denbighshire, was founded as a result of the preaching of Rev, George Sayce, minister of Chester Street Church at Wrexham from 1821 to 1847. At first he preached in the open air near "The Cross" and then in houses which were made available to him. In 1826 a cottage and garden were purchased for £50 and here preaching services were held and a Sunday School started. The cottage soon became too small and it was decided to build a chapel and schoolroom. The Sunday School at this time numbered 120 and was the only one in Holt. Raising the money for erecting a chapel was not easy. Miss Rowe, who had attended the home meetings, left £20 for the erection of a Baptist chapel in Holt. Mr. Sayce had to travel through fourteen counties with a collecting book and by this means raised a large sum of money which together with a loan of £250, Miss Rowe's legacy and a grant from the Baptist Building Fund in London met the expenses. The chapel was opened on 29 April 1828[316] and was repaired in 1894 at a cost of £105.[317]

On Census Sunday 1851 there were 17 scholars in the morning, 17 adults plus 15 scholars in the afternoon, and 70 adults plus 30 scholars in the evening.[318] In 1915, together with its mother church at Chester Street, the church joined the North Wales Union of the Lancashire and Cheshire Baptist Association. The last mention of the church in the minutes of the Chester Street Church was in 1936 and the church appears to have closed about 1939. The building is now used as a furniture store.

Former Holt Baptist Chapel 2003

Ministers

Branch of Wrexham, Chester Street 1828-1900	*1828-1900*
Joint Pastorate with Wrexham, Bradley Road, and Lodge Brymbo	*1900-01*
Branch of Wrexham, Chester Street	*1901-c. 39*

Hook-a-gate

Hook-a-gate (Hooker Gate) is a hamlet in the Township of Whitley and Welbach in the parish of St. Chads. It is 3 miles SW of Shrewsbury. In 1807 Rev. James Palmer and others made application for the registration of a meeting house as a place of worship for Baptists in the village of Hookagate.[319] In 1819 at the Shropshire Annual Meeting Brother Meabury was appointed to supply several places including 'the Hook-a-gate'.[320] Bagster's *History, Gazetteer and Directory of Shropshire* (1851) mentioned the existence of a small Baptist chapel, 'near to which the colliers worked till within the last few years'.

One of the memorial stones in front of the entrance to Claremont Baptist Church is to Josiah and John Wilson. The inscription reads:

SACRED TO THE MEMORY OF
Josiah Wilson
who departed this life 18th August 1851
also
James son of the above who died in infancy 1821
....
ALSO OF

JOHN WILSON of Smithfield Road son of the above
who died 15th November 1884

John Wilson, who was interred in the General Cemetery, Shrewsbury, was a Sunday School teacher at Hook-a-Gate and a member at Claremont at one time being a Deacon and Church Treasurer. His son Josiah, who was also a Deacon of Claremont until he was afflicted by total blindness, [321] does not appear to have been associated with the work at Hook-a-gate.

At the Annual meeting of the Shropshire Association in June 1877 Mr. C. Nutsey of Claremont Street, Shrewsbury reported that as the small chapel at Hook-a-gate had been 'long unused for religious purposes' the Trustees proposed to sell it. It has not been possible to identify the site of the chapel

Horsebridge

According to *The Baptist Handbook* (1883-95) there was branch of the Pontesbury church at Horsebridge, a hamlet on the B4387 road from Minsterley to Westley.

Ightfield (Mossfield Chapel)

Ightfield is a village situated 4 miles SE of Whitchurch. The work in the village was commenced by a deacon of Oswestry English Baptist Church and a chapel was opened there in 1844.[322]

Another chapel was opened in 1847:[323]

> IGHTFIELD, SALOP. A new meeting-house was opened here, Oct 3, with sermons by Messrs Manning of Bristol college[324] and Minshull of Prees;[325] the Lord's Supper was administered in the evening. The congregations are good and there is much promise of usefulness. Until recently evangelical religion was unknown in the village and neighbourhood but, by the labours of a few individuals, a congregation has been collected, a sabbath school formed, and now a chapel erected and opened.

The chapel was on the east side of the Ightfield-Millenheath road about half a mile south of Ightfield village and some fifty yards north of Maltkin Farm. The baptistry is said to have been in the aisle and to have been covered when not in use. The 1858 marriage certificate of Charles Gresty (son of William and Ann buried here) records that he was 'married according to the Rites and Ceremonies of the Congregationalists.' The officiating Minister was Samuel Minshull.

The small burial ground contains seven memorial stones and also a tomb with the following inscription:

Sacred to the memory of James Edward Yeadon
Beloved Pastor of the Baptist Churches of Whitchurch
and Ightfield (1862-1870) who entered into his reward
6 Sept 1870 aged 33 years

Remember I have tried to preach Jesus

The last person to be interred on this site died in 1936.

On Census Sunday 1851 there were 36 present in the morning and 59 in the afternoon. The average attendance over 12 months was given as 75 plus 25 Sunday scholars. [326] The church was first listed in *The Baptist Manual* 1852 when it had 21 members. By the following year it had united with the church at Whitchurch and the church of Whitchurch & Ightfield was a founder member of the reorganized Shropshire Association in 1853. From 1874 it was listed in *The Baptist Handbook* as a branch of Whitchurch. The Ightfield church closed in 1937 and the building was then used as a store. The building has since been demolished but the burial ground remains.[327]

Ministers

From 1853 the pastor of Whitchurch was also pastor of Ightfield.

Ironbridge

Rev. John Thomas, of Old Chapel, Broseley, registered a dwelling house at Ironbridge in the parish of Benthall for worship by Baptists in 1811[328] but a church was not formed there. According to *The Baptist Handbook* (1894-96) there was branch of the Birch Meadow, Broseley, at Ironbridge.

Knighton (Norton Street) [329]

The border town of Knighton is known in Welsh as *Trefyclo*, although road signs nowadays refer to it as *Tref-y-Clawdd*, 'town on the dyke', a reference to Offa's Dyke nearby. Although there was a Baptist cause in Knighton in 1742-3[330], the church did not survive and there is no record of Baptist work in the town until 1833. In that year a woman who kept a school in Knighton opened her cottage so that Baptists might meet there for worship. Services were led by Rev. James Jones of Rock Baptist Chapel, Mr. Jacob Price who later went to America, and Mr. Thomas Harvard, who later became Pastor of Maesyrhelem Chapel.

In 1835 a meeting was held in the old Town Hall, where the town clock now stands. Three ministers took part in the service, namely, Samuel Blackmore, of Kington, Benjamin Price, of Newtown, and W. Jenkins, of Dolau Nantmel. Shortly after this Mr. W. S. Mayo, a currier, who was a prominent Baptist in Radnorshire[331], held meetings in his home. Meetings were held subsequently in various other places but Mr. Mayo's high Calvinist views divided the congregation. It was then that Mr. William Davies made his home available for services. He was one of the two Baptists who had begun the work at Gravel, Radnorshire.

In the period 1858-60 the Baptist cause began to prosper in Knighton and in 1860 Rev. T. L. Davies of Presteign (Presteigne) formed the Baptist church there. By 1862 it had joined the Old Welsh Association. The church has in its possession a Bible which was used in its services in 1862. The church was served by visiting preachers including Rev. Thomas Jones of Bettws-y-Crwyn, the son of Rev. James Jones of Rock. A chapel was built in Norton Street and this was opened on 29 September 1865.

During the first twelve years the church had five ministers. Rev. David Evans became the first minister but his ministry lasted exactly six months. Nothing is known about Mr. Griffiths, who followed him. The next minister Rev. John Jones, from Llangwm, Monmouthshire,[332] was a rigid Calvinist who delighted 'to expatiate on the doctrines of grace'. When he left to become minister of Speen, Buckinghamshire, the church asked Mr. Mayo to supply the pulpit. As 'the church was established on Strict Baptist principles, and the deeds specify an adherence to the truths of the Gospel', he joined the church and became an office-holder (elder or deacon?).[333] In 1871 the church called to the pastorate Rev. David Lewis, who was the first pastor of the church at Neyland, Pembrokeshire. After a ministry of two years he moved to Talgarth, Breconshire.

In October 1873 two evangelists came to Knighton from Bristol to conduct evangelistic services in the different chapels in the town. As a result twenty-three people were baptized in the Baptist chapel on 12 October by Rev. James Williams of Evenjobb. Rev. James Gay of Coxall took part in the service and afterwards he became the pastor of the church. Sadly for the last eighteen months of his pastorate he was a very sick man and suffered much pain. While on a visit to Gravel to fulfil a preaching appointment, he was caught in a storm, got soaked to the skin and contracted pleurisy, and on 3 September 1877, he passed away at the early age of thirty-seven.

Stability to the young church was provided by the forty-one year pastorate of William Williams from 1878 to 1919. He founded a branch church at Knucklas in 1897. Sadly, Mr. Williams died under tragic circumstances.[334]

Knighton Baptist Chapel, Norton St.

Old Workshops, Station Road, Knighton
Intended as the site for a new Baptist Chapel and Manse

In 1894 the church, which described itself as 'The Society of Particular Strict Communion Baptists' acquired a carpenter's workshop and a house at the corner of Station Road and Bowling Green Lane for the erection of a new chapel and a manse. However, by a majority vote the church decided to develop the existing premises at Norton Street and the site was never fully used as a chapel. The site was sold in 1921 when it became a carpenter's workshop again.[335]

Those who disagreed with the decision not to proceed with the development of the Station Road site left the Norton Street church and formed a second Baptist church in the town in 1901. This dispute weakened the Norton Street church and it was not until 1922 that the Norton Street premises were completely refurbished and the galleries erected. The interior of the present chapel is notable for its absence of the big seat (*sêt fawr*), where deacons of Welsh Baptist Churches would sit facing the congregation during services. The original entrance to the chapel was closed and a new entrance was made into the building from Russell Street, although the church is still called, Knighton, Norton Street. The re-opening services were held on 15 April 1923.

One member of the Norton Street church, David John Lewis, entered the Baptist ministry after training at Manchester Baptist College. In 1970 Miss Susan Evans, SRN, SCM, was commissioned for missionary work with the Baptist Missionary Society. She later became the Society's Welsh Representative and a member at Newbridge-on-Wye before marrying Mr. David Wilson, FRCS, who is currently Church Secretary of Presteigne Baptist Church.

Ministers

Evans, David.	(6 months)
Griffiths, -	
Jones, John H.	10.1867-70
Lewis, David	1871-3
Gay, James	1873- 03.09.77
Williams, William	08.1879-04.11.1919
Pugh, John	03.1920-22.10.40
Rowson, Thomas (*Honorary Pastor*)	1930- 8.11.34
Richards, David John	12.1941- 66
Baker, Patrick John, BD	1968-79
Brown, Conway Carrington Russell	1980-82
Wood, Stephen Ralph, BD	1983- 03.2003
Rich, Maggie (Margaret S.), BA	13.08.2005-

Knighton (Victoria Road)

A second Baptist church was formed in Knighton in 1901 and it joined the Shropshire Baptist Association that year. A chapel was erected in Victoria Road in 1904. By 1908 the church had 78 members and 100 scholars. The first minister, Rev. Thomas Rhys Broad, was appointed in 1915.

The Annual Meetings of the Shropshire Association were held at Victoria Road 7 and 8 June 1909 and hospitality was provided at the Chandos Hotel by the proprietor, Mr. David Davies, who was the Church Secretary.

When the church closed some members joined the church at Norton Street, while others joined the Methodist Church. The building was sold to the Council for use as a Community Centre. The proceeds were deposited with the West Midland Baptist Association, the investment interest being sent to a church in Radnorshire chosen by the Radnorshire and Montgomeryshire Baptist Association.

In 1986 the Methodist Church at Knighton was in need of a replacement building and they acquired the building from the Council and it is now Victoria Road Methodist Church.

Knighton Methodist Church formerly Victoria Road Baptist Church

Ministers

BROAD, Thomas Rhys	1915-22
NIELD, Samuel	1923-25
EVANS, William Samuel	1926-30
JOHNS, B. D.	1933–37
BROWN, John	1940-45 (and Aston-on-Clun 1944-57)

Little Drayton

Although Little Drayton is now part of Market Drayton, it was for a long time an independent community. At the time of the 1851 Religious Census there was a chapel there, which had been erected in 1815. Services were held every fortnight and there was no stated minister. The average attendance was 20. [336] Nothing further is known about this cause.

Llandrinio (Sarnwen Chapel)

It seems that Rev. John Palmer of Shrewsbury began the work in the parish of Llandrinio. The Ministers and Deacons of the Baptist churches at Shrewsbury, Oswestry and Wellington acquired land in 1810 at Sarn Wen in the parish of Llandrinio.[337] The upper room of a cottage was opened for use as a meeting house[338] in March 1815. An account of the opening of the chapel at 'Llandrenis (*sic.*)' was published in *The Baptist Magazine* in May 1815

The cause at Llandrinio probably remained a preaching station of the Shropshire Itinerant Society until a church was formed in 1829 and it continued to supply preachers until one of its preachers, David Crumpton, was called to the pastorate in 1836. 'He was a strict Calvinist, a good preacher, had a good voice, and able to start the hymn-tunes well. He was very sympathetic with his neighbours and helpful either in the fold-yard or in the garden; if a doctor was needed he was only too pleased to be called on to prescribe.' [339]

Another preacher supported by the Shropshire Itinerant Society was William Owen. He was baptized by Rev. Joseph Ashford, of Welshpool, in the River Vyrnwy in May 1826. He became a member of the Llandrinio church and preached there for four years. There was great regret when he left to become pastor of Madley, Herefordshire, where he was ordained on 3 November 1836.[340]

In 1851 the census return was made by John Evans, the 'Baptist Lay Leader'. He reported that the church had 100 free seats and had an average congregation of 20. He made the following additional remarks on the census form:

> Sir, I confess myself ignorant of many things but this I know that God has exalted one to the British throne of true protistant spirit. May the Lord evermore preserve her royalty that truth may appear and Error flee away.[341]

The church was received into the first Shropshire Baptist Association in 1830.[342] By 1853 the church had united with that at Maesbrook and the united church joined the re-organized Shropshire Association when it was formed that year. From 1874 it was a branch of the English Baptist church at Oswestry. By 1902 the chapel was no longer in use and it became a dwelling house known as Wiltshire House. However, at the Annual Meeting of the Shropshire Association in June 1910 it was agreed that 'the event of the proposed re-opening

Wiltshire House (formerly Llandrinio Chapel)

of Llandrinio Chapel, a grant be made for the expenses of Supplies, the amount to be fixed by the Executive'. As far as is known, the chapel was not re-opened and in 1922 the Charity Commission authorised the Trustees to sell the house and land for not less than £225.[343]

There was a small burial ground on the left of the chapel. The gravestones were removed and the ground levelled. The inscription on the one remaining gravestone reads as follows:

> To the memory of
> ELIZABETH wife of WILLIAM
> THOMAS late of Rhantregunwen
> who departed this life 2nd Novr 1832
> Aged 52 Years

The schoolroom was demolished and the space now forms part of a garden at the rear of the property.

Ministers

CRUMPTON, David	1836-41 (and of Sweeney Mountain from 1837)
EVANS, John (Lay),	1851
United Maesbrook and Llandrinio church	*1853-74*
Branch of English Walls, Oswestry	*1874 until its closure*

Llanhedric

The only information available about a Baptist chapel at Llanhedric is found in a newspaper article about the retirement of Rev. William Jenkins:

> As reported in a recent issue of the Express, the Rev. W. Jenkins has resigned the pastorate of the Baptist Churches at Sarn, Churchstoke [i.e. Cwm] and Llanhedric (Clun).
>
> Three distinct presentations have subsequently been made at these three churches. Llanhendric was first to offer its bounty, when at the close of a preaching meeting Mr. Newman, Three Gates, took the chair and called upon the daughter of Mr. and Mrs. Bright, of Burlow, to formally make the gift. Miss Doris Bright, in a happy little speech, handed over a sum of money and declared that it was one of the happiest days of her life in making the presentation of the purse. Miss Ada Bright then presented the pastor with a handsome volume in equally felicitous terms. ...[344]

Llanhedric is not far from Whitcott Keysett and there is a footpath between the two places.

Longford

Longford is 1 mile SW of Newport. There was a Baptist chapel there that was enlarged in 1849/50[345] but nothing further is known of the work there. The chapel did not make a return for the 1851 Religious Census.

Lord's Hill and Snailbeach[346]

In the late eighteenth century Snailbeach and the district around were thriving because the lead mines, which had been originally worked by the Romans, had been re-opened. Miners were recruited from Cornwall, South Wales and Derbyshire to extract the ore and many of them were Baptists.

The Baptist church at Snailbeach began with help from the Baptist church at Dog Lane, Shrewsbury. In 1788 Rev. William Smith preached at a house near Westbury. His successor Rev. John Palmer preached the Gospel in the villages of Yockleton, Pontesbury, Habberley, Minsterley and Snailbeach. Three converts were baptized in Shrewsbury in 1796. In 1810 John Palmer baptized four men and three women in the brook at Minsterley and they joined the Shrewsbury church. They would walk to the town thirteen miles there and thirteen miles back for communion services.

The monthly journey to Shrewsbury for the communion service proved too trying, especially for the older members. So in November 1817 some twenty-three persons resident in Snailbeach, Minsterley and Pontesbury wrote to the Shrewsbury Church asking for permission to form themselves into a separate Church. Accordingly, on the 4 January 1818 a Church was formed at Snailbeach and the meetings were held in a blacksmith's shop at the Snailbeach Mine. The first Pastor was Rev. Joseph Lakelin, who came from Burslem, Staffordshire. Unable to find accommodation at Snailbeach he was obliged to live at Pontesbury. He went on horseback to preach at Minsterley, Wrentnall and Snailbeach each Sunday.

In 1832 Edward Evans came from Newtown and for

the first year of his ministry at Snailbeach, as was often the case at the time, he was 'on trial'. As the Snailbeach church was flourishing and it was evident that it was necessary to build a permanent meeting-house. Edward Evans travelled up and down the country soliciting financial help for this purpose. The 4th Marquis of Bath owned all the land in Snailbeach and he refused to have a nonconformist chapel on his estate, but the 6th Earl of Tankerville provided a site for the chapel at Lord's Hill. This was purchased without delay and there was sufficient land on which to build a chapel and a Manse, and to leave a portion for a burial ground. A flight of steps North West of the chapel leading down to a small stream appears to indicate where baptisms first took place. A later external baptistry lies south west of the chapel. A modern baptistry was installed in the chapel in the 1860's. The chapel, which was built in 1833 and enlarged in 1873, was much smaller than the present building, the pulpit being placed at the side adjoining the Manse, which was subsequently incorporated into the chapel. A new cottage for use as a manse was built alongside the chapel about 1873.[338] The gallery of the chapel can be reached either by means of stairs within the chapel or by crossing a small bridge from the hillside by the side of the chapel.

Lord's Hill Chapel

Lord's Hill Chapel showing balcony entrance

Samuel Hughes, a lead miner from Crows Nest Dingle, Snailbeach, saw Edward Evans and others building the chapel. This lead to a conversion experience and he became a local preacher and hymn writer. However, he thought that Evans lacked inspiration and became a 'speckled bird', seeking satisfying preaching in Shrewsbury, Broseley, and Little London, near Wolverhampton.[348] Evans 'was an ardent follower of [John] Gill and [Abraham] Booth, in his Calvinistic views, and was never ashamed of giving expression to them'.[349] Ill-health forced him to resign the Snailbeach pastorate in 1866. He moved to Nantwich and it was reported that 'though unable to take a regular pastorate, he will with others endeavour to raise a Baptist cause in the town'.[350] The Baptist chapel there had been re-opened in 1862 and Rev. J. B. Lockwood, pastor from 1864, accepted a call the following year to General Baptist church, Infirmary-street, Bradford.[351] It is surprising in view of his ill-health and his Calvinist theology that the Nantwich church now called Edward Evans as pastor. He continued as pastor until 1869 until 'he was compelled, by reason of declining health and bodily infirmity, to resign his charge'.[352]

On Census Sunday 1851 the Snailbeach church had two congregations. At the Lord's Hill Chapel there was an afternoon congregation of 240 (including 90 Sunday scholars), while at Perkins Beach the morning congregation was 65.[353]

The church played a major part in the lives of many miners. At the Conference of the Old Association held at Lord's Hill in June 1884 the following resolution was passed:

> That this Conference deeply sympathises with the Church at Lord's Hill, under the trying depression of trade in the district through the partial stoppage of the mines, and sincerely hopes that help may be rendered to many families who are thus thrown into distress.

Tragedy hit the local community when on 6 March 1891 the steel rope of the eight foot cage used to convey the miners to the lead seams broke, and seven workmen were killed, four were lay preachers and three were Sunday School teachers.

The 7th Earl of Tankerville, who was major landowner in the area, stayed in the area about 1907 trying to promote mining and provide work for local miners. He and his wife actively supported mission work and he both preached and sang in Lord's Hill Chapel.

For many years a feature of the church life was its hearty singing, both by the choir and the congregation. One of its conductors was Mr. Joseph Evans JP, who also served as the organist at the Lord's Hill chapel. He was choirmaster for over sixty-five years.

Whilst services were always well attended, the chapel would be filled to overflowing for special events such as Easter, Whitsuntide, Sunday School and Church Anniversary Services and Harvest Festivals. Peggy Chidley (born 1917) recalled that the church attracted a congregation from a wide area:

> There was more people I've heard dad say used to come down the road from the Vessons. You'd see the lamps, oil lamps coming. Dad used to reckon there was almost as many people came from over the back side of the hill as there was went from the village.[353]

In the 1930's (?) one of the members bought the old ore house, one of the mine buildings in the village and gave it to the church for a meeting place. This was used during hard winters and for mid-week meetings. It is sometimes referred to as Snailbeach Chapel.

The Lord's Hill Chapel re-opened on Good Fridays when Members and Sunday School children together with parents and friends would assemble at the Crow's Nest to form a group which would march to the Chapel headed by the Snailbeach Brass Band. Before they assembled, Mr. Parry, the local grocer, would scatter a large tin of sweets for the children to gather up. The march began at 3.00 p.m. and hymns and well-known choruses would be sung en route, the chapel being reached at 4.00 p.m. when tea would be taken. An evening service, with appropriate hymns and message would commence at 7.00 p.m.

The chapel and minister's house on 'God's Little Mountain' in Mary Webb's novel *Gone to Earth* are the Lord's Hill chapel and manse.[355] W. Reid Chappell in his book *The Shropshire of Mary Webb* (1930) wrote,

> If you ever want a bright cheerful musical and devout hour of genuine Nazarene Christianity take a long slow ascent through the green thickets and over the stony ways with the good people of Habberley or the sharper climb in company with the faithful of Plox Green to Lord's Hill Chapel.

In 1950 a film based on the novel *Gone to Earth* was made at the Chapel and in the District. At the time the chapel was poorly attended.[356] Repairs to the chapel were carried out and the chapel was re-opened on Thursday, 24 September, 1953 when the preacher was Rev. E. W. Hayden of Shrewsbury.

Peter Davies, who lived at Little Ness, near Shrewsbury, recalls in his book *A Corner of Paradise* a cycle ride that took him to Snailbeach and Lord's Hill. At Snailbeach a couple invited him into their home and gave him a drink. They were Methodists but attended Lord's Hill Chapel. The husband, a retired miner and a local preacher, was preparing to lead the mid-week meeting at the Chapel. That a Methodist was in a position of leadership at the Chapel suggests that in the period after the Second World War the Chapel had moved away from its Particular Baptist heritage. Since 1967 the lay pastor has been Peter Hallihan, who works for the Trinitarian Bible Society. The church now practices 'close communion' and it was the last church in the Shropshire District to do so.

The church left the Baptist Union in 1968 and when the West Midland Baptist Association merged with the Worcestershire Baptist Association to form the Heart of England Baptist Association on 1 January 2001, it did not join the new Heart of England Association.

The Lord's Hill Chapel ceased to be used over ten years ago but after extensive renovations were carried out with the help of English Heritage, the chapel was brought into use again. The harmonium, which had been used up to then, was scrapped and hymns are now sung unaccompanied.

Ministers
Until 1868 the church was known as Snailbeach but it was listed in *The Baptist Handbook* from 1867 to 1869 as Snailbeach, Lord's Hill and from 1870 as Lord's Hill, Snailbeach

Joint Pastorate with Minsterley	*1826-32*
Lakelin, Joseph, Senior	1826-32
Evans, Edward	1832-66 (ordained 1833)
Phillips, Thomas T.	1866-77
Jenkins, William	1878-92
Jones, W. L.	1892-1901
Parker, Alfred	1900-04
Joint Pastorate with Pontesbury	*1907–42*
Joint Pastorate with Brockton and Pontesbury	*1949– 66*
Hallihan, C. Peter (Lay)	1967-

Ludlow

The first reference to Baptists in Ludlow is in an appeal for thorough reform made by Baptists to the Army officers who in 1659 replaced Parliament, five months after Richard Cromwell's death.[357] However, there is no further mention of this cause.

In September 1811 Rev. John Palmer went to Ludlow 'in compliance with the earnest and frequent Solicitations of Several Persons there and preached in a Room Licensed in the Square in the Town.' Afterwards services were taken by Rev, Thomas Griffin, the Pastor of the church at Kidderminster, and students under instruction of Rev. Samuel Kilpin at Leominster. The Claremont Minutes record the baptism of eight people at Ludlow on the Lord's Day, March 1812:

> No Cold Bath to be procured in the Town –Snow on the Ground. The weather very bad & the Rivers very high, it was judged imprudent and unsafe to attempt to baptise out of Doors. Mr. Thos Thegsall very kindly lent us free use of his Malt House and Cistern-House. The ordinance was administered with great Solemnity and Propriety. Many who witnessed it were Much affected. Bro^r^ Palmer preached on the occasion and Bro^r^ Griffin Baptised

In the afternoon those who had been baptized were received into membership of the Shrewsbury church but advised to seek their dismissal to form a church 'of the same faith and order' at Ludlow.[358] The church thus formed was received into the Shropshire Association in 1813[359] but it did not survive for long, possibly even closing as early as 1815.

At the Shropshire Association meeting in October 1839 'it was resolved that Br. Kent apply to the Trustees of the late Mr. Goff to make enquiry respecting the establishment of a school in Ludlow'. However, nothing came of this enquiry.

It was not until 1874 that a Baptist church was formed again in Ludlow and on 28 June that year eighteen members signed the "Record of the Church of Jesus Christ meeting at Rock Lane Chapel, Ludlow". The church restricted membership to baptized believers and observed close communion.[359] Above the entrance to the chapel was a stone with the inscription 'Ebenezer 1868' but it is not known who first began work at the chapel.

Mrs. Ann Bennett, a widow, conveyed to Rev. William Owen, of Narbeth, Pembrokeshire the premises comprising the chapel, cottage and a pigsty. She wished the property to be 'placed in Trust for the use of Christians in public worship holding the Scriptural View of "Believer's Baptism" by immersion'. To carry out her wishes on 25 May 1877 Mr. Owen conveyed the property to various Trustees, who included James Evans, draper of Ludlow, and Rev. Thomas Evans of Pontesbury. During her lifetime Mrs. Bennett was to be paid ten pounds per year.

In December 1879 a fortnight's evangelistic meetings were held with several speakers and fifteen 'came

Rock Lane Chapel after closure and before demolition

Ludlow Baptist Church Rockspring Centre

forward and declared themselves on the Lord's side.' Mr. James Evans, a draper of King Street, acted as lay pastor at the time, but other members of the Church shared in the Church services. Baptisms were administered in the Gospel Hall, kindly lent by the Brethren.

On Wednesday, 16 June 1880 the foundation stones of the Schoolroom were laid to accommodate a hundred Sunday school scholars. During the 1880's there were many conversions and baptisms, which now took place in the baptistery in the schoolroom.

There is a gap in the church records between the 1880's and 1901. However, the minutes of the Shropshire Association's Autumnal Meetings held in November 1885 record that:

> Some conversation took place concerning the Baptist interest at Ludlow and the Chairman, Mr. John Jones and the Secretary were appointed to confer with the Baptist Friends there.

By 1893 the Chapel had passed into the hands of the Brethren and at a meeting of the Association's General Committee held in March,

> It was resolved that a recommendation should be addressed to the Trustees of the Chapel urging them to appoint additional Trustees, who should be accredited Members of Baptist Churches, and that a small rent should be charged to the Brethren now

occuping (*sic*) the Chapel as an acknowledgement that it is the Property of the Baptist Denomination.

In April 1901 the leaders of the church, significantly known by the Brethren term the 'Oversight' discussed the possibility of the work becoming a Baptist church again. The following month the Oversight decided to form a diaconate and they proposed that the existing Oversight should become deacons. At a church meeting held at the close of the morning service on 2 June 1901 the members of the Oversight were duly elected deacons and this can be considered to be the date when the present Baptist church was formed. At a deacons' meeting held on 28 June it was decided to advertise in *The Christian* for 'a minister with private means' but this did not lead to a ministerial settlement.

The church had a strong interest in overseas missions. So in 1902 it gave a gift of ten shillings to the Baptist Missionary Society and gifts of fifteen shillings each to the Baptist Zenana Mission, Brother George in South Africa and Brother Thomas Wales on the Island of St. Vincent, West Indies. The church decided 'to fall in with other Baptist Churches by holding simultaneous collections on Mar. 23 towards the Baptist Centenary Fund.'

The relationship between the church and the Shropshire Association developed slowly and by 1902 the church had joined the Association.

The church discussed the terms of admission to membership in 1928:

> It was felt that all candidates should if possible be baptized but that we do not make it a fixed rule in receiving from other churches, or conscientious objection to the same.

During the early 1930's several evangelistic campaigns were held and in 1937 a further schoolroom was added thus completing the premises. Membership in 1907 had risen to 35 whilst there were 70 Sunday School scholars. From its foundation in 1901 until the 1940s the church was without a settled Pastorate and faithful laymen mostly undertook the work of the church.

In 1944 as a result of the development of the local housing estate the members were led to appoint a full time Minister, the Rev. George Hayes, during whose ministry the membership greatly increased and in subsequent years, it has always been the intention to have a settled Pastor. However, there have been pastoral vacancies of varying length, the longest being one of nearly six years. Philip Hayden, son of Eric Hayden (minister at Claremont, Shrewsbury, 1952-56) became pastor at Ludlow in 1983. When he died from cancer at the early age of 34, he left his widow and family without their own home. To solve this problem the West Midland Baptist Association launched an appeal which raised over £46, 000 from 145 churches.

The church building had suffered a great deal from vandalism and other problems. In 1989 the South Shropshire District Council began an extensive programme of refurbishment in the Sandpits community, which had been sadly lacking in the provision of a Community Centre. The local authority approached the Baptist Church with the suggestion that, in return for the sale of their building, the Church might be based on the proposed new centre on a long-term peppercorn lease, together with a flat with three bedrooms. The Church would be responsible for the use and upkeep of the buildings. The Church Members felt divinely led to pursue the suggestion and after dealing with the apparent difficulties of funding, building work began in the summer of 1993. At the same time the fellowship called a full time Minister, Rev. Ken Paskin, to the Church and Centre and his induction took place on 16 April 1994.

The new Church buildings were officially opened on the 1 July 1995. The membership of the Church, now known as Ludlow Baptist Church, trebled over the next four years. Mr. Paskin was called to another pastorate at the end of 1999 and after a short interregnum Rev. Jonathan Edwards was inducted on 22 July 2001.

Ministers

Ludlow – First Church (Rock Lane Missionary Chapel)

Evans, James (Lay)	1874-
By 1893 the chapel had passed into the hands of the Brethren.	

Ludlow – Second Church (formed 1901)

Hayes, George	1944-47
Baker, Frederick Arthur	1948-51
Tyrrell, Trevor Grahame Rupert	1952-61
Popham, Sister Margaret Joan	1961-64
Magill, Sister Daisy Joan	1964-66
Iles, Derrick Joseph (Lay)	1967-68
Davis, John Paul	1969-75
Waltham, Colin, BSc	1977-81
Hayden, Philip, BA (Lay)	1983-06.88
Paskin, Kenneth Richard	1994–99
Edwards, Jonathan, BA, BD	2001-

Madeley (Ænon Chapel)

There was Baptist work in Madeley in the eighteenth century. In 1748 and 1773 a collier's house in Coalbrookdale and a clockmaker's in Madeley were licensed for dissenting worship, perhaps for Baptist worship. Except for Quakers and Methodists, the only protestant dissenters' meeting recorded in eighteenth-century Madeley was a Baptist one mentioned in 1760. From 1818 a congregation used a former club room on Lincoln Hill, which was probably an offshoot of Old Chapel, Broseley.[361] In 1850-1851 the *Baptist Manual* lists a church at Madeley, although no other details are given. It is possible that those who belonged to this church formed the nucleus of the Particular Baptist church that was formed on 26 October 1856.

The Shropshire Baptist Association, which had been reorganized in 1853, played an important role in developing Baptist work at Madeley. When a District Meeting was held at Broseley in April 1854 it was recognized that Madeley was 'a very important sphere of labor owing to its large & increasing population'. At the District Meeting at Shrewsbury in October 1854 'Brethren Lawrence and Crumpton were appointed to visit Madeley &, if possible, make arrangements for opening of a place for Divine Worship there and the preaching of the Gospel in connection with the Association The Ministers present engaged to supply in their turn'. Ministers continued to supply the Home Mission Station at Madeley until June 1855. The Association then proposed that there should be a joint pastorate with Dawley but the Dawley church did not agree to this arrangement as they felt they needed the undivided attention of their Pastor. Joseph Morgan, who had been Pastor of the Donnington Wood church, made an important contribution to the developing work at Madeley and in October 1855 he asked the Association for help to enable him to pay the brethren supplying there. In the financial year 1855-56 the Association paid the following for the work at Madeley:

Rent and cleaning of Room at Madeley	£5 2s 0d
Lighting of Room at Madeley	5s 0d
Mr. Joseph Morgan for entertainment of Ministers, supplying at Madeley	£1 7s 0d
Wine for Ordinance at Madeley	7s 7d
Expenses of Committee at Madeley	5s 0d
Travelling expenses of supplies at Madeley	£7 8s 6d

During the first part of 1856 Mr. M'Carthy supplied at Madeley and at the 1856 Annual Meeting it was 'decided that Mr. McCarthy be requested to continue his services at Madeley 'to afford an opportunity of judging whether or not his labours be acceptable and useful'. However, at the District Meeting on 7 October it was reported that 'Mr. M'Carthy's labors (*sic.)* had ceased, he not being acceptable on account of his indistinct articulation'. The Home Mission Secretary, Rev. A Tilley of Bridgnorth, was asked to write to Rev. T. Thomas of Pontypool Academy requesting him to send a student to supply the pulpit for one month. It was decided that if a church were formed at Madeley with a settled Minister, the Association would provide £20 per annum towards his support. This arrangement no doubt led to the decision to form the church later that month.

The Breviates of the Annual Meeting held at Wrexham in June 1857 record:

> Mr. Evan Jenkins, late student at Pontypool, has received and accepted a call to the pastorate, and his labours have been blessed with an increase in the congregation, and to the comfort of the church. His support is derived from the voluntary and united contributions of friends on the spot, the associated churches, and the Baptist Home Missionary Society, London.

By June 1858 the church had joined the Shropshire Association.

On 25 August 1857 Mr. J. H. Hopkins of Birmingham, a leader in the Midland Baptist Association, laid the foundation stone of the Baptist chapel. Rev. C.T. Keen of Bridgnorth, Rev. T. Howe of Shrewsbury, Claremont, and Rev. Josephus Judson of Wellington conducted the service. A collection on the site raised £7, and Mr. Hopkins was presented with a silver trowel to mark the occasion.

Seven months later, on 2 April 1858 (Good Friday), the new chapel was officially opened. It was named Ænon (*Now John also was baptizing at Ænon near to Salim, because there was much water there; and they came, and were baptized. John 3:23*). The chapel was built of yellow brick and slate with cast iron window frames and a very graceful classical front.[362] The total cost of the land and building was £490. By the opening day £150 had been contributed, leaving a debt of £340, a considerable liability for the membership of thirteen. The preacher at the opening service was the Rev. Charles Vince of Graham Street Baptist Church, Birmingham, considered to be the ablest Baptist preacher in the Midlands.

On that Easter Sunday three services were conducted by Dr. Thomas Thomas of Pontypool and the collections for the day amounted to £33. The next day there was a tea party, followed by an evening service, at which Rev.

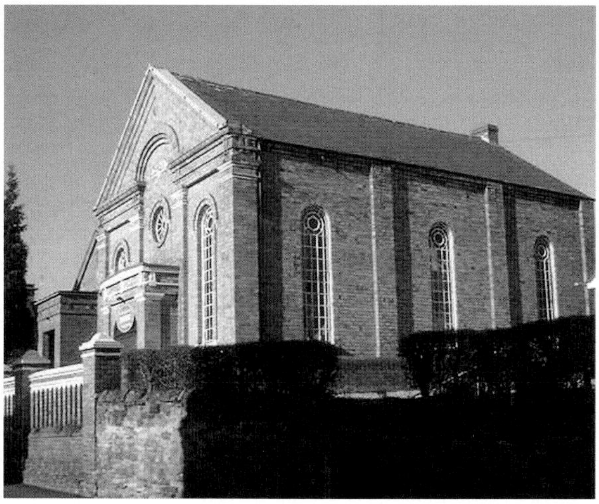

Ænon Chapel

Evan Jenkins was formally recognized as first pastor. Rev. Henry Lawrence of Shrewsbury presided. Dr. Thomas delivered the charge to the minister and there were addresses by Rev. C.T. Keen and Rev. T. Skemp of Dawley Bank.

The first year in the new chapel produced encouraging results, for the membership increased by five to eighteen. In 1860 attendance at the Communion Table was opened to non-members by a majority of five at a meeting attended by fourteen members. By 1867 the membership had risen to forty. On 29 December 1869 a bazaar was held to celebrate the removal of the final debt of £100 on the chapel. Unfortunately the membership did not rise further, but steadily fell until in 1898 it was back again to eighteen.

The years 1863 to 1865 are recorded as being an unsettled period. In May 1863 the Rev. Evan Jenkins resigned the Pastorate, feeling 'that a change in the ministry was desirable, that he had done his work here and that he did not have the cordial sympathy and support on the part of some of the leading members which appeared to be necessary for future success'. The church, however, requested that he should continue as pastor but he declined to do so. In January 1864 Mr. Webb, a student of Pastors' College, supplied the pulpit for a month and at the end of the month a church meeting unanimously invited him to the pastorate, but he declined their invitation. Later that year Mr. Knight from Pastors' College became the pastor until he removed to Bury. Rev. Evan Jenkins was then invited to resume his ministry. This he did until he resigned again in 1868, only to return again as Pastor in 1872 for a year and then again from 1876-81. During the intervening years, 1868 to 1871, the Pastor was Joseph B. Sargent. In 1872 the churches at Madeley and Oakengates united to support a minister, and Rev. Thomas Smith of Whitebrook, Monmouthshire, was chosen as pastor. He remained for four years, and this was the first of several joint pastorates with other local Baptist Churches.

In 1881 Rev. E. Spanton, minister of Dawley, was requested to provide supplies for the pulpit and to conduct meetings. From 1882-1888 Rev. Thomas Whittle was minister of Madeley and Shifnal. For the next seventy years most of the ministers shared their pastorate with that of Broseley.

The vestry at the back of the church had always been used as a Sunday School, but it was very small and totally inadequate. In 1931 a schoolroom was built next to the church at a cost of £800. Rev. E.G. Cole of Shrewsbury opened it on 30 September 1931.

In the 1930's the chapel had a thriving Girls' Life Brigade. The 1st Madeley Company was run by Mrs. Emmie Moore, Miss Dorothy Moore and Miss. Ivy Dorsett, and met every Monday evening in the schoolroom. They had a summer camp every year at seaside resorts such as Borth where they went with the Wolverhampton Battalion. Rev. Alberic Clement, whose first pastorate was Madeley and Broseley, later became Home Secretary of the Baptist Missionary Society.

One of the results of the formation of the New Town of Telford was the opening of a Pastoral Centre at Woodside in December 1969. This was first the responsibility of the Madeley minister, Rev. Gordon Tubbs, but in the later 1970s neither Ænon chapel nor Woodside had a Pastor. Then in 1980 Bridgnorth Baptist church appointed a full-time pastoral worker to take charge of Woodside.[363]

In 1968 Madeley Church was also affected by the development of Telford when the manse was subject to compulsory purchase and subsequent demolition. The church received £2000 compensation that was invested by the Baptist Union. This grew to £15000 and was used towards the refurbishment of the chapel in the year 2000. In this refurbishment the rotting floor, pews and organ were removed. A new floor was laid and carpeted, the walls replastered and new lighting was installed. Chairs were purchased to provide comfortable and flexible seating for eighty people and new entrance doors were fitted. The whole of the interior was then repainted in attractive colours. The total cost was £22000.

Mr. Bruce Grocott, MP for Telford, reopened the refurbished chapel on February 26th 2000. This was followed by a day of celebration shared by congregation, friends and members of local churches. The day culminated in an evening service at which the speaker was the Rev. Brian Nicholls, General Superintendent of the West Midland Area of The Baptist Union.

In January 2003 the church had a membership of 32 and held two services every Sunday including a morning Sunday School. There was a Monday morning "drop-in" meeting for a chat over a free cup of coffee and a Bible Study class every Tuesday evening.

The church supports ecumenical work in the area through the South Telford Association of Churches.

Although the church has never had a large membership, it has for nearly a century and a half been a witness to the Christian faith in Madeley High Street. Since the refurbishment of the chapel in 2002 the membership has grown to 57 in 2007. The 1st Madeley Boys Brigade was formed in November 2006.

Ministers

JENKINS, Evan	1857-63
KNIGHT, W. H.	1864-65
JENKINS, Evan	1865-68
SARGENT, Joseph E.	1868-72
JENKINS, Evan	1872
Joint Pastorate with Oakengates	*1872-78*
SMITH, Thomas L.	1872-76
JENKINS, Evan	1876-78
JENKINS, Evan	1878-81
WHITTLE, Thomas	1882-88 (with oversight of Zion, Shifnal, from 1883 and Donnington Wood from 1885)
Oversight of Shifnal, Zion	*1889-90*
Joint Pastorate with Old Chapel, Broseley, and Zion, Shifnal	*1893-95*
PLATTEN, T.	1893-94
Joint Pastorate with Old Chapel, Broseley	1896-1904
JONES, Lemuel	1895-1900
HALL, W. S.	1910-11
Joint Pastorate with Oakengates	*1917-20*
HAMPTON, Percy	1917-20
WOOD, Alfred John	1924-27
Joint Pastorate with Old Chapel, Broseley	*1929-54*
MORGAN, Thomas Lloyd	1929-38
CLEMENT, Alberic Samuel, BA	1941-44
LEIGH, John Samuel	1949-54
MONKLEY, Douglas Reginald	1955-59
BAKER, Frederick Arthur	1960-63
RUSSELL, Sister Winifred Mary	1965-67
Joint Pastorate with Woodside Pastoral Centre, Telford	*1970-76*
TUBBS, Gordon Lionel	1970-76
FOXALL, Francis Berwick	10.1982-09.88 (ordained 04.88)
GREEN, Edwin (Lay)	2001-03
OSMUND-SMITH, Keith	2002-

Maesbrook[364]

Maesbrook is a small hamlet, 6 miles S of Oswestry on the B4398 road between Llanymynech and Knockin. In 1844 a chapel, known as Ænon Chapel, was erected at Maesbrook Ucha and on Census Sunday 1851 the afternoon congregation was 35 and the evening congregation 43. By 1853 the church had united with that at Llandrinio. From 1865 until 1867 Maesbrook was a branch of Welshpool. By 1874 the church at Maesbrook and Llandrinio was in 'a languishing state' and the Oswestry church meeting decided that Maesbrook and Llandrinio church should unite with the Oswestry church and that a preaching plan should be drawn up.

The church flourished in the nineteenth century but as people, chiefly agricultural workers, left the district, the attendance at services gradually declined, resulting in the closure of the church in 1976. The building, which was beside the village hall, has been demolished.

Ministers

United Maesbrook and Llandrinio church	*1853-74*
REES, T.	01.05.1859 -
Branch of Welshpool	*1865-67*
Branch of Oswestry English Walls	*1874-76*
SOPER, W. Leonard (Lay)	1973

Market Drayton[365]

Towards the close of the seventeenth century Baptists had met near Market Drayton at The Hurst Farm in the village of Wistanswick but the meetings there appear to have ceased in the early part of the nineteenth century. Mr. and Mrs. Bayley who lived at Market Drayton moved in 1778 to Whitchurch and began Baptist work there. Their pastor, Rev. John Hinmers, began meetings in Market Drayton in the house of Mr. William Wynn in the Newtown area. It was at his house on 19 August 1817 that a 'society' was formed as an offshoot of the Baptist church at Whitchurch. It was decided to look for a more central meeting place and it was agreed to rent a room in Frogmore Road, which had previously been used as a day school. This was opened on 25 September 1817 when Mr. Hinmers preached. The first baptism in Market Drayton took place in July 1818 when Mr. Hinmers baptized a candidate in the River Tern.

The former Baptist Chapel, Shropshire Street

Rev. Robert Carr, who became pastor of the Market Drayton Independent Church in 1816, resigned his pastorate the following year as he had come to Baptist convictions. He moved back to his home city of Liverpool and it was there that he received a call to be pastor of the Baptists at Market Drayton.[366] After much thought and prayer he decided to accept and he became the first settled Baptist Minister in the town.

The rooms at Frogmore Road could not now cope with the increased congregations and it was decided to build a chapel in Keeling's Lane (later known as Back Lane and now as Salisbury Road). The building was opened for public worship on Sunday, 16 August 1818 with Robert Carr as the preacher. The chapel had its own burial ground, which is shown on the modern Ordnance Survey map.

The Quarterly Meeting of the ministers of the Shropshire Association was held at Whitchurch on 24 and 25 December 1817. It was reported that two deacons had been ordained at 'Drayton' on 22 December by Mr. Hinmers with the imposition of hands and that 'it is expected that a church will soon be formed'.[367] On 29 November 1818 the church was indeed formed with 45 members. It is not known how long Robert Carr remained at Market Drayton but Rev. George Parsons succeeded him. Unfortunately, he was accused of wrongdoing and was dismissed from the pastorate. The next pastor, Rev. Edward Blackstock, a long-time friend of William Gadsby, was often invited to preach elsewhere and William Gadsby and a number of other Manchester ministers would preach in his absence.

Although Whitchurch had founded the Market Drayton church, the new church did not join the Shropshire Baptist Association. In January 1822 just before Blackstock became the pastor the church passed a resolution opposing the Evangelical Calvinism associated with Andrew Fuller:

> In the fear of God, and thro' His grace upholding us, to withstand the doctrine of Fuller, and to oppose all such who broach errors opposite to the truth of God.

Blackstock subsequently adopted open communion views and this was to cause difficulties in subsequent pastorates.[368] He was succeeded in the Market Drayton pastorate by Thomas Littleton, who has been described as 'a diligent and truly experimental preacher for thirty-six years - it is said - without one Sabbath's intermission'.[369]

During the pastorate of James Simmester the church joined the strict communion West Midland Association. A number of Manchester ministers were Trustees of the church and during Mr. Simmester's ministry the church appealed to them for financial help. Efforts to keep the chapel open proved unsuccessful and it closed in 1843 and he became an itinerant preacher.

During 1855 arrangements were made by the Association to re-open the Baptist chapel as a Home Mission station and to put the building in trust for the denomination. This was made possible through the generous giving of Messrs. T. and G. Dunn and Mr. G. Morgan of Hatton. The chapel was re-opened on New

Year's Day 1856. During the summer vacation of 1856 Mr. Jeavans, of Stepney College, was invited to supply the pulpit and £5 was given to him for his services. In December 1856 John Griffiths Phillips became a Home Missionary at Market Drayton.

At the Annual meeting of the Association in June 1857 it was reported that

> Several ministers had been invited to Market Drayton but one circumstance or another had prevented them from settling there. Mr. Brame (late student of Regent's Park) attended the association meetings as representative of the station; he stated that it was his full conviction that if an active and devoted minister could be obtained for the station he had no doubt of its ultimate success; that he considered it a wide and important sphere of labour, and only regretted that his present state of health forbid his continuing his ministrations there.

By November 1857 Rev. John Sissons was serving at Market Drayton and the Mission Station was formally constituted as a Particular Baptist Church on 6 December 1857. Like some other Shropshire Baptist churches the new church practised open communion, welcoming to the Lord's Table those who had not been baptized as believers.

Rev. Joseph Burroughs succeeded John Sissons but difficulties arose and he resigned the pastorate. He decided to remain in the town and a second Baptist church was formed with Mr. Burroughs as pastor. He died at the age of 75 in December 1870. His will directed that Providence Chapel should be sold and the proceeds given to Baptist Home Mission. With the sale of Providence Chapel, the division among the Baptists in Market Drayton came to an end and thereafter they met as one church.

.

In 1860 members invited a student of Pontypool Baptist College, Thomas Clark, who had been a successful preacher in the chapels in the Welsh Valleys, to preach at Market Drayton on the first Sunday of January 1861. He found the church in a very low spiritual state but he recognized the opportunities for progress in the faith. He was duly inducted as pastor and served until 1905. In 1870 it was decided to build a new place of worship in Shropshire Street.

Rev P. A. Pepperdene succeeded Thomas Clark and remained at Market Drayton until 1910 when he received and accepted a call to a church in the United States of America.

In 1945 the church left the Shropshire District and joined the North Staffordshire District of the West Midland Baptist Association.

Following a period of decline, especially among young people, the church closed in 1955 and the building was duly purchased for use as business premises. It was used for a while as the Artisan Ballroom and is now a Kingdom Hall of the Jehovah Witnesses.

In the summer of 1970 a "Sunday Club" was begun at Red Bank House, the home of Mr. and Mrs. John Smith, who had been agricultural missionaries with the Baptist Missionary Society in the Indian State of Orissa from 1956 to 1965. In June 1972 a communion service was held at the end of Sunday Club, the service being conducted by Rev. Jack Moorman, from Indianapolis, Indiana, USA, who was serving as pastor of Wem Baptist Church. Those involved in the work at Market Drayton adopted the name of 'Market Drayton Evangelical Fellowship.' By January 1973 there was agreement that the Fellowship should become a Baptist church. Discussions took place about further development of the work with Mr. Moorman and he told them of Ferrell Kearney who wished to move from his work in Iceland to a pastoral situation in the United Kingdom. He came to Market Drayton in June 1973 and was recognized as the pastor of Market Drayton Baptist Church. In August the Sunday morning service was moved to the Beacon Community Centre, while evening meetings remained at Red Bank House. By the end of October there was criticism of Mr. Kearney's preaching, its content, style and presentation. He resigned on 13 November 1973 and John Smith subsequently became honorary Pastor.

As yet the new Market Drayton Baptist Church had not been formally constituted. This took place on 8 November 1976 and 10 people became the founder members. John Smith was appointed as elder. After some initial hesitation the church joined the Shropshire District of Baptist Churches.

In the late 1970's membership decreased rapidly owing to many families leaving the district and in May 1981 it was decided to cease holding services at the Beacon Community Centre and to return to Red Bank House. By the end of the summer of 1982 the church consisted of just two families, seven people in all, including a baby. There seemed to be no prospect for a viable Baptist work in Market Drayton and the final service was held on the July 25 1982 at Red Bank House. John Smith and his family joined the local Anglican Church and, after ministerial training, he was ordained in the Church of England and served as a Non-stipendiary Minister.

Ministers

Market Drayton - First church 1818-1843

Carr, Robert	1817- at least 1818
Parsons, George-	03.12.1821-
Blackstock, Edward	10.03.1822 –01.25
Littleton, Thomas	21.08.1825-12.05.33
Roycroft, -	04.04.1835-30.01.37
Simmester, James	25.05.1839-12.43

Market Drayton - Second church 1857-1955

Brame, W. R. (*Home Missionary*)	- 06.1856
Phillips, John Griffiths (*Home Missionary*)	12.1856 -
Sissons, John	1857 - 03.10.58
Burroughs, Joseph	1858 –60
Clark, Thomas	1861-1905
Pepperdene, Philip Arthur	1905-10
Tipton, E.	1911-19
Arnold, W. J.	1919
Joint Pastorate with Audlem, Cheshire	*1920-34*
Brindley, Harry	1920-24
Johnson, George James	1925-36
West, Arthur Herbert, BA, BD	1939-44
Lewis, David Richard (*Honorary*)	1953- 9.04.55

Market Drayton - Third church, Providence Chapel, Shropshire Street 1860-1870

Burroughs, Joseph	1860-08(or 09).02.70.

Market Drayton - Fourth Church 1973-1982

Kearney, Ferrell (*Honorary*)	13.06.1973-30.11.73
Smith, John Thomas, MPhil (*Honorary*)	1973-82

Ministerley

The first Dissenting minister to have preached in Minsterley is said to have been Rev. John Palmer. He preached first at the Bridge Inn on 26 December 1794. As soon as an opening had been made, he invited Independent ministers to join him in the work. In 1805 Thomas Howly, Esq., a member of the Baptist church at Shrewsbury, fitted up, at his own expense, part of a farm house, which was still sometimes called "the old chapel" even at the end of the nineteenth century. The rent for this room was paid by Baptists and Independents jointly and the ministers of the two denominations officiated on alternate Sundays. In the following year Chapel House was built and licensed as a dissenting meeting-house. Although considerable friction arose from time to time because of differences about baptism, this arrangement continued until 1833 when the two denominations agreed to separate. That year the Independents built their own chapel in the village, while the Baptists built a chapel 'close to Snailbeach mine'.[370]

The Independents formed their church at Minsterley in 1805, while the Baptists did not form their church until 1817. Twenty-one members `of the Shrewsbury church were dismissed to form the Baptist church and the Shropshire Itinerant, Mr. W. Mayberry, was called to be their pastor.[371] By 1823 the Minute Book of the Shropshire Baptist Association called the church 'Minsterley and Snailbeach'. The second and final pastor was Rev. Joseph Lakelin. By 1852 he was living at Snailbeach and he became a member of Pontesbury Baptist Church (Chapel Lane).

Ministers

Mayberry, W.	1817-
Lakelin, Joseph, Senior	1826- *c.* 39 (Joint Pastorate with Snailbeach - 1832)

Montgomery

Baptist work in Montgomery began when services were held in the Town hall on Friday. 28 May 1897 and the preacher was Rev. T. E. Williams, of Newtown.[372] The first baptisms took place in Lymore Park on Sunday 27 June when he baptized six candidates.[373] The Minutes of the Annual Conference of the Radnorshire and Montgomeryshire Baptist Association on 3 June record:

> The Conference heard with great pleasure, through Rev. T. E. Williams Newtown, that at last a cause had been started at Montgomery, under very

> favourable circumstances and bright prospects, and was resolved that the ministers of the Association should give a Sunday each free to the place. It was also agreed that Mr. Williams should correspond with the ministers and make the arrangements.

In 1898 the church called Charles Parry Thomas, a student at Aberystwyth College, to be its first minister. Land was acquired from the Earl of Powis in Princes Street as a site for a chapel. Messrs. Shayler and Edmunds prepared the plans for erecting a building at a cost of £1700.[374]

The site was far from ideal as it had been an old cesspool and the building made of red and yellow Ruabon bricks needed to be buttressed to prevent its collapse. In 1910 the Annual Meeting of the Radnorshire and Montgomeryshire Baptist Association approved a proposal that the church should hold a bazaar with the aim of raising £300 towards the reduction of the building debt.

Benjamin Withers, who was a member of the church and an Assistant Preacher of the Radnorshire and Montgomeryshire Baptist Association, was called to the pastorate of New Wells Baptist Church in 1900. Sadly he had to resign the pastorate through ill health two years later and is believed to have died in 1903.

The initial promise of the church was not fulfilled and after World I the church was in a low state. Richard Pryce Jones, a member of Sarn Baptist Church, became Church Secretary in 1922 and then Lay Pastor a year later. He also served as Free Church Chaplain of the Infirmary of Forden Union Workhouse. He passed the Baptist Union Examination and was ordained. When he left Montgomery in 1929 the Area Superintendent, Rev. J. Ivory Cripps, wrote to him, saying 'Apart from your pastorate, it is quite certain that the cause would have become extinct'

The departure of R. P. Jones meant that in order for there to be stipendiary ministry at Montgomery it needed to be linked with another church. The West Midland Association explored the possibility of a joint ministry with Welshpool but the Welshpool church concluded that the distance between the churches made this impractical. In 1931 the churches of Montgomery and Brockton called J. L. Baines as their pastor. The churches shared ministry until 1939. The church closed *c.* 1940/41 and the building was used as a food store in World War 2. It was demolished in 1966 and a bungalow was built on the site.

Richard Pryce Jones

Ministers

THOMAS, Charles Parry	1898-1901
ROLLASON, Alfred Percy Harold	1902-05
Joint Pastorate with Sarn and Cwm	*1915-16*
EVANS, William John	1920-21
JONES, Richard Pryce	01.1923- 30.06.29
Joint Pastorate with Brockton	*1931-39*
BAINES, John Leslie	1931-32
WICKS, Benjamin John	1934-36
JAMES, Eric	1936-39

Montgomery Chapel

Morville

Morville is situated 3 miles WNW of Bridgnorth. John Thomas, of Broseley, registered a dwelling house for Baptist worship in 1811[375] but a church was not formed there.

Much Wenlock

John Thomas, of Broseley, registered a dwelling house in Much Wenlock for Baptist worship in 1811.[376] A small Particular Baptist congregation was meeting in Much Wenlock in 1851. On Census Sunday there were 20 in the congregation. It was reported that the average congregation was 40 with 12 Sunday scholars.[377]

Newdale

Newdale (or New Dale) was a hamlet in the parish of Wellington, 2 SE of Wellington. The village, together with a foundry and a Quaker meeting house, was built by Abraham Darby and his partner Thomas Goldney *c.* 1760. Although the name remains on the Ordnance Survey map for Telford, Ironbridge and the Wrekin, there are now no houses there. According to *The Baptist Handbook* for the period 1877 to 1893 the Dawley church had a branch at Newdale.

Newport

The church came into being through the meeting together of a number of Baptist families in the area and the church was formed in 1992 with a nucleus of 15 members. The church joined the West Midland Baptist Association and the Shropshire District of Baptist Churches. A Covenant Service took place at Burton Borough School Hall on the 27 March 1993.

As there was no building available for church services, meetings were first held in a school hall, but the fellowship soon moved to the Scout Hut in Longford Road. Two elders, Mr. Peter West and Mr. Roy Ellis, led the Fellowship.

In 1996 the church moved to Water Lane into a building, which had been the Telephone Exchange and then the offices of Newport Town Council. It was then that the church decided to apply for membership of The Baptist Union.

Newport Chapel

In 1998 and early 1999 the Fellowship became increasingly aware of the need for a pastor and so sought the advice of the West Midland Baptist Association. The outcome was a successful application for a Home Mission Grant to help support a part-time minister. Rev. Malcolm Thorpe became their part-time minister in November 1999.

As the church at present has no baptistry, baptismal services are held at Donnington Wood Baptist Church. An extension to the church was built in 2006/ 2007. Malcolm Thorpe retired in December 2006.

Minister

Thorpe, Malcolm Edward Charles	1999 -2006

Newton (see Craven Arms)

Oakengates

Rev C. R. Cameron, perpetual Curate at Wombridge 1808-1856, strongly resisted the nonconformists and, apart from the building of a Wesleyan chapel at Ketley Bank, no chapel was established in the parish during his time. Baptists began meeting in the public auction rooms at Oakengates and a church was formed in 1866. At the first meeting of the reorganized Association in 1867 three of the ministers present were asked to supply the pulpit. A chapel with seating for 200 was built in Stafford Road and opened on 5 September 1868.[378] The first pastor was Samuel Couling from 1870 to 1872 but in 1873 it united with Madeley to call Rev. Thomas Smith as Pastor. Thereafter the church normally had pastoral oversight by being linked to another church. During the Second World War the work declined and the chapel had closed by 1945.

Former Oakengates Baptist Chapel © 2003 Janice Cox

Ministers

Couling, Samuel	1870-72
Branch of Madeley	*1872-78*
Chapman, David Charles	1878
Joint Pastorate with Donnington Wood	*1889-1903*

Oakengates Ministers *continued*

TOWLER, Edward	1889-94
MAURICE, William	1896-1901
BONSER, William	1901-03
Joint Pastorate with Zion, Shifnal	*1907-08*
THURSTON, Victor E. (*Baptist Union Colporteur*)	1907-08
Joint Pastorate with Madeley	*1917-20*
EVANS, E.J. (*Lay*)	1936

Oldbury

A Particular Baptist Church was formed at Oldbury (then in Shropshire) in 1815 and a building 'in the form of a vestry' with about 100 seats was erected in Canal Street in 1816. In 1834 a new building was erected in front of the first building and this was capable of seating 250 to 350 persons.

The church joined the Midland Association in 1818[379] but left to join the West Midland (Strict) Baptist Association in 1841. When this Association closed the church did not belong again to a Baptist Association.

On Census Sunday in March 1851 the morning congregation was 40 with 21 Sunday Scholars; the afternoon congregation was 50 with 31 Sunday Scholars, and the evening congregation 70. The average congregation was 45 to 50 in the morning, 50 to 60 in the afternoon and 65 to 80 in the evening. The minister at the time was William Sheldon, a cordwainer and currier who lived at Spon Lane, West Bromwich.[380] R. F. Chambers mentions that a Mr. Brooks was pastor in the early days, and that it was a flourishing cause in the 1870's, having a large school. The church closed in 1953 and the building has now been sold.[381]

Ministers

BROOKS, -	
WHITE, Luke	1827
SHELDON, William	1851(?)-61

Ollerton

Ollerton is a hamlet 3 miles SE of Hodnet. In 1851 there was a Baptist chapel there and attendance on Census Sunday was 35 plus 15 Sunday scholars. [382]

Osbaston (see Rolla (The Rollaw))

Oswestry (English Church) [383]

The town of Oswestry (Croesoswallt in Welsh) is situated on the borders of Wales and England and, in consequence, many of its inhabitants are conversant with the languages of both countries and places of worship have been built to meet their respective needs. Rev. John Palmer and other ministers preached in Oswestry and its neighbourhood for some years before a Baptist church was formed in 1806. Eight members of Dog Lane Baptist Church, Shrewsbury were dismissed in August 1806 to form the new church. [384] A chapel was erected on English Walls and opened on the 5 September 1806. The church became a founder member of the Shropshire Association. In 1809 the fellowship adopted, as was usual at the time, a Calvinistic Declaration of Faith and Practice.

In November 1817 Thomas Cooke, who had been a member of Cannon-street Baptist Church, Birmingham, became the church's second pastor. The church grew numerically and spiritually and preaching in the villages was 'well attended'. A Sunday School was opened and a penny-a-week society was formed in aid of the Baptist Mission.[385] In July 1818 it was decided to enlarge the chapel and this was done, the building being re-opened for services on 1 November.

On Census Sunday morning the general congregation was 92 and there were 22 Sunday scholars, while in the evening the congregation was 107. It was reported that as the church had been without a regular minister for 18 months the congregations had much declined.[386] However, when the congregations increased again, consideration was given to the building of a new church with a greater seating capacity. The matter was on the agenda for a number of years until a decision was reached to erect a church on the west side of Salop Road, a main thoroughfare from Shrewsbury to the town, and alongside the site of a half timbered house known as Blackgate. Plans were passed for the Church to be built of Cefn stone, rock faced with Broughton stone dressing, and with a clock tower rising to a height of seventy feet The Church had a seating capacity for 400 adults (500 for a mixed congregation), a baptistry made of marble and at the rear, three vestries of convenient size.

The Mayor, A. Wynne Corrie Esq., laid the first memorial stone on 14 June 1891, and it was situated on the right of the main entrance. The ceremony was preceded by a service in the afternoon at which many notable personages as well as Ministers from local churches were present. The total cost of the Church

Salop Road showing houses (later demolished) to make room for the Baptist Chapel

Salop Road showing Baptist Chapel following demolition of houses (shown opposite)

was between £3000 and £4000 but the amount due had already been reduced by £1000 by the time the Church opened for worship, mainly through the generosity of members and friends.

The first services for Worship took place on Sunday 6 March 1892; prayer meetings being held at 7.00 a.m. and 10.00 a.m. preceding the 11.00 a.m. service conducted by Rev. T. J. Wright of London. Chairs had to be provided in the aisles and chancel for the evening service. The English Walls chapel was then closed but centenary services marking its opening were held at the Salop Road Church in 1906. A schoolroom was added to the new premises in 1909.

In 1976 the churches at Welshpool and Kerry called Rev. Wilfred Chapman to a joint pastorate and he told his church at Bluntisham that he had accepted this call. However, at the last moment the Kerry church decided to withdraw from the arrangement. It was then that the Oswestry church linked up with Welshpool to form a joint pastorate and this arrangement continued until 1986 when the churches went their separate ways.

Miss Margaret Sweeting took early retirement from her work as a Health Visitor and she served as Lay Pastor for two years from May 1988. During her pastorate there were serious problems with the church building but her ministry was significant in the renewal of church life. She encouraged the church members to believe that the church had a future.

When the number of regular worshippers at the Salop Road Church declined and the building deteriorated, services were held in the schoolroom, and fellowship meetings in the week in various houses. The inability of the congregation to maintain the Salop Road Church prompted a search for smaller premises. A large house, 'Graylands', in Western Avenue was purchased and adapted for worship, with upstairs accommodation for the Minister. The last service in the Salop Road building was held on 5 November 1995 and the first service at 'Graylands' took place on 12 November. Rev. Peter Hayes, Minister of Dawley Baptist Church, led a Service of Dedication for the new building on 19 November.

Mr. Ivor Waddelow, a local veterinary surgeon, had been Church Secretary at Oswestry from 1970 to 1982 before he left the area to train for the Baptist ministry at Bristol Baptist College. Following ordination he served at Ilkley Baptist Church from 1984 until his retirement in 1993. In 1995 he was invited to return to Oswestry and served as part-time minister from 1995 until he retired for a second time in 1998. He went to Bristol to live and then was called to Victoria Park Bristol and served there until he retired for the third time in 2001 from the Baptist ministry. When he retired from Oswestry, Rev. Stuart Warren, who returned to England from Canada, succeeded him as part-time minister.

From 1995 there was a slow but steady growth in church life and the premises at 'Graylands' became too small. A modern single storey commercial'

Graylands in 2003 (now a private house)

property, formerly used as a warehouse was purchased and, after it had been renovated, it was opened as a worship and outreach centre on 8 June 2002. This new Baptist Church called Cornerstone stands at the corner of Lower Brook Street and Roft Street. The name 'Cornerstone' was chosen to indicate that Jesus is the Cornerstone of all the church seeks to do. From January 2003 until November 2004 Rev. Jan and Rev. Steve Worthy, leaders of Agape Ministries for Church Growth, joined the church's leadership team as part-time evangelists. Rev. Ken Sykes became the minister in November 2006.

Cornerstone Baptist Church (front view)

Cornerstone Baptist Church (rear entrance)

Ministers

Pain (or Paine), William	04. 1807 (ordained 27.01.08)-1.07.11
Cooke, Thomas	27.11.1817-at least 1827
Clarke, Robert	1838-11.45
Gabriel, Henry	1846 - 11.49
Crumpton, David	30.10.1852-13.09.57
Wilks, Edward Davies	1858-81
Archer, George	1882-92
Thompson, Malcolm Macmillan	1896-04
Elder, James Clark	1905-
Dight, Edward Henry	1915-16
Hardin, Edwin	1917-20
John, John Llewellyn, BA	1921-25
Byatt, Horace Robert	1926-34
Cox, Bert Albert	1934-36
Edwards, John Glynn, BA,	1938-39
Saunders, Reginald Dyke, BA	1939-42
Owen, Gwilym Washington, BA	1946-55
Watkins, Myrddin	1958-64
Williams, Cyril James	1965-76
Joint Pastorate with Welshpool (known as the E. Montgomeryshire Group 1976-1981)	*1976-86*
Chapman, Wilfred	1976-81
Lewis, Anthony James Leonard	1981-86
Sweeting, Margaret, SRN, SCM, HV (Lay)	05.1988- 08.90
Waddelow, Ivor Reginald, MRCVS	1995-98
Warren, Stuart Malcolm, MA	1999-02
Worthy, Janice (*Part-time Evangelist)*	01.2003-11.04
Worthy, Stephen Alan (*Part-time Evangelist*)	01.2003-11.04
Sykes, Charles Kenneth, BA(Ed)	2006-

Oswestry (Penuel Welsh Church) [387]

For a long time a number of the Welsh members of the English Baptist Church at Oswestry had wanted to establish a Welsh cause in the town. In March 1860 they requested their dismission to the Welsh Church at Cefn Mawr, near Wrexham. They felt that the English Church 'would not be much weakened by their withdrawal'.[388] Their first meeting had been held the previous month in a room, previously used as a commercial school, behind No. 58 Willow Street, near the Woolpack public house. The first baptism took place in the English chapel in March that year[389] and by March 1861 fourteen people had been baptized. Later the congregation moved to a room in Plough Bank.

For its first four years the church was a branch of Seion, Cefn Mawr. In 1870 Gethin Davies, Classical Tutor at Llangollen College, gave help to the cause and was ordained in the room where the church had been meeting He served as pastor until 1874. In 1872 the members purchased and moved to a building belonging

Original Trustees Penuel Chapel

William Williams *coal merchant*
Henry Parry *plasterer*
John Griffiths *carpenter*
John Williams *clerk on Cambrian Railways*
Charles George Bailey *bookseller*
Robert Roberts *silk merchant*
David Roberts, Weston Rhyn *farm bailiff*
Thomas Roberts, Weston Rhyn *farrier*
Gethin Davies, Llangollen Theological College
Edward Davies, Cefn Mawr *contractor*
Dan Ellis, Acrefair *postmaster*

to the Independent Methodists in Rope Walk on Pistyll Croft, Beatrice Street.

In 1883, David Jenkins, of Cardiff accepted the call to ministry at Penuel and stayed until 1886. Following his departure, the church decided to purchase a piece of land for approximately £200, to build a new chapel and two houses in Castle Street opposite the old building. One of the houses was used as a manse.

In 1893 the Rev. David Rees became minister and stayed for 18 years. The Rev. David Griffiths followed him and he remained as pastor until his death in 1920. There was then a gap of almost twenty years before the Rev. E. Bryn Jones was inducted as minister at Penuel, which was now linked to two Montgomeryshire churches, Bethel and Seion, Llanfyllin. After a successful ministry of nine years, he left for Penygroes, Carmarthenshire.

In 1948, the Rev. Boaz R. Williams became minister. At first he continued to be responsible for Bethel and Seion, Llanfyllin, preaching at Llanfyllin one Sunday a month. However, from 1955 he assumed responsibility for three small churches at Gefailrhyd, Moelfre and Llansilin in Denbighshire.

In 1956, Oswestry Town Council unveiled plans to demolish the church and the two adjoining houses, in order to redevelop the surrounding area. However, the members of Penuel objected strongly to this proposal and eventually the church and the two houses were saved from demolition. In celebration of their victory, and in thanksgiving, the chapel was repaired and re-decorated by the members at a cost of £600 in 1961.

The Rev. Boaz Williams died in September, 1973 and his widow, Mrs. Katie Williams, with the help and support of a small number of members and visiting ministers, continued to keep the church open for worship until it eventually closed in 1983.

Former Oswestry Welsh Chapel

The building was sold and is now used as a carpet warehouse.

It had been well supported. In 1908 it had 88 members; in 1934, 46 members; in 1956, 61 members and in 1960, 63 members.

Penuel joined the North Wales Eastern Association in 1865 and the Denbighshire, Flintshire and Merionethshire Association in 1883.

Of the other Welsh churches associated with Penuel, only Seion, Llanfyllin and Salem, Llansilin remain but they have 5 and 6 members respectively.

Ministers

Branch of Seion, Cefn Mawr, near Wrexham	*1860-64*
Davies, Gethin	1870-74
Jenkins, E. David	1883-86
Lewis, Benjamin (*Student Pastor*)	1888-89
Rees, David	1893-1911
Griffiths, David	1913- 29.05.19.
Joint Pastorate with Bethel and Seion Llanfyllin, until 1955 and then with Gefailrhyd, Moelfre and Llansilin	*1938-73*
Jones, Eleazer Owen Bryn, BA, BD	1938-47
Williams, Boaz Richard	1948- 09.09.73.

Ovenpipe (see Tankerville)

Perkins Beach (see Lord's Hill and Snailbeach)

Plealey[390]

Plealey is a hamlet 1¼ mile ENE of Pontesbury. At the beginning of the nineteenth century there were Baptists living in the area that included the villages of Plealey and Pontesford and as their numbers were growing it was felt desirable to provide accommodation for worship nearer their homes. The houses of Richard France and Edward Owen in Plealey were licensed in 1824 and 1825 respectively as Dissenters' Meeting houses. The men folk in the villages were chiefly employed on farms or in the local coalmines.

On 13 October 1828 Richard France, then an Independent (or Congregational) adherent, applied for, and obtained, a licence to build a chapel in the village of Plealey. The property however, was never vested in Trustees and when Richard France changed his views on baptism, it became a Baptist chapel and he prohibited Congregational Ministers from officiating at any service from 1830 onwards.

The Congregationalists then withdrew from the chapel and with their brethren at Pontesbury who had previously attended Minsterley Congregational Church, built a place of worship in Pontesbury and this was opened in 1839.

Plealey Chapel had been registered as a Baptist chapel but in 1851 it became a Wesleyan Methodist Chapel, and has remained a Methodist chapel ever since.

Plealey Methodist Church

Pontesbury (Chapel Lane)[391]

Rev. William Smith, who served at Shrewsbury from 1783 to 1789, engaged in village preaching and occasionally preached at a house near Westbury. His successor at Shrewsbury, Rev. John Palmer, preached at various places in the district including Minsterley, Snailbeach, Habberley and Pontesford. However, the first record of the preaching of the Gospel in Pontesbury is in 1820. This took place in the house of Samuel Heakin, a member of the Baptist Chapel in Shrewsbury and services were held on Sundays and weeknights. The preachers were Rev. John Jones Benyon, an Independent Minister of Dorrington, and Rev. W. Mayberry of Snailbeach. When Mr. Mayberry left the neighbourhood Mr. Liddell succeeded him for a time.

In November 1817 some twenty-three people living in Snailbeach, Minsterley and Pontesbury wrote to the Shrewsbury Church asking for permission to form themselves into a separate church. Accordingly, on the 4 January 1818 a church was formed at Snailbeach.

The first Pastor of the church at Snailbeach was Rev. Joseph Lakelin. As he was unable to find accommodation at Snailbeach, he was obliged to live at Pontesbury. The only service he could conduct at Pontesbury was on a Monday evening at the home of Samuel Heakin. However, he felt that the spiritual needs of the people in that village demanded a more regular ministry and he sought financial help from the Trustees of the Goff Charity. They promised to send a man to teach the young and preach the Gospel if a suitable room could be found. A house was rented for six months and Mr. John Francis of Caerleon, South Wales, was sent to work in the village. In this he was supported by four members of the Snailbeach Church, who resided in the village.

As the work grew there was a need to build a meeting-house and a minister's residence. A meeting-house was erected and the following account of its opening appeared in *The Baptist Magazine* in 1828:

> On April the 15th, 1828, was opened a place of worship for the use of the Baptist denomination at Pontesbury, near Shrewsbury. The Rev. Mr. Cooke, Oswestry, preached in the morning; and Rev. Mr. Kent, Shrewsbury, afternoon, and night. Collections were made, and notwithstanding it was an extremely wet day, £11 2s, was realized. The place has cost £300, and near £100 was subscribed in the neighbourhood, with the exception of a few pounds in Oswestry and neighbourhood. This place is lent to the Trustees of the late Mr. Goff to teach a free school in, and their Schoolmaster is a Baptist minister, who preaches in it twice on Lord's days, and other places adjacent. More than eighty

Pontesbury Baptist Chapel

> children in the day school, and seventy in a Sabbath School. The friends of education and conversion of sinners, no doubt will lend their assistance to clear away the remaining part of the debt. It will seat 300 hearers, is well attended, and the prospects are encouraging.[392]

On the 11 October a Particular Baptist Church was formed and on the following Tuesday, 14 October Mr. John Francis was ordained as its pastor. [393]

The progress of the Church was not to be smooth and in 1841 the Church was in such an unsettled state as a result of internal dissent that it was dissolved and another Baptist Church was formed elsewhere in the village. The dispute seems to have been about Evangelical Calvinism. However, several of those who had been members of the original church decided to form a new Church fellowship. So on the Lord's Day February 12 Rev. Manoah Kent of Shrewsbury 'gave twenty nine baptized believers the right hand of fellowship, and thus recognized them as a Christian Society.' During the month of March Mr. Joseph Willis supplied the pulpit and this led to his receiving a unanimous call to the pastorate. He served until he was forced to resign because of ill health in June 1847. He was succeeded by a Welshman, Edward Roberts from Pontypool College and the church grew during his pastorate, despite his difficulty in preaching other than in his native tongue. On Census Sunday 1851 there were 155 present and 62 Sunday scholars in the morning. There were 64 at the afternoon Sunday school and 180 in the evening. The evening congregation was below the average of 240 owing to the stormy weather. [394]

When Edward Roberts resigned the pastorate, the Church issued a unanimous invitation to Mr. Jones of West Bromwich, Staffordshire. As he was unwilling to give an immediate answer Mr. Joseph Smith, the son of Rev. James Smith of Shrewsbury, was asked to supply the pulpit. Mr. Jones did not accept the call and the church then unsuccessfully approached two other ministers. On Sunday 4 January 1852 the Church invited Mr. Smith to the pastorate and he immediately accepted, commencing his work as pastor on Sunday 18 January.

On 25 March 1852 the members adopted articles of Faith and Rules (sixteen in number) which restricted membership and attendance at the Lord's Table to believers baptized by immersion. Joseph Smith, however, favoured open communion and at a members' meeting on 28 June 1852 he proposed that ''Members of Christian Churches who consciously hold different views upon the subject of Baptism to our own, should be permitted to participate in the privilege of the Lord's Supper.' Each member present spoke and the motion was passed with a majority of 9 to 2. However, to prevent dissatisfaction on the part of those not present, a final decision was deferred until the following Sunday. The motion was then agreed to with one member abstaining, but the decision was reversed before the year was out. Whether the Church's change of mind resulted in the resignation of its pastor at the end of the year is not known. The issue of open communion was finally resolved in 1861 when the Church by a majority passed the following resolution:

> That Paedobaptists – being accredited Members of the several bodies of their particular denominations – holding evangelical doctrines be admitted to the Lords table – but not to membership.

It was not until 1919 that the Church, with one abstention, decided that as the Trust Deed contained no restriction as to the qualifications for membership

> The membership of Pontesbury Baptist Church be open to all who profess faith in the Lord Jesus Christ as their personal Saviour and desire to follow him in his teaching and life.

In 1854 a plot of land situated on the opposite side of the road and a short distance away from the Chapel was purchased for use as a burial ground, but it is now closed due to lack of room for any further interments.

On 5 January 1865 John Harrison of The Bog, who had been 'an acceptable preacher in connection with the Calvinistic Methodists' was baptized at Pontesbury by the former minister of Pontesbury Baptist Church, Rev. Joseph Smith, and received into membership. The Old Association Circular Letter in 1866 reported that he had 'taken charge of the church at Sarn'. Strangely, his membership and that of his wife Anne was never transferred to Sarn.

A joint pastorate was formed with Lord's Hill Church in 1906 and the first minister was Isaac Brook of

Manchester Baptist College, who was ordained on 10 October 1907.

Among the many Pastors at Pontesbury mention must be made of the Rev. Thomas Evans, who was lovingly called 'The Bishop'. A former student of Haverfordwest Baptist College he came to Pontesbury from Waterford, where he had worked under the Irish Home Mission. He left Ireland in poor health in 1864. He came to Pontesbury in April 1866 and his ministry lasted for 38 years. He passed away on 19 June 1913 at the age of 74 and his body was interred in the Baptist Church burial ground. As each child left the morning service, he would hand out a sweet. As they were not wrapped in any paper the handing out on a hot summer day could be a "sticky" business!

In 1926 the flooring of the Church was renewed to bring it to the level of the vestibule entrance and also to reduce the steps to the choir seats. As the final boards were being lifted two bodies were found lying in the culvert which ran under the Church from the small graveyard outside the eastern wall. The coroner had to be notified so that work could be completed.

The Church went through a period of some difficulty in 1948 and the Church closed for public worship from 30 December. At a Church Meeting held on 14 February 1949 there was a majority decision to re-open for worship and this took place on Easter Sunday, 17 April 1949. Later that year a joint pastorate was formed with Lord's Hill and Brockton with Rev. Payson Burley, a grandson of C. H. Spurgeon as Pastor.

The Church purchased 4 Brook Villas for use as a manse and it was occupied in 1962 until, in 1985, a more modern house was purchased in Brook Rise. An extension to the church was built in 2006. Bill Kimbery retired in May 2007

Ministers

Francis, John	14.10.1828-09.41
Church dissolved in 1841 and reformed on 12.02.1842	
Willis, John	05.1842-06.47
Roberts, Edward	14.10.1848-0 5.10.51
Smith, Joseph, Junior	18.01.1852-12.55
Lewis, David	04.05.1856- 05.57
Dore, James	18.10.1857- 27.03.64
Evans, Thomas	01.04.1866-29.03.04
Joint Pastorate with Lord's Hill	*1907-48*
Brook, Isaac	19.05.1907- 01.13
Bradford, Arthur Ernest	26.03.1913-26.10.13
Brook, Isaac	25.03.1914- 26.09.15
Newton, John	24.10.1915-09.17 (ordained 05.03.16)
Saunders, Frederick James, BA, BD	07.09.1917-28.05.22
Wynn, Frederick	26.10.1922-15.10.27
Bowen, John Llewellyn	07.04.1929-19.06.38
Harlick, Israel	2.10.1938-27.09.42
Harlick, Israel	27.10.1947-27.10.48
On 30.12.1948 worship ceased but the building was reopened for worship on Easter Sunday, 17.04.1949	
Joint Pastorate with Lord's Hill and Brockton	*1949-66*
Burley, Payson Cunningham	08.09.1949-01.55
Jarman, Sister Margaret Florence	01.09.1956-07.09.61
Garner, Peter	23.09.1961-30.06.66
Chapman, William John	1968- 71
Aitken, Robert Wilson	05.03.1973-30.08.77
Hair, Jack	10.11.1977- 02.07.80
Fisher, Brian (*Student Pastor*)	1980-84
Hibbs, Kenneth	1984-89
Cumming, Norman Frederick, MA (*Student Pastor*)	1989-92
Dowling, David William	1994-01
Kimbery, Wilfred David (Bill), BA	21.07.2001-05.2007

Pontesbury (Second Church)

In 1841 a second Particular Baptist Church was formed in Pontesbury and it met in a private house. It joined the short-lived West Midland Baptist Association and was never in membership with the Shropshire Association. Its only pastor was R. Jones. On Census Sunday 1851 there were 29 in the afternoon congregation and 26 in the evening.[395] The Church appears to have closed about 1855, since in that year the Pontesbury Baptist Church Minute Book records:

> On Lord's Day May 6 Mary Davies (who was a member of the Second Baptist Church until the

time of its dissolution) received the right hand of fellowship and became a member of the Church.

Previously, John and Susanna Philpott, who were 'Formerly Members of the Second Baptist Church' were received into membership in July 1851, although the following year they transferred their membership to Snailbeach.

Minister

Jones, R.	1854

Prees

Prees is 5 miles S of Whitchurch. There were Baptists there in the early nineteenth century, since a chapel 'newly erected' was licensed for worship in 1809[396] but nothing is known about the subsequent history of the Baptist society there. However, recently Wem Baptist Church has begun a 'church plant', known as Prees Baptist Fellowship, in the village which is 5 miles from Wem. As the other churches in Prees have no youth work the Wem church began youth work in the village hall. In August 2002 a Holiday Bible Club was held over 5 days and there was an average attendance of 165 4-11 year olds. Then on 8 September 2002 the Fellowship held its first Sunday morning service.

Prees Heath

Prees Heath is 2½ miles NNE of Prees. Baptist work began there in 1856 when some Baptists rented a building with house attached, which was situated on the corner of the roads leading to Ightfield and Claverhall. From 1874 Prees Heath was a preaching station or branch of the church at Whitchurch, which purchased the chapel and the house in 1905 for £150. The work went into gradual decline and the Whitchurch minutes recorded in February 1925:

> With regard to Prees Heath the difficulties were very great and services had been irregular.

The work closed *c.*1984 and both the chapel and the house were subsequently demolished.

Minister

Walley, Alfred Edward (Lay)	1915-19

Quatford

The village of Quatford is 2 miles SSE of Bridgnorth. A Baptist chapel was erected in 1825 and on Census Sunday there were 25 in the evening congregation.[397]

Rolla (The Rollaw)

In 1803 Mr. Birch, who was a Baptist and owner of The Rolly (Rolla) Farm at Osbaston, obtained subscriptions to build a chapel on his farm. The opening services were conducted by Mr. Edgerley, the Elder of the Scotch Baptist Church at Shrewsbury, and also by Mr. Appleton, also from Shrewsbury.[398] There is no further information about Baptist work at Rolla until at the quarterly meeting of the ministers of the Shropshire Baptist Association at Whitchurch on 24 and 25 December 1817 - Baptists at the time did not celebrate Christmas (!) - it was reported that there was the prospect of a small church being formed at 'The Rolla', where Mr. Thomas Thomas, a member of the Shrewsbury church, regularly preached.[399] In following July five members of the Claremont church living at Rolla and Welshampton (?) requested their dismission to form themselves into a church.[400]

Mr. Thomas had also supplied Welshpool and at the Annual Meeting of the Association on 5 and 6 May 1819 he was requested to 'give attention to Llandrinio and Rolla' and the Treasurer (of the Itinerant Committee) was ordered to pay him £5 per quarter. The 1823 List of Particular or Calvinistic Baptist Churches, published in *The Baptist Magazine*, gave the name of Thomas Thomas as the pastor of the church. It was never large, the highest membership being 8 in 1824 and the lowest 6 in 1826. At the Annual Meeting in Shrewsbury on 30 June and 1 July 1829 it was reported that as

> The friends of both the Rolaw and Landrinio (*sic*), are yet without a minister, and have expressed a wish that Brother Little should come and have oversight among them for a short time on probation, it was agreed that he should be invited to supply them for three months commencing on the first Sunday in August next.

The church closed by 1839 if not earlier. Unfortunately the chapel was never conveyed to trustees with the result that when the farm was sold, the new owner demolished the building. Baptist work, however, was re-established in the area at Maesbrook two miles away in 1844.

Minister

Thomas, Thomas	1823

Rowley (see Brockton)

Ruyton of The Eleven Towns

A dwelling house at Ruyton, 9 miles SE of Oswestry, was licensed for worship in 1809[401] but a church was not formed there.

Sarn

The village of Sarn is situated in the Vale of Kerry (Dyffryn Ceri) on the A489 road between Newtown and Churchstoke Until 1860 Sarn was in the parish of Kerry (Ceri) but that year the ecclesiastical parish of Sarn was formed. Sarn, or 'The Sarn' as it is called by its older inhabitants, was in the county of Montgomeryshire until the county became part of the new county of Powys in 1974.

The earliest record of Baptist activity in the Kerry parish is in the Visitation Returns for 1804 when the Incumbent wrote that

> There are some dissenters (Anabaptists, few in number) in the Parish, their numbers of late have not increased ... There is no Chapel belonging to the Dissenters in the parish.[402]

The Dissenting Registrations for the Kerry Parish are incomplete but they include the registration of the house of Evan Bowen, The Lower House, in the township of Gwenithrew[403] and so this may well be the place where the first services were held. However, the early preaching did not result in the formation of a church. Services at Sarn were begun again by Rev. John Jones of Newtown.[404] In 1827 Joseph Davies built the chapel in the village. He is buried near the chapel's porch and the inscription on his tomb reads:

> In memory of Joseph Davies, Gent.
> formerly of Black Hall and afterwards
> of Newtown in this County,
> who died Feb 11th 1857 Aged 84 years.
> He erected this Chapel at his own expense and here and at other places for 60 years he preached the gospel gratuitously and for the same period he honorably sustained the office of Deacon in the church at Newtown.[405]

The original chapel was a simple brick building but at a later date the side facing Kerry was clad with slate to protect the building from the weather and an entrance porch was built. The inside of the chapel was modified in 1906. Until then the pulpit was immediately inside the door and so any latecomers had to enter the building in full view of the congregation! The pulpit was moved to its present position facing the entrance and the text 'O worship the Lord in the beauty of holiness', painted on a metal sheet, was fixed on the wall over the pulpit. New pews were provided, but those to the left of the pulpit were not fixed so that they could be moved to face the congregation for Anniversary services. The chapel was fitted with a new floor and two new stoves were provided for heating. The total cost of the renovations amounted to nearly £180. The largest donation of £25 towards the cost was given by David Davies Esq., MP. To mark the re-opening of the Chapel after its closure for three months, services were held on Tuesday evening 18 September 1906, on the following Wednesday with a public meeting in the afternoon and a preaching service in the evening, and on the following Sunday with three services. In addition to the minister, Rev. William Jenkins, who preached at the morning and evening services on the Sunday, no less than seven other ministers, including the former pastor, Rev. John Harrison, preached at these services.[406]

In 1938 a Schoolroom and Minister's Vestry was built, the money being given by Miss Mary Withers, formerly of Pantllwyn (Pant-y-llŵyn), Sarn, in memory of her parents, sisters and two brothers.

The chapel does not have a baptistry. In the early days baptisms took place in a brook near the City Lane, then at Trefeen (Tre-ffîn) and Bahaithlon in a brook where there was a sluice-gate to form a washing pool for sheep. During the twentieth century baptisms have also taken place in the Baptist churches at Kerry and Montgomery. For the most recent baptism a portable baptistery was erected inside the Sarn chapel.

Like many other Baptist churches in the nineteenth and twentieth centuries, Sarn found it difficult to provide adequate financial support for the ministers and their families. According to family tradition Rev. Edward Owen (1854-63) supported himself by working as a carpenter. The church accounts were clearly a matter of concern during Rev. Edward Lawrence's ministry (1893-95). There were probably similar concerns in earlier ministries but no records are available. During the twentieth century maintenance of stipendiary ministry was only made possible with the help of the Baptist Union Home Work Fund (later renamed Home Mission Fund). The Home Mission Fund Grant Application in 1972 illustrates the perilous state of the church finances. That year the church paid car expenses of £73.50 for garage repairs but no other ministerial expenses and they offered no ministerial expenses for the following year. Nevertheless the church was given a Home Mission Fund Grant in 1973. The last full time pastorate ended in 1984. Since 1989 part-time or retired ministers have served the church.

Sarn Chapel

Trefeen showing the stream where baptisms took place

It was probably during the ministry of Rev. Arthur G. Jones that the church adopted open communion. In 1899 the Radnorshire and Montgomeryshire Baptist Association required its member churches to practice close communion. So the church left the Welsh Association and joined the Shropshire Baptist Association, which later united with the West Midland Baptist Association. However, in November 2000 the church decided not to join the new Heart of England Baptist Association but to rejoin the Radnorshire and Montgomeryshire Association. While retaining its membership with the Baptist Union, the church rejoined The Baptist Union of Wales. The English Assembly was held at Sarn in June 2005, when Rev. Michael Collis became President of the Assembly.

Although Sarn has never been a large church several men, who have been members, have entered the Baptist ministry. David Richard Owen, the son of Rev. Edward Owen, and Henry Harrison[407], the son of Rev. John Harrison, became Baptist ministers. Richard Pryce Jones became the lay pastor of Montgomery Baptist Church and, following his passing of the Baptist Union Examination, he was ordained.

During the pastorate of John Harrison a young man named Charles Joseph, who was born at Stanton-upon-Arrow, Herefordshire, came into the district seeking work. His search was fruitless and when he arrived one day at the Blue Bell Inn crossroads between Sarn and Churchstoke, he was so disconsolate and unsure of his future that he decided to throw his walking stick into the air and to follow the way it fell. It pointed towards Sarn and there he found employment as a farm labourer. He began to attend services at Sarn Chapel and was led to Christ by Rev. John Harrison, who baptized him in the brook near Lower View, City Lane. After he moved to Birmingham to work as a builder, his membership was transferred to Latimer Street Baptist Church. In their letter of commendation the Sarn church said that he had been an acceptable preacher in the villages. He was encouraged to preach and to train for the ministry at Pastors' College. He had a distinguished ministry becoming President of the Baptist Union of Great Britain and Ireland in 1914.

Ministers

Branch of Zion Baptist Church, Newtown	*1826-37*
JONES, John	1826-31
TROW, Edward (Lay)	1831
JONES, John	1837-51
OWEN, Edward	1854-63
WILLIAMS, Isaac Thomas	1864
HARRISON, John	1865-84
DAVIES, William	1885-87
BAKER, Stephen James	1888-90
DAVIES, David Burwyn	1891-92
LAWRENCE, Edward	1893-95
JONES, Arthur George, PhD	1895-98
JENKINS, William	1899-1916
JOHN, John Llewellyn, BA	1916-21
MORGAN, Thomas Lloyd	1922-29
MORGAN, Richard Cynddylan	1931-35
DAVIES, David Glyn	1934-39
BAKER, Frederick Arthur	1939-47
DAVIES, William Penry Rowland, BA	1948-56
EVANS, Brian, DipTh	1958-63
DAVIES, Robert	1963-73
NICKLIN, Harold William	1974-20.5.1975

Sarn Ministers *continued*

Davies, William Penry Rowland, BA	1975-80
McHaffie, James	1980-84
Wood, Geoffrey	1989-92 (Moderator 1992-95)
Collis, Michael John, BA, BSc, MTh, PhD	1998-

Shifnal (Aston Street)

The first Baptist church at Shifnal was formed in 1700. In the *Evans List*, compiled in 1716-1719 the church at Shiffnall (as the name was then spelt) is said to have a congregation of 36 hearers, which included 6 voters for the county. In 1798 *The Baptist Annual Register* reported

> Mr. Harrisson, a member of Mr. Pearce's church, Birmingham, long in the ministry, having retired from business, in 1795 settled at Beckburry, his native village, about four miles from Sheffnall; since when he has regularly given his labours gratis every fortnight, and sometimes oftener. He also has supplied Wolverhampton. Their hearers doubled within these years, and they propose to build a gallery, if it can be prudently done.

.

Mr. Harrisson was subsequently ordained since his will describes him as the Reverend Thomas Harrisson of Beckburry. [408]

The Church Book in 1810 records payments made to various visiting preachers, including Mr. Price. Since Mr. Smith was paid for supplying at Wellington when Mr. Price was baptizing at Shifnal, he is to be identified with Rev. Richard Pryce of Wellington. Samuel Hollis was ordained as pastor on Christmas Day 1813. [409] He did not live at Shifnall, since the Church Book for the period 1813-20 refers to the payments for entertaining him and also stabling for his horse at the Red Lion. He was taken ill on 24 March 1822 and thereafter the church was supplied by visiting preachers. [410]

William Humphries was one young man who was baptized by Samuel Hollis and joined the Shifnal church. He moved to Bilston, where he joined the Baptist church and was encouraged to preach in the surrounding villages. Then at the age of about 21 he went to Horton College to train for the Baptist ministry. [411]

The meeting-house used in the time of Thomas Harrisson was no longer used by 1815, since there is a licence that year for the use as a place of worship of a joiner's shop in Aston Street, lately in the occupation of William Morris.[412]

The church joined the Midland Baptist Association in 1794 and the Association's Annual Meeting was held there in 1798.[413] The Church left the Midland Association to become a founder member of the Shropshire Baptist Association in 1808. The Association's Annual Meeting was held there in 1811 and prayers were offered by Brethren Fereday (or Ferriday) and Waldron, who supplied at Shifnall.[414]

The Shropshire Association met at Shifnall in May 1820 and Samuel Hollis wrote the Association's Circular Letter in 1820 on the subject of 'The Doctrine of the Resurrection'.[415] The church paid £1 13s 6d for entertaining 15 Ministers at the Red Lion.

The church left the Shropshire Association by 1841 and several left Aston Street Chapel to form the second Baptist Church. On Census Sunday 1851 the Aston Street congregation was 31 in the morning and 13 in the afternoon. [416] The church seems have continued until about 1877 and the chapel was sold to the District Council for £90 in 1902.

Ministers

Harrisson, Thomas	1795-98+
Hollis, Samuel	25.12.1813-22
Tunnicliffe, Jabez	1829- 31
Jones, R.	1840
Taylor, -	*c.* 1854-62
Evans, H.	1863-68
Baugh, Timothy,	1868
Branch of Dawley	*1875-77*

Shifnal (Zion)

A theological disagreement at Aston Street Chapel in October 1841 led to the formation of a second Baptist Church in Shifnal in 1842. Rev. David Payn of Bridgnorth, the Secretary in the County for Baptist Home Mission met with those who had left the Aston Street chapel and agreed to provide preachers on condition that they raised £4 10s per quarter.[417] A new chapel was opened in Old Shrewsbury (later known as Victoria) Road on 15 March 1844. The cost was above

£600 and over half of the cost was raised by 'friends on the spot'.[418] On Census Sunday the morning congregation was 110 (including 59 Sunday scholars) and the evening congregation was 13.[419]

The church closed about 1890 but it reopened in 1891. In 1898 the Bridgnorth church sent Mr. V. E. Thurston to Shifnal to help them and when he was welcomed at the Shropshire Association's Autumnal Meeting in November that year, Mr. W. Ledsham, of the church at Whitchurch, said that 'Mr. Thurston must have been a most worthy and courageous man to take up the work at Shifnal'. However, the following year he moved to Ryeford. The church then made contact with the Pioneer Mission seeking a pastor but without success. However, in 1907-08 Thurston served as pastor of the churches of Oakengates and Shifnal. The last church member died in 1920[420] and the church closed about 1921. The building was subsequently used as a magistrates' court in the 1940's but in 2005 a firm of architects in Shrewsbury are seeking to obtain lottery funding for the retention of the building and the adjoining former fire station.

The former Baptist Chapel in Shrewsbury Road

In front of the building are two tomb stones with the following Inscriptions[421]:

> In affectionate remembrance of Charles King who died March 1870 aged 76 years. He died in the hope of a glorious immortality through Jesus Christ our Lord.
>
> Jane, wife of Charles King, Born March 1st 1777. Baptized August 27 1809. Died April 19 1855

Ministers

Butcher, J.	1852
Clems (?), C. H.	1868
Baugh, Timothy	1872-74
Under the oversight of Pontesbury	*1875*
Under the oversight of Dawley	*1876-78*
Branch of Madeley	*1884-90*
The church closed but was reformed in 1891	
Joint Pastorate with Madeley and Broseley, Old Chapel	*1893-95*
Thurston, Victor E. (Lay)	1898
Joint Pastorate with Oakengates	*1907-08*

Shrewsbury (Claremont)

There are no written records of the early history of the Baptist church in Shrewsbury but the Rev. Josiah Thompson, minister from 1718 to 1725 wrote:

> There is reason to believe that it is the oldest congregation of Protestant Dissenters in this Kingdom, and that it hath kept up its Church state here through all the changes of two centuries. From some family papers now before me there appears to have been a number of Baptists here, in or before the year 1620, but when formed into the Church state or who was their pastor is not known.

In a letter to the Rev. Joshua Thomas of Leominster, he wrote

> There were many Baptists both in Shrewsbury and at Pershore in the reign of Queen Elizabeth. My great-grandfather, Mr. Thomas Seymore [i.e. Thomas Seymour, Senior], was born of Baptist parents at Shrewsbury, 1627.[422]

It is on the basis of these claims that the Claremont church claims a foundation date of 1620. However, it is important to note that he did not know when the society was 'formed into the Church state', i.e. when the church was actually formed. Owen and Blakeway[423], the historians of Shrewsbury, rejected the statements of Thompson and their conclusions have never been refuted. They concluded that the only statement on which they could rely on was that of Thomas Phillips, a deacon of the church and historian of Shrewsbury, who wrote in 1779 about the Baptists in Shrewsbury,

A society of this denomination, appears to have been known in the time of the Common-wealth, and before that time, there were a number of them here, but whether they met together as a distinct society is not certain.[424]

John Barker in his book *Shrewsbury Free Churches* said that the first minister of the church was a Mr. Penry who died for his principles in 1578 but Penry died in 1593 and any connection between him and Shrewsbury has never been established. The available evidence, therefore, shows that there were Baptists in Shrewsbury in Commonwealth times and the date of the foundation of Claremont should be in the 1650's.

Janice Cox has identified a number of Baptists among the Dissenters in Shrewsbury in the period 1660-1669. They included Richard Newton, his son Habakkuk and William Browne. William Browne was a comb maker and a member of the Mercers Company. He was prosecuted before the Shrewsbury Quarter Sessions on at least 22 occasions between September 1663 and January 1685/6 for not attending church. He was also bound over to attend the Quarter Sessions on several other occasions. On 19 April 1685 the Mayor and some other officials raided a secret conventicle held at his house. There were five women present and William Browne was heard reciting the Scriptures, namely the Epistle and the Psalms. At the following Quarter Sessions he was fined £20, a very large sum in those days.

Richard Newton, a glover, was prosecuted at the Quarter Sessions at least 24 times between March 1660/1 and January 1685/6 for not attending church. He was also bound over to the Quarter Sessions on several occasions. His daughter Tabitha Hill was a member of the Baptist church in Shrewsbury in 1718. His son Habakkuk, also a glover, appeared before the Quarter Sessions on several occasions between July 1683 and January 1685/6 for not attending church. He was presented to the Lichfield Consistory Court in 1685 for not frequenting his parish church and was excommunicated.[425]

The Shrewsbury church was Arminian in its theology and in 1692 the members approached the General Baptist Assembly about the views of Richard Newton, although there was no subsequent contact between the church and the Assembly.[426]

Upon Complaint made from the Brethren Meeting in and about Shrewsburry of persons teaching & maintaining Doctrines Contrary to the Articles of ffaith The Assembly have Agreed That a Letter should be sent to our Brother Brown and the rest of our Brethren there & another Letter to our Bror Newton touching the same the Letters in yse terms

Ffrom the Assembly of Messengers Elders and Brethren Mett at London ye 17th of the 3d. month 1692

To our Beloved Bror Brown & the rest of our Brethren in the ffaith & Order of the Gospell Meeting in & about Shrewsburry wishing & Increase of all graces &c.

Whereas we did in our Answer to your last year lett you know That wee Caused the Confesion of our ffaith to be reprinted & published by us all & did agree to hold Comunion with all such as should subscribe the said Articles of ffaith and walke accordingly & that in Case any within our Comunion should Broach Opinions contrary to the Said Confession of ffaith and will not be reclaymed to leave it to the Discretion of the Church or Churches concerned for their Reformacon And Whereas we, are Informed that you are troubled wth. Severall persons who teach & maintaine Socinianisme or Doctrines contrary to the Articles of our faith Our Advice unto you is That you call in the assistance of the Sister Churches in your parts & take such method to reclaim them as shall be judged most Necessary & so wee bid you heartily farewell.

To our Beloved Bror Richd. Newton liveing in Shrewsbury wishing grace mercy & Peace.

Whereas we have been Informed that you have to our Griefe troubled the Churches abt. You by teaching & maintaining those Opinions that are Contrary to the Articles of our faith lately reprinted & subscribed by us & Notwithstanding wee sent the last year to Desire the Contrary you yet psist herein wee againe Nevertheless to testifye our affections to you & desire of your welfare send this to Desire & perswade you to forbear & Desist troubling of the peace and welfare of our Brethren But if you should persist in these errors which we pray that you might not we have sent Advice to our Brethren what to do in that Case.

In 1707 the Baptist congregation had no regular minister and they sent a pressing invitation to the pastorate to Rev. Nathan Davies of Cwm, Radnorshire, saying 'we sometimes have not a meeting, in three, or four or six months'. He, however, chose to remain at Cwm, probably because he could live more comfortably on his own land.[427] When the John Evans List of Dissenting Ministers and Congregations was compiled, the minister was Robert Watkins and the congregation consisted mainly of farmers and tradesmen. There were 50 Hearers, 2 Voters for the County and 3 Burgesses.

It is not known where the church met in the early years of religious toleration but in 1712 an empty warehouse belonging to Mr. Thomas Seymour, Junior, in Dun's Shut[428] was licensed as a Baptist meeting house. Subsequently a new meeting-house was built in Still Yard Shut (now Golden Cross Shut) and licensed in 1736. This meeting-house was retained until it was sold in 1829, although it was used after 1780 as a Sunday school and day school.[429]

In 1748 the church called to the pastorate, William Morgan, an assistant minister of the Particular Baptist church at Blaenau, Monmouthshire.[430] On Morgan's death in 1753 the church turned once again to a Welshman, Rees Evans, originally from Newbridge (Pontnewydd), Radnorshire, who had trained at Bristol College.[431] However, the pastorate was not a happy one and the pastorate ended in 1757 as a result of 'the very bad behavior of his wife and the ill-will of some of the members.'[432]

During the ministry of Rev. Rees Evans there were difficulties as he held General Baptist views and most of his congregation were Particular Baptists. This led to his resignation in 1757 when he moved to Tewkesbury. Rev. Charles Rogers, who came from Exeter, followed him but he did not stay long and returned to Exeter. Theological tensions arose again during the ministry of his successor, Rev. John Pyne, who had been minister since January 1762. Feuds between him and his congregation reached such a pitch that he was dismissed on 13 September 1773. A number of the members of the congregation seceded to form a General Baptist Church with him as their pastor.

It is not surprising that when the Quaker evangelist, Mrs. Abiah Darby, visited Shrewsbury in 1766 she found there 'several of those called particular baptists' whose 'narrow opinion' would 'not admit that free Grace is offer'd to all'.[433]

After the bitterness of the split in 1773 the church began to seek another pastor. On the recommendation of Hugh Evans, Principal of Bristol Baptist Academy, in the autumn of 1773 the church extended an invitation to John Sutcliff. They told him that their church was 'a decaying interest', but they were hopeful that the Lord would 'yet appear for his people' and 'cause a revival to take place.' They asked Sutcliff to come 'for a month or two, or more.' Eventually he agreed to go to Shrewsbury the following June after he had finished his studies at Bristol. During Sutcliff's final year at Bristol John Sandys supplied the church but when Sutcliff came to Shrewsbury he found that the majority of the congregation were still hankering after Sandys. Sutcliff stayed there until January 1775 when he left for Olney, where he was to exercise a notable ministry. The following year the church called back John Sandys to be their pastor and he served there until 1781.[434]

During the ministry of John Sandys the congregation left Still Yard Shut and built a new meeting-house in Dog Lane. There was a large congregation on the opening day, 22 September, 1780, but lean years followed. When John Palmer came to Shrewsbury, he began to attend the Baptist church there. Unfortunately, the death of several subscribers together with others losing much of their property as a result of business failures in the town resulted in the meeting-house being shut. There was a debt of £200 and it was expected that the building would have to be sold. However, at the request of the remaining congregation John Palmer began to preach to them. On the advice of Joshua Thomas, of Leominster, he dissolved the existing church and formed a new Particular Baptist Church with a Calvinistic Declaration of Faith. He began his ministry in the autumn of 1793 and was ordained as pastor on 13 April 1796. His first task as pastor was to liquidate the debt on the place of worship. The Baptist Case Committee had given its approval to the church collecting money and summoned John Palmer to London for this purpose. This meant an absence from Shrewsbury of five months.[435] The church grew under his ministry and the chapel was enlarged in 1810. In 1820 Dog's Lane became known as Claremont Street.

Little has been recorded of the work of John Palmer's wife. Susannah, although it is known that she used to visit the poor and sick members of the church. She was accompanied in this by Mary Downing, who married James Penney in 1816. James and Mary Penney sailed to India to work with the Baptist Missionary Society. She died there on 24 December, 1829.[436]

John Palmer's health began to fail in 1820 and a Mr. Carr was appointed to assist him, but in November 1821 when the church considered his appointment as Co-Pastor there was only a small majority in favour and 'he did not feel he could accept.[437] Palmer was forced to retire in 1822 and he died on 15 May 1823 and was buried in a vault in the chapel. His widow Susannah moved to Wallingford, where she died on 28 July 1844, aged 78.

Claremont Chapel erected 1780

Interior View of Claremont Chapel erected 1780

In 1822 Manoah Kent, a student of Bradford Academy, accepted an invitation to the pastorate after having served three months on probation. The records are scanty until 1828, when 13 members withdrew and applied for their dismission to form a second church in Castle Foregate. They seemed to have disagreed with the teaching of the Pastor. Their departure did not bring an end to controversy and in 1833 the whole case was submitted to arbitration by 'indifferent persons'. The 'body of the church' chose Rev. William Steadman, DD, of Bradford, Rev. Samuel Saunders of Liverpool, and Rev. John Jackson of Bath. The opposing side chose Messrs William Rushton, Junior, J.J. Godfrey and William Holden, all of Liverpool. William Rushton was the author of *A Defence of the Particular Redemption* (1831), which opposed the views of Andrew Fuller.[438] It seems that the dispute at Claremont was about high Calvinism. The legal decision, written by Thomas Blackburn, Esquire, found in favour of Rev. Manoah Kent.[439] Some did not accept the arbitration award and were subsequently 'excluded' from the membership. The arbitration award apparently cleared the air, for the church entered on a period of extraordinary prosperity.

Manoah Kent resigned in 1844 and a letter was sent to certain well known gentlemen asking if they could recommend a minister 'who was removable'. The church eventually called Rev. John Baxter Pike, a son of the General Baptist leader, Rev. John Gregory Pike, and he served at Shrewsbury for two years. He served in both Particular and New Connexion Baptist churches and it seems that the willingness of Claremont to call him to the pastorate is a sign of how far the church had moved away from the Particular Baptist views of John Palmer.

On Census Sunday 1851 the morning congregation was 149 with 51 Sunday scholars, while the evening congregation was 268.[440] The church was not to have another long pastorate until that of Rev. Thomas Howe (1852-67). Unfortunately the records of this period are somewhat scanty, as he kept his own minute book and took it away with him on his departure. On 6 October 1872 the fellowship meeting at St John's Hill amalgamated with the Baptist Church at Claremont Street to form a church to be known as 'The Claremont Street Baptist Church.' Rev. Robert Shindler, friend and biographer of C. H. Spurgeon, became the first pastor of the united church.

Rev. Robert Shindler

By this time the chapel was falling into disrepair. In 1874 the need was so urgent that a support had to be placed beneath the ceiling to prevent its falling on to the pulpit. The Sunday school was also calling for improved accommodation. The Church Members met specially and agreed that:

> A new Chapel and School room be erected and an appeal for funds be made at once to the general public of Shrewsbury and District, but that the building scheme and appeal be deferred until the arrival of a Pastor.

When the Rev, W. Wright Robinson accepted the Call in 1876 the scheme was quickly put into effect. The old Church was demolished, a mortgage of £1,000 obtained and the present building[441] was erected in 1877-8 at a cost of £2,500. Before a baptistry was installed in the church, baptisms took place in the River Severn.

At the turn of the twentieth-century the church was at a low ebb and did not respond to the challenge of the ministry of Rev. D. M. Davies (1897-1904). However, with the coming of Rev. T. W. Hart (1906-12) prosperity returned to Claremont and the debt of the building was paid off.

Claremont Baptist Church 2003

In the 1970s some churches moved to a strongly Reformed theology and the Claremont church received such teaching during pastorate of Rev. Alvin Shuttleworth. After he left in 1985 one deacon and a few members, with several long-standing attenders, left to form Shrewsbury Evangelical Free Church, which is committed to Reformed theology and outside denominational structures.

Ministers

Travers, Samuel	Probably 1691/2 (or 94)-99
Watkins, Robert	*c.* 1699-
Thompson, Josiah	1718-25
Morris, Robert	1726
Sedgefield, John	1742-45
Oulton, John, Junior	1745-48
Morgan, William	1748-53
Evans, Rees	1753-57 (ordained 1754)
Rogers, Charles	1759-60
Pyne, John	1762-13.09.73
Sutcliff, John (not ordained)	06.1774-01.75
Sandys, John	1776-81 (ordained 1777)
Wykes, - ,	1782-83
Smith, William	1783-89
Palmer, John (Supply)	1793-94
Church re-formed 21.09.1794	
Palmer, John	1794-07.22 (ordained 13.04.79)
Carr, - (*assistant*)	1820-11.21
Kent, Manoah	12.06.1823-44
Pike, John Baxter,	1844- 01.47
Williams, W. P	14.12.1848-
Smith, James	02.02.1851-01.02.52
Howe, Thomas	10.1852-67
Angus, Henry	1867-72
Shindler, Robert	1873-75
Robinson, William Wright	1876-85
Williams, George Nathaniel	1886-8
Thomas, Hector Vortigern	1888-90
Maurice, William	1891-96
Davies, David Morgan, BA	1897-1904
Hart, Thomas William	1906-12
Compton, William Henry	1912-21
Cole, Ernest George	1923-38
Galbraith, W.	1939-45
Wooster, Claude Hué	1946-52
Hayden, Eric William, MA	1952-56
Francis, Matthew, MA, BLitt	1957-63
Davey, Walter C.	1964-12.70
Shuttleworth, Alvin, BD	09.1971-85
Collard, Philip Bruce Charles, BA	09.08.1986-96
Welch, Timothy Bernard, BA, MTh	1997-31.10.2003
Smith, Timothy (Lay *assistant*)	09.2001-
Crosland, Charles Edward, BD	11.2004-

Shrewsbury (Barker Street)

A General Baptist church was formed in 1773 when John Pyne was dismissed by the Shrewsbury church. A number of members of the congregation seceded to form a General Baptist church in Barker Street with him as pastor. He moved to Bewdley in 1781 and this probably caused the church to close.

Minister

Pyne, John	1773-81

Shrewsbury (Sandemanian or Scotch Baptist) [442]

Edward Pike, a Sandemanian Baptist, licensed a 'tenement or room in Hills Lane', [i.e. Cole Hall Chapel] as a meeting place in 1800. He was succeeded by John Edgerley in 1803 and then by the Scottish minister John Hinmers in 1808, under whom the society flourished. Cole Hall Chapel became 'too small and inconvenient' so they decided to build their own chapel in Castle Court, Castle Street (the chapel was built on top of two vaults which had been used as part of the House of Correction) which was licensed at Easter 1811. However, a dispute between John Hinmers and the rest of the congregation led to a split and he left to join the Baptist church at Dog Lane, Shrewsbury and became in 1814 the pastor of the church at Whitchurch, Salop. A 'respectable portion' of the congregation returned to Cole Hall Chapel, where they were meeting in 1815. By 1837 the congregation was described as 'nearly extinct' and it did not appear in the 1851 Census.

Ministers

Pike, Edward,	1800
Edgerley, John	1803
Hinmers, John	1808

Shrewsbury (Castle Foregate, later St. John's Hill) [443]

Rev. John Palmer preached in the Castle Foregate area of Shrewsbury but was unable to plant a new church there. However, in July and August 1827 a split began to emerge between Claremont Street Baptists and their new minister, Rev. Manoah Kent, John Palmer's successor. A group wanting Rev. Thomas Hassall of Haverfordwest as their minister now sought to establish a church in the Castle Foregate area. They said that the Claremont Street Chapel would not accommodate sufficient people and the vast population of the Castle Foregate was 'ill-served'. The breakaway group met in the area and on 28 February 1828 a new Baptist church was formed. 15 members of the new church received their dismission from Claremont Street and one from Birch Meadow, Broseley. The members erected a chapel, which was opened on Good Friday, 9 April 1830. Rev. Manoah Kent preached one of the sermons, reconciliation of the two factions having taken place two days earlier.

Unfortunately, for the new congregation the chapel was in the way of the proposed railway line from Shrewsbury to the north and so in the 1840s it was taken down. The congregation then met temporarily in a large room in a building in St. Austin Street, where it had 66 and 81 on the two services on Census Sunday 1851.[444] In 1858 they leased the former Friends Meeting House on St. John's Hill and on termination of the lease they were required to fill up the baptistry and restore the boarded floor.

When William Hawkins, formerly a member at Brentford, was ordained as pastor on 27 December 1836, his father-in-law, Rev. J. A. Jones, gave the charge to both the minister and the church.[445] He moved to Bradford-on-Avon in 1840. A report of the baptism of five people in 1849 stated that 'this little Cause has had to go through many deep waters, and has experienced many trials'.[446] When William Hawkins returned in 1860 he found the cause in a very low state.[447] He was succeeded in 1863 by Timothy Baugh who came from Broseley, Birch Meadow, and on 24 April 1864 Edward Evans, the pastor of Snailbeach, had the joy of baptizing his son at St. John's Hill.[448] Several short pastorates followed and in 1872 a Strict Baptist magazine commented that the church was lost to the denomination.[449] Most of the congregation then joined Claremont Street Baptists in October 1872, but those who did not wish to do so hired a room in Marine Terrace, English Bridge for a while.[450] They later met in the Forester's Hall, Wyle Cop, but without a permanent meeting place of worship their number soon dwindled. There is now no Strict Baptist cause in Shrewsbury.

Ministers

Sangster, A.	1830
Hassall, Thomas	1831-36?
Hawkins, William	27.12.1836 - 03.40.
Fowler, J.	1842
Arnesby, George	1844-50
Lawrence, Henry	22.09.1858-
Hawkins. William	04.1859-63
Baugh, Timothy	12.07.1863-64
Wyard, George, Junior	06.1866-
Manning, James	1871-72

Shrewsbury (Coleham, later Wyle Cop)

This congregation was established in Coleham through the zeal of Rev. John Williams in 1859.[451] When he moved to Holyhead, the church called to the pastorate Rev. C. F. Vernon from Thaxted. During his pastorate a chapel was erected at Wyle Cop and John Williams laid the foundation stone in August 1863.[452] Mr. Vernon served as pastor for two years. He resigned the pastorate to devote himself to open air preaching, remaining in Shrewsbury until 1866 when he moved to London for family reasons.[453]

Another short pastorate followed and then in 1865 the church called Daniel Jones from Haverfordwest College.[454] The work at Wyle Cop proved to be more difficult and when he left Shrewsbury in 1868 a denominational magazine reported a gift to him of 'a handsome purse and twenty sovereigns'.

> Mr. Jones has been pastor at Wy-le Cop (*sic.*) Baptist church for nearly four years; and during this time he has succeeded against many and great difficulties in doubling the number of members, and in largely increasing the attendants.[455]

Walter Satchwell, a Congregationalist, changed his views on baptism and after being baptized at Wyle Cop by Rev. William Wotton, he served as pastor of Wyle Cop (1874-76).[456] However, the cause did not flourish and it ceased to meet by November 1885.

A Committee of Deacons and Trustees was appointed to manage the property. The chapel was first let to the Blue Ribbon Army[457] and then to the Salvation Army. By June 1888 the property had passed into the hands of the Baptist Building Fund who intended to offer it for sale. However the Shropshire Association's Wyle Cop Sub-Committee wished to reopen the chapel and had requested the Baptist Union to send a Minister. The Deacons of Claremont opposed the actions but after a full discussion at the Association's Annual Meeting it was agreed to make an effort to reopen the chapel and to raise £50 for this purpose. In November that year the Sub-Committee reported that 'Negotiations with the Deacons of the Claremont Church had fallen through. The Building Fund had decided to put the property up for sale.' However, by the next Annual Meeting in June 1899 it was reported that the building had not been sold. So the Association decided to seek the co-operation of the Deacons of the Claremont Street Church in taking steps to reopen the chapel and offered the Building Fund a rent of £10 per annum. This proved impossible and at the 1890 Annual meeting it was reported that the moveable furniture of Wyle Cop Chapel had been given to the churches of the Association. The building was subsequently used as a warehouse and is now an antique shop.

Ministers

Williams, John	1859-61
Vernon, Charles Frederick	12.09.1862-63
Smith, J.	1864
Jones, Daniel	1865-68
Jones, Thomas	1869-73
Satchwell, Walter	1874-76
Berry, John James	1876-79
Llewellyn, Lewis	1880-83

Shrewsbury (Crowmoor)

During the pastorate of Rev. Eric Hayden at Claremont it was decided to build a church hall on the housing estate of Crowmoor. A site was obtained and the building was opened on Saturday, 19 July 1958. Miss Gwenoline Edwards, a member of Claremont, both donated and lent Claremont money to enable the building to be erected. It was planned to build a church next to the hall as soon as funds permitted. The hall was used firstly for Sunday School work but the first Sunday services were held there on 12 October that year.

An enthusiastic band of helpers from Claremont organized the Sunday School and Church Services, the Pastor taking an evening service once each quarter. Missionaries in training were invited to Crowmoor to gain experience and to visit the homes on the Estate and all gave splendid service, whilst two Deacons from Claremont liaised between the two places of worship.

In 1962 a Deaconess, Sister Heather Hunt, was appointed to assist the Rev. Matthew Francis during his ministry. Until 1978 Claremont and Crowmoor had a common membership but that year Crowmoor became an independent church. Mr. Ron Lycett was inducted as Lay Pastor on 9 September 1972 while teaching at Grange School and the church appointed Elders. In September 1997 he became a full time pastor with Ron Davies, one of the Elders. During this time the church grew very quickly. The congregation had to move from the church building for Sunday services by 1980, meeting in the Music Hall.

By 1983 the numbers were such that the congregation had to divide into two, half returning to the Crowmoor building, the other half becoming Barnabas Christian Fellowship with its own leadership, although the Crowmoor and Barnabas leadership still met regularly together.

Opening of Crowmoor Baptist Mission
Front Row L to R: Mr. Herbert G. T. Gee, JP (Senior Deacon, Claremont, Shrewsbury), Rev. Charles Hardiman (West Midland Area Superintendent), Mrs. E. Moore (Former President, West Midland Baptist Association), Mr. John Hamer (Deacon Emeritus, Claremont, Shrewsbury), Miss Gwenoline M. Edwards (Claremont, Shrewsbury)
Back Row, L to R: Mr. Wilfred P. Roberts (Church Secretary, Claremont), Mrs. H. G. James (President, Shrewsbury Free Church Council), Rev. Matthew Francis (Minister, Claremont, Shrewsbury), Mr. F. I. Roberts (Treasurer, Claremont, Shrewsbury)

Crowmoor Baptist Church in 1998

By 1986 the Crowmoor building was again too small. During this time there was a planning blight on the Crowmoor site. Other properties were sought including redundant Anglican, Methodist and Presbyterian churches but all proved unsuccessful. It was in 1987 that Ron Lycett sensed that God was telling him that his ministry was soon to end. At his request he, with his wife, went on sabbatical leave in 1988. Within two months of the church granting this leave the local Council gave permission to build a new church. Begun in September 1977 it was officially opened on 17 September 1988 by Mr. Lycett. He left in July 1989 to plant a new church in the Cannock Chase area He also began a teaching ministry in Ghana and Nigeria.

The Barnabas Christian Fellowship moved in 1985 to the Wakeman School and later to rooms over a public house situated between Mardol and the public car park in Hill's Lane. Since October 1996 the Fellowship has met in the former Territorial Army Centre in Coleham, which was purchased. The Barnabas Centre, as the work is now known, did not join the Shropshire District of the West Midland Baptist Association.

Ministers

Pastors of Crowmoor Mission (under oversight of Claremont, Shrewsbury)	
Hunt, Sister Heather Elise	1962-64
March, Roger Edgar (Lay Assistant)	1968-70
Lycett, Ronald Edwin (Lay)	09.1972-76
Pastors of Crowmoor Baptist Church	
Lycett, Ronald Edwin (Lay)	1976-07.89
Crichton, George	1993-2006

Snailbeach (see Lord's Hill)

Stoke Upon Tern[458]

In 1669 a number of Particular Baptists met together for worship and fellowship at Hurst Farm, a residence of the Low family situated in a secluded setting between the villages of Wistanswick and Allerton where the boundaries of three parishes met. Thomas Low attended the 1689 and 1692 Particular Baptist Assemblies in London.[459]

There is no trace of any building being erected at any time but there was a baptistry that was 'spring fed'. The Rector of the parish reported to his Bishop in 1669:

> They have more company than the parish church ... one of them gathered at a meeting fifteen shillings, at three pence per pole (head), for his paines.

The Hurst Farm

Clearly 60 people attended a meeting. The meetings were held at 'the houses of Thomas Low and his sonne'. The 'teachers' were 'Thomas Low and his sonne, illiterate persons'.[458] They may not have been scholars, but in his will of 1695 Thomas Lowe's books were valued at £1 10 s. They included Henry Ainsworth's *Annotations upon the five books of Moses and the booke of Psalmes,* a Bible with a concordance, 'Mr. Shepherd's Works in one volume, and a large Concordance, now in the hands of my brother James'.

As far as can be ascertained, the members refused to register their place of worship under the Toleration Act 1672 and it was not until 1745 that a licence for worship was granted.

It is uncertain when the meetings at the Hurst began but it is possible some members of the society were living in the parish from the time of the Civil War. A book, sold at the Hurst in 1891 but published in 1657, contains the note 'I have been banished now almost two years, but never to this day knew the cause of it, neither hath there been anything laid to my charge.'

It seems that the Hurst meeting was the origin of similar meetings in the Frodsham meetings of Cheshire, for the Hurst Minute Book records 'General Meetings' at Bostock and Frodsham.[461]

There was a burial ground in the Clover Croft in Child's Ercall parish. Local tradition speaks of gravestones but they have long since disappeared. It is supposed that over 60 burials took place, the last one being in the early 1800s.

Minister

Parker, -	1705-12+

Stoney Stretton

Stoney Stretton is a hamlet 7 miles WSW of Shrewsbury. In 1851 there was a Baptist meeting there under the leadership of George Darrall, the manager of Westbury Colliery, with an average congregation of 30.[462]

Sweeney Mountain

In 1831 Thomas Jones, a grocer, of Oswestry, purchased land at Sweeney Mountain, near Oswestry, for the erection of a School room and for preaching the Gospel. The land and building, with the necessary expenses, cost £118 11s 10d.[463] A church was formed on 10 August 1837 and David Crumpton of Shrewsbury, who was pastor of Llandrinio, was also ordained pastor of Sweeney Mountain that day.[464] From 1874 the church became a branch of the English Baptist Church at Oswestry. In the middle of the twentieth-century numbers declined and, as the condition of the building itself deteriorated it was decided to close the church about 1984. The building was sold and it is now a private house.

Tall Trees (Former Sweeney Mountain Baptist Chapel)

Minister

Crumpton, David,	10.8.1837-

Tankerville

The hamlet of Tankerville is 2 miles distant from Snailbeach. In the steep valley below was the Tankerville mine, both the hamlet and the mine taking their name from the Earl of Tankerville, who owned much of the Stiperstones hills. The mine was on the site of an earlier eighteenth century mine called the Ovenpipe Mine. From 1874-75 the Lord's Hill church had a branch at Ovenpipe and then in 1879 the church opened a branch at Tankerville. The Tankerville branch was last listed in *The Baptist Handbook*, 1920.

Vernolds Common

According to *The Baptist Handbook* (1875-82) there was branch of the Newton church (Craven Arms) at 'Vernot's Common'.

Wellington[465]

It seems that there were Baptists in Wellington in the eighteenth century. Robert Morris, a mercer, who was the minister of the Baptist church at Shrewsbury, licensed his newly built house in Wellington in April 1730 for use as a meeting-house. Although no denomination was specified in the Licence it is reasonable to assume that it was used by a Baptist society. His house, now known as Portway House, was formerly known as Chapel House. It stands in Plough Road (formerly Chapel House Road) near the centre of Wellington.[466]

Portway House (Chapel House)

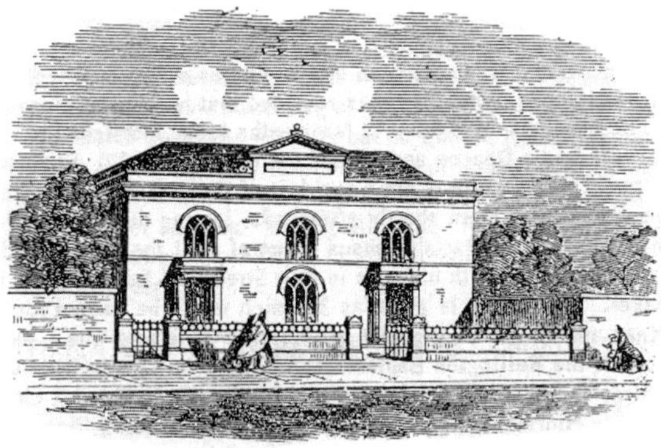

The Baptist Chapel, Wellington c. 1850

By 1772 there were no Baptists or Presbyterians in the parish but by 1799 as a result of the preaching of Rev. John Palmer there were a few Baptists. They were members of the Shrewsbury church and met at Chapel House. In March 1807 they requested the Shrewsbury church to grant them their dismissal in order to form a separate church in Wellington. The seven members who signed the letter referred to meetings held locally on Sundays and Tuesday evenings. Palmer continued to give valued assistance and encouragement to the church, travelling to Wellington to preach and administer communion.

The church was a founder member of the Shropshire Baptist Association founded in 1807. That year a Baptist chapel was opened in Back Lane (now King Street) and it was registered as a meeting house on 11 April 1809. Dissenters' meeting-houses did not have to be registered if the number of worshippers was less than 20. So the date of registration may indicate that it was only 1809 that the number of worshippers reached 20. In 1809 the church called its first pastor, Rev. Richard Pryce from Wrexham.[467]

By 1824 there were 52 members and the chapel was rebuilt in brick in 1828 with seats for 340. On Census Sunday in 1851, the morning attendance was 60 and the evening attendance 100.[468] The chapel[469] was enlarged in 1897 but closed in 1920 when the members joined the Congregationalists on Constitution Hill.

Wellington Union Free Church

Congregationalism came to Wellington some 100 years after Robert Morris licensed his dwelling house for worship. The first Congregational church had a life of some 60 years before ceasing to exist some time in the 1880's. A second church was formed in 1898 and a new chapel was opened on Constitution Hill on 18 May 1900.

During the First World War there was a strong desire to form some sort of union with the Baptists. Following discussions both churches agreed to unite to form a Union church. On 5 March 1920 a public tea was held to mark the official formation of Wellington Union Free Church with 80 members being present. The first Members' Meeting for the new church was held on 12 March 1920 when the new church's constitution was approved. Since 1918 the Pastorate has alternated between the two denominations, but in 1978 the Congregational adherents became Members of the United Reformed Church formed in 1972. Members today are part of a single membership roll encompassing Baptist and United Reformed Church traditions.

Ministers – Wellington Baptist

Pryce, Richard	1809- at least 1811
Keay, William	1820- *c.* 55 (ordained *c.* 1836)
Grainger, Henry Gabriel (*assistant)*	11.1849 – *c.* 51
Clark, Thomas	1853-55
Judson, Josephus	6.06.1856-73
Jones, Joseph	13.09.1874-78
Morgan, Joseph Brown	1880-85
Jones, Samuel	1886-88
Reid, Henry	1889-97
Hardin, Edwin	1898-1910
Pickles, Frank	1911-16

Ministers – Wellington, Union Free

The denomination of the Ministers is indicated as follows: (B) Baptist, (C) Congregational, and (URC) United Reformed Church	
Williams, George Nathaniel (B)	1918-26
Anglin, Harry Thomas (C)	1927-34
Morgan, Glyndwr, BA (B)	1935-43
Thomason, John Kenneth (C) but became (B)	1944-49
Hosier, Albert Edwin (C)	1952-57
Newton, Edwin Howard, BA, BD (B)	1960-66
Pidcock, Dennis Ryan, BA (C)	1967-72
Outen, Francis Alan, BA (B)	1973 -78
The church joined with United Reformed churches at Oakengates and Madeley churches to form the Wrekin Group	*1978-84*
Appleby, Eric Corrigan (URC)	1978-84
Foreman, Henry (Harry), BA, BD, MA (Ed), PhD (B)	1985-26.04.92
Foreman, Colin Edward (URC) & also Telford Youth Chaplain	1994-99
Stringer, Mary (B)	2000 -12.05

Welshampton

Welshampton is 2¼ miles E of Ellesmere. The first reference to a Baptist church there is in *The Baptist Magazine* in 1831, in which the date of formation of the church is given as 1820. Its first and only minister was James Fenn. Very little is known about this church, although there is a report of a baptism of a blind person in September 1844 and another person in January 1845.[470] On Census Sunday 1851 the services morning, afternoon and evening were 10, 15 and 22 respectively.[471] The average Sunday School attendance was 15. The church was last listed in *The Baptist Handbook* 1873.

Minister

Fenn, James	1820–1835

Welshpool

The Baptist cause at Welshpool (Y Trallwng), Montgomeryshire, began in 1811 when Mr. Crumpton rented a room for twenty-one years and fitted it out for worship. According to local tradition this room was in No. 4 Mount Street, now called Ellenydd, on the main road through Welshpool.[472] The Shropshire Itinerants supplied the place once every fortnight, but after ten years there seemed no prospect of a church being established. However, Joseph Ashford, Junior, returned to his native town and he was appointed by the Shropshire Itinerant Committee to supply the place regularly and this he did for eighteen months. The work progressed and on August 11 1820 Rev. John Palmer formed a new church from members dismissed from his

Ellenydd, No. 4 Mount Street

Welshpool Baptist Chapel, Chelsea Lane

church at Shrewsbury. The newly formed church gave a unanimous call to Mr. Ashford who was then ordained to the pastorate.[473]

On 4 and 6 April 1828 'a plain and commodious place of worship, 46 feet by 30 inside' was opened in Chelsea Lane. The collections at the opening service amounted to £27. The erection of the building incurred a debt of nearly £700. As a result the minister could receive no remuneration and was compelled to attend to his secular calling to maintain his family. The Hon. George Henry Roper Curzon (later 16th Lord Teynham) preached at the morning and evening services on 6 April. Mr. Crumpton of Shrewsbury preached in the afternoon.[474] The church received a grant of £60 towards the cost of the building from the London Baptist Building Fund.[475]

Joseph Ashford remained at Welshpool until 1829/30 when he moved to Kensington Baptist Church, Brecon. He was 'an energetic man, a diligent pastor, and an acceptable preacher.' His stay was short there and he became pastor of Donnington Wood Baptist Church from 1830 to 1835. Rev. Henry Morgan, who had served briefly at Kensington Baptist Church, Brecon, succeeded Joseph Ashford. By June 1831 the Welshpool church had left the Shropshire Association and joined the South-east Welsh Baptist Association. According to the List of Particular Baptist Churches in Wales, compiled by Joshua M. Thompson and published in *The Baptist Magazine*, 1831, the church at a branch at Lodge but the whereabouts of Lodge is not now known.

At a church meeting held on 10 August 1833 it was decided to dissolve the church as the members had experienced 'manyfold (*sic.*) trials of late, the statement of which would be neither agreeable or pleasant to ourselves, nor profitable to others'. At this meeting it was decided to ask Rev. Thomas Hassall of the 2nd Baptist Church Shrewsbury to assist in reforming the church fellowship. Mr. Joseph Ashford, Senior, who had served as a deacon in the original church continued as a deacon. The fact that the church approached Mr. Hassall rather than Rev. Manoah Kent of the Claremont Street church suggests that the sympathies of the church lay with those who adopted a more conservative standpoint on theological matters.

In 1836 the re-constituted church called to the pastorate, Abraham Jones, a former student of Bristol Baptist College[476] and he remained at Welshpool until 1842 when he became minister of Providence Baptist Chapel, Brook, Chatham, Kent.[477] The following year Joseph Drew from Newtown, who was an Assistant Preacher of the Old Association[478], began work in the church and in six months the church grew from 29 to 50 members.[479] In 1845 he was ordained to the pastorate,[480] but later that year he accepted the pastorate at Newbury. At Welshpool two short pastorates followed and it was probably financial difficulties that led to the closure of the church in 1849. According to local tradition, the chapel was then used for storage, the pulpit and pews being removed.

In 1856 the church was re-opened by a remarkable Baptist layman George Thorne. He was an Inland Revenue Inspector, who came to the town on being appointed as Collector for the Welshpool or Mid-Wales District. He had previously opened a Baptist church at Neath and then, despite much opposition, a Baptist church at Peterhead, Aberdeenshire.[481] On coming to Welshpool he immediately set about collecting money to pay off the debt on the building. A good congregation soon gathered and he became the pastor. In the original building the pulpit and the baptistry faced the entrance in Chelsea Lane. However, George Thorne reorganized the building so that the pulpit was now on the wall at right angles to the entrance. When he was promoted to the Stourbridge district, the ministers of the town presented him, at a public meeting with an address expressive of their love for him and their sorrow at his departure.[482]

Just before George Thorne left the district, his nephew John Wright Thorne moved to Welshpool from Greenwich. He and his wife Sarah were received into membership on 8 November 1860. That Sarah Thorne was received into membership at the same time as her husband is of interest as she had not been baptized. Probably there was an understanding that she should be baptized and George Thorne baptized her on Christmas Day. When George Thorne left his nephew John Thorne succeeded him[483] and he remained at Welshpool until he accepted a call to the church at Dawley Bank in 1864. He refused the church's first invitation but accepted a second invitation and was recognized as Pastor there on 24 July 1864.[484]

David Griffiths, who was pastor from 1906 to 1909, had become blind at the age of 6½ years but he never allowed his handicap to frustrate him. After a pastorate at Colwyn Bay he served for 22½ years as Free Chaplain to the National Institute for the Blind.

When the Shropshire Association was reorganized for the second time in 1867, the Welshpool church rejoined. However, in 1870 it joined the Old Welsh Association again. The church joined The Baptist Union in 1843. In 1867 the church at Maesbrook became a branch of the Welshpool church.

Welshpool Baptist Church is the only Nonconformist church in the town that still meets in its original building.

Ministers

ASHFORD, Joseph, Junior	1820-29
MORGAN, Henry James	1830-34
Church was dissolved and re-organized 10.08.1833	
JONES, Abraham	20.7.1836-42
NORGROVE, John Corban	1841- 08.1842
DREW, Joseph	1843-45 (ordained 1845)
CARPENTER, Charles	1845- 09.47
BELL, Samuel M.	1848-49
The church closed in 1849 but was re-opened 22.09.1856	
THORNE, George	22.09.1856-60
THORNE, John Wright	1861-64
ALFORD, James Drewitt	1864-66
Joint Pastorate with Maesbrook	*1865-67*
GRIFFITHS, T.	1866-67
EVANS, John	1869-71
JENKINS, Jabez	1873-75
OWEN, R.	1878-85
HARRIS, H.	1887-88
JONES, Samuel	1889-90
ROWSON, Thomas	1891-05
GRIFFITHS, David	1906-09
DOUGHTY, Charles Henry	1910- 28.09.19
WILLIAMS, Idris, BA	29.09.1922-28.02.24
EVANS, John Henry	08.07.1924-30
ROBERTS, Emrys	1931-34
Joint Pastorate with Llanfair Caereinon, Montgomeryshire	*1938-43*
BASSETT, Brinley	1938-43
CLEAL, Clifford Haynes, MA, BD *(Oversight)*	1972-75
Joint Pastorate with Oswestry with Maesbrook and Sweeney Mountain (E. Montgomeryshire Group)	*1977-80*
Joint Pastorate with Oswestry and Sweeney Mountain	*1981-86*
DONOHOE, Stewart (Lay)	11.2000-08.2003
FANTHAM, Keith	2006-

Wem[485]

This church had its birth through the ministry of Rev. John Palmer of Shrewsbury. He first visited Wem in 1810 and, together with James Fenn, was responsible for bringing together others 'who were Dissenters'. James Fenn was dismissed by letter from his Shrewsbury church to Wem on 2 May 1813. The Minutes of a Church Meeting held on 30th December 1814 read:

> Four persons had their dismissal to form a Church of the same Faith and Order at Wem and the first recorded meeting held there took place on the 3rd January 1815.

No. 45 Cripple Street was registered for worship in 1813 as was a meeting house at the same address in 1814. Successive Baptist chapels stood on the same site, now known as Market Street, until the Church acquired the former United Reformed Church premises in Chapel Street in 1988. Interestingly, this chapel's burial ground contains a memorial to Rev. William Jones 'minister of the gospel in this town',[486] who was the minister of the Baptist church from November 1851 until his death the following June at the early age of 40. On Census Sunday 1851 the attendance at the two services was 22 and 45.[487]

In 1853 the church called to the pastorate J. B. Rotherham, a former Wesleyan preacher, who after reading Alexander Carson's book on baptism[488] had been baptized as a believer by Rev. William Leng, of Stockton-on-Tees. While at Wem Rotherham came into contact with the congregation of the Disciples of Christ at Shrewsbury and he arranged for a visiting evangelist, Mr. Francis Hill, of Sunderland to conduct a service in Wem Baptist chapel. In 1854 Rotherham resigned the pastorate and joined the Disciples of Christ[489] and became an evangelist for The Disciples.

The foundation stone of a new chapel was laid on 21 July 1870, the cost of the building being £1,056. It was of a "T" shape design and the limited space had been well planned.

A special feature of the Church had been its strong interest in missionary work and here reference must be made to the pastorate of A. E. Walley, JP (1920-1950). Pastor Walley had been actively connected with the Church since 1918 and his residence at Lighteach Farm became 'open house' for the entertaining of missionaries as well as for visiting preachers, also for meetings, etc., and the family produced active workers in the Church.

Henry Eckford, who served as a deacon and Church Treasurer, became noted for his contributions in the horticultural world. He gave special attention to the growing of sweet peas and eventually introduced no less than 115 varieties. He became a well-known personality and was awarded the Victoria Medal of Honour of the Royal Horticultural Society. He was given a silver teapot by horticulturalists from all over the world and the address given to him not only mentioned his horticultural achievements but also 'his beautiful Christian character'. He died on 5 October 1905 and two art windows were erected at the back of the pulpit to his memory.

In 1988 the church acquired from the United Reformed Church, the former Independent Chapel, in Chapel Street and the windows in memory of Henry Eckford were transferred to the new premises in 1991.

Wem joined the Shropshire Baptist Association in 1815 and became a member of the West Midland Baptist Association in 1916. In 1896 Wem joined the Free Church Council which had been formed

Wem Baptist Chapel, Market Street (until 1991)

Wem Baptist Chapel (formerly Wem Independent Chapel)

in that year. The church was unable to accept the Swanwick Declaration 'Not Strangers but Pilgrims' and it withdrew from membership of the West Midland Baptist Association and the Baptist Union in 1989. It became a member of the Fellowship of Independent Evangelical Churches in February 1991.

Ministers

Fenn, James	1815-
Phillips, John	22.10.1816 -
Muckley, William	1821-23
Gough, Walter	11.07.1825-30
Stephens, John Goddard	1830-30.06.36
Hinmers, John (*Honorary*)	1835
Griffiths, J.W.	1839
Jameson, -	1841-42
Corken, William Duncan	1843 - 24.01.45
Pugh, William	25.12.1850 -51
Jones, William	16.11.1851-27.06.52
Rotherham, Joseph Bryant	1853 -54
Osborne, W.	1854-09.57
Morgan, Edward	1860-62
Corby, T.	1862-63
Hughes, Hugh	1867-76
Richards, Richard	09.10.1876-80
Sear, George	29.11.1887-17.09.95
Roberts, David William	03.05.1896-1900
Watts, Isaac	1900-04
Cowling, Thomas Henry	08.1904- 01.09
McLeod, J. L. Keith (*temporary pastor*)	1910
Boulton, Charles Sumner	1910-16
Bennett, William,	16.03.1917- 08.20
Walley, Alfred Edward, JP (Lay)	1920-50
Toms, Kenneth Henry	1950-54
Burch, Walter W.	1954-57
Chapman, William John	1960-68
Iles, Derrick Joseph	1968-71
Moorman, J. A.	1972-74
Jones, Colin David	30.11.1974-09.96
Wright, Philip Michael	1999-

Whitchurch

The work at Whitchurch began when Mr. and Mrs. John Bayley, who were members of the Baptist church at Shrewsbury, moved there in 1778. John Bayley opened his house for worship, which he conducted by reading the scriptures and speaking from a chapter to a few of his neighbours who met with him. After this he arranged for Rev. John Palmer of Shrewsbury and Rev. Richard Pryce of Wrexham to preach once a month on Whitchurch and Tilstock, a village 2½ miles distant from Whitchurch. [490]

Soon afterwards their meeting place was removed to a house in Jarratts Yard supposed to be at Green End. A church was formed in 1808 when eight persons received their dismissal from the church at Shrewsbury and on the 1 March 1809 James Yates was appointed its Pastor. In 1813 John Bayley registered for worship a building, which he owned in Green End, which had previously been used as a malt kiln [491] and it was opened for worship on 11 January 1814. [492] Then in October 1824 a new chapel was opened to the west side of Green End. On Census Sunday 1851 there were 104 present (including 58 Sunday scholars) and 93 were present in the evening. There were 64 Sunday school scholars in the afternoon. [493]

Between the years 1862 and 1889 considerable improvements were made to the chapel.[494] New windows were put in, gas was installed and the premises enlarged by extending towards the street and forming an entrance lobby with a schoolroom above.

James Yates was present at the first Annual Meeting of the Shropshire Association in 1809[495] but by 1835 the church had ceased to be in membership with the Association. However, by that date it had joined the Baptist Union and it was then the only Shropshire church in membership with the Union. When the Association was reorganized in 1853, the church became a member.

In October 1874 the church called to the pastorate Mr. W. Carey Walters on the assumption that 'his Theological Teaching will be substantially in accord with Baptists as represented by his own father; the Rev[d] A. Maclaren of Manchester, and Rev[d] C. H. Spurgeon and Dr. Landels of London'. To prevent any misunderstanding the church asked him to give 'an early communication of his general views of the doctrines of Christianity as he may deem of vital importance'. The church was satisfied with his reply and he commenced his ministry at Whitchurch on 3 January 1875.

Up to 1875 the church had only admitted to its membership those who had been baptized on profession of their faith but the church then decided it was willing to receive as members those 'who whether by conviction or other sufficient cause cannot be baptized'. In January the church received Mrs. Sophie Walmsley, the wife of a deacon, as 'an unbaptized member'.

Carey Walters exchanged his pulpit with Rev. J. B. Bradnock, Unitarian minister at Nantwich. He subsequently resigned his pastorate and formed a Free Christian Church (Unitarian) in the town. '5 members all unbaptized left with Mr. Walters plus 2 baptized members'.

Following the departure of Mr. Walters a number of short pastorates ensued. Difficulties arose during the pastorate of Rev. Isaac Lloyd (1879-83) because he refused to allow 'any unbaptized person to have a voice and a vote in church business'. The church enjoyed considerable blessing during the ministry of Rev. Edward Ebenezer Lovell (1899-1913). At the end of his ministry there were 62 members at Whitchurch and 11 members at Ightfield, with 95 scholars at Whitchurch, 12 at Ightfield and 10 at Prees Heath. The last pastorate ended in 1938 and with the decline in numbers services ceased about 1945. The chapel building found a new lease of life as the Whitchurch Institute.

Ministers

Yates, James	01.03.1809-12
Hinmers, John	02.05.1815-
Phillips, John	11.04.1822-15.04.48
Joint Pastorate with Ightfield	*1848-76*
Bontems, William	25.10.1848-11.55
Harvey, J.	1859-60
Yeadon, James Edward	13.07.1862-06.09.70
Wylie, Alexander, MA	02.10.1870- 04.73
Walters, W. Carey	03.01.1875-11.76
Joint Pastorate with Ightfield and Prees Heath	*1877-1937*
Hall, Henry	1877-79
Lloyd, Isaac	1879-10.06.83
Reid, Henry	1884-85
Reid, Henry	1886-89
Adams, John Swancott	1890
Williams, Samuel Turner	1892-96
Jones, Albert Edward Owen	1896-98
Lovell, Edward Ebenezer	1899- 19.06.13
Rignal, Charles	1914-17
McMillan, Peter	07.03.1920-26.12.20
Collett, James George, ATS	26.06.1921-25
Wright, Samuel Thomas	17.02.1926-38

Whitcott Keysett

There was a Baptist congregation meeting a house in the village at the time of the 1851 Religious Census. [496] Thomas Jones, the pastor of Bettws-y-Crwyn, who moved to Whitcott in 1851, may have held meetings in his home until his death in 1873. A church at Whitcott was formed in 1876. Its minister, J. H. Wait, became minister also of Coxall in 1881 and it was a branch of Coxall until it closed in 1886.

Minister

Wait, John Henry	1876-1886 (also Coxall from 1881)

Woodside, Telford

To meet the spiritual needs of families moving into Telford several 'Pastoral Centres' were planned with the expectations that the denominations would cooperate together. The first was the Dawley Pastoral Centre in 1967 using the Methodist premises. The Hereford Diocese and Madeley Parish Church paid for a purpose-built pastoral centre at Sutton Hill in 1967, while the West Midland Baptist Association paid for a pastoral centre at Woodside. Each pastoral centre had an area for worship but also facilities for other Christian activities linked with the local community. The foundation stone of the Woodside Pastoral Centre was laid by the General Secretary of the Baptist Union, Dr. David Russell, on 5 October 1968.

Woodside remained an essentially Baptist venture with an afternoon service at 2.00 p.m. to enable members of the Madeley church to attend. The Madeley church held its evening service at the centre for a time in the early 1970s. The Baptist Union gave an Initial Pastorate Grant enabling Rev. Gordon Tubbs to serve as minister of Woodside and Madeley from 1970 to 1976.

In 1979 the work at Woodside needed a fresh start and the thriving Bridgnorth church appointed as a full-time worker, Philip Moody, a former London City Missionary, who had worked on the Thamesmead Estate. The Bridgnorth church and the West Midland Baptist Association each provided £2000 for his stipend. The services were then held at 11.00 a.m. and 7.00 p.m. Woodside was reformed as an independent church of 29 members in January 1982. However, there were tensions in the fellowship concerning the importance of the charismatic gift of prophecy and Philip Moody left the church at end of 1983. The growth of the church stagnated in the later 1980s and the church closed in December 1992. The building was leased to the Telford and Wrekin Council in 2004.

Minister

Joint Pastorate with Madeley	*1970-76*
Moody, Philip Geoffrey (Lay)	01.04.1979-12.83

Wrentall[497]

James Freme of Wrentall House opened a Baptist chapel c. 1840. It had an average congregation of 26 in 1851 when it was served from Pontesbury. The chapel closed *c.* 1875 and was used as a village hall after Freme's death. The building was re-opened as a chapel by the Primitive Methodists in 1910 but closed in 1986. It has now been converted to residential use.

Wrexham (Chester Street)[498]

The English Baptist Church in Chester Street is in direct descent from the oldest "gathered" community of Dissenters in Wrexham. The original Dissenting congregation worshipped in a barn situated behind the Talbot Inn in Queen Street. From the time when Rev. John Williams became a Baptist in 1715, the Baptist element in the congregation increased. After his death in 1725 the church looked for a Baptist pastor, able to preach in both English and Welsh. It was not until

The Old Baptist Chapel demolished in 1875. (Drawing based on an old photograph)

Wrexham, Old Meeting, Chester Street

1740 that Rev. Evan Jenkins, who had been an assistant minister at Penygarn,[499] settled at Wrexham. Because those baptized as infants could be members of the Wrexham church, the church could not join the Welsh Association. However, Evan Jenkins was a frequent preacher at the Association meetings. He was one of those who 'could preach in English and repeat [the sermon] in Welsh'.[500] During his ministry land was purchased at Chester Street in 1747.

After the death of Evan Jenkins in 1752 at the age of 39 there was no settled preacher until Rev. David Jones, of Moleston, Pembrokeshire, became the pastor in 1755. At Cefn Bychan, where he regularly preached, some came to hear him from the top of Glyn Ceriog, and invited him visit them there. At Glyn Ceriog a congregation was formed and they wished to erect a chapel there. The cost of erecting chapels at Glyn

Ceriog and Wrexham was beyond the resources of the congregations. So as was usual at the time, David Jones raised money on preaching tours. In 1762 it became possible to erect chapels at both places. The Wrexham church was known as the "Old Meeting", a term that is still used in official records and on the church's headed notepaper. Sadly, 'something of a disgraceful nature took place between him and the church' and he left to become an itinerant preacher. [501]

The Baptists at Cefn Bychan continued to be members of Wrexham until 1786. About that time, or possibly sometime earlier, fellowship was established between the Wrexham church and that at Brassey Green, near Bunbury, Cheshire.

In 1773 Joseph Jenkins, the son of Rev. Evan Jenkins, accepted a call to the Old Meeting and he immediately re-organized the church. The members adopted a Calvinistic Declaration of Faith and Church Covenant. The Trust Deed of 1778 requires that the minister must be a Baptist. Joseph Jenkins preached at the Welsh Association meetings, principally in English on five occasions. He remained in the town until 1794 when he moved to London.

Joseph Jenkins was succeeded by Robert Roberts, a deacon of the church, who adopted Sandemanian views. Under his ministry the congregation declined until services ceased to be held regularly and the church became temporarily extinct. The church was revived when three Baptists from elsewhere moved into the town. They were Mr. John Ratcliffe and his wife, Mary, from Manchester and Mr. Richard Pryce, from Newtown, Montgomeryshire. Mr. Ratcliffe contacted Rev. John Palmer of Shrewsbury who came over to Wrexham several times. On 25 September 1805 he baptized 5 people, who together with 6 others became foundation members of the new Particular Baptist Church. On 20 November Richard Pryce was ordained as the pastor and John Ratcliffe became a deacon. The church became a founder member of the Shropshire Baptist Association.

Richard Pryce resigned towards the end of 1809. As the church was now said to be 'in a destitute state', it applied to the Tutor of Bradford Academy for assistance. Thomas Barraclough was recommended to the church and he spent some time there during the summer and the autumn that year. He received a pressing and unanimous invitation to become the pastor and he was ordained there on 31 January 1810. The fortunes of the church revived but sadly he caught a severe cold when attending a funeral and he died in June 1811 at the early age of 29.[502]

After the death of Thomas Barraclough the church declined numerically until Rev. John Palmer, encouraged George Sayce, a member of his church and a tallow chandler, to move to Wrexham in 1817. He was not ordained until 1821.[503] During his ministry the church grew and he was able to establish a daughter church at Holt as well as supporting missions at Bowling Bank, Gresford and Wheatsheaf. On Census Sunday 1851 there were 75 adults and 45 scholars in the morning, 40 scholars in the afternoon, and 118 adults in the evening.[504]

The chapel met the needs of its members for many years and in April 1875 a 'Day of humiliation and prayer' was observed to thank God for his work at Chester Street over the years. About this time, it was felt that the fellowship should undertake the building of another place of worship in the area. The last services in the chapel were held in May 1875. The site was cleared and a new chapel was erected upon it at a cost of £1,700. The first service was held on the 7 October 1876.

Unfortunately, the foundation stone of the new chapel is now badly weathered so that the name of the minister who laid the stone cannot be read. He was Dr. John Prichard (or Pritchard), who was minister of Penybryn English Baptist Chapel, Llangollen, from 1861 until his death in September 1875. The original inscription on the foundation stone was: [505]

BUILT 1762

O THOU THAT INHABITEST
THE PRAISES OF ISRAEL
OUR FATHERS TRUSTED IN THEE
LAID BY
REV. J. PRITCHARD, DD, AUG 31 1875

When there was the probability that the Shropshire Association would become part of the West Midland Baptist Association, the Chester Street Church decided that it should leave the Shropshire Association and transfer to the North Wales Baptist Union. After such a long association with the Shropshire churches, this transfer, which took place in September 1915, was very reluctantly agreed to by the Shropshire Association.

In 1902 it was realised that after a period without a pastor, the membership of the church had begun to decline considerably. So the church called a student from Rawdon College, Lewis John Harvard. He was not very strong physically and he left in 1908 to become co-pastor with Rev. John Thomas at Myrtle Street, Liverpool. The Welsh Revival of 1904-1905 does not appear to have had any marked influence on the Chester Street Church, even though there was much interest taken in it throughout the Wrexham district. Since 1966 the church has been served by lay pastors.

Ministers

Independent Ministers served the church at first but c. 1715 Rev. John Williams became a Baptist and subsequent pastors been Baptists.	
Evans, John	1667/8-00
Thomas, Jenkin	1702-08
Williams, John	12.07.1715-05.10.25
Jenkins, Evan	1740-23.03.52
Phillips, Henry, (*assistant)*	1751-53
Jones, David	1755-70
Jenkins, Joseph, MA	1773-94
Roberts, Robert (not ordained)	1794-02
The Baptist cause became extinct but was reconstituted on 25.09.1805	
Pryce, Richard	20.11.1805-09
Barraclough, Thomas	31.03.1810- 20.06.11
Sayce, George	1817-45 (ordained 27.06.1821)
Clare, Joseph	27.09.1846-53.
Brooks, Thomas	27.09.1853-54
Griffiths, Enoch	08.1856- 07.12.57.
Ashworth, Abraham	01.1859-
Lyon, John	21.04.1861–65
Williams, Isaac Thomas (*Supply*)	1865
Perkins, Frederick	O8.09.1866-30. 11..68
Brasted, John Bangley	1870
White, W. (*Supply*)	10.1871-72
Williams, R.	1872
Thomas, Samuel David	1874-82
Jenkins, David Rhys	1879-86
Hudgell, Philip Augustus	17.04.1889-15.11.91
Thomas, John Hobson	14.08.1892-99
Harvard, Lewis John	1902-08
Morris, Lewis	1909 -21
Greenwood, Vincent	1924-27
Watkins, A.J.	1933-47(?)
Himbury, David Mervyn, BA, BD	1950-51
Drake, Ralph, BD	1953-57
Thomas, William Derek, BA, BD	1965-68
M'Caw, Martin Trevor, BA, BD	1971-77
Heap, Stephen Irvine	1980-86
Thomas, Nigel Bruce	1993-96
Wells, John Leslie (Lay)	1996-09.2004
Evans, Kenneth (Lay)	01.05.2005-

Wrexham (Bradley Road)

During the latter part of the nineteenth century a large number of people came to reside in the Newtown area of Wrexham, Denbighshire, and in conjunction with the Free Churches in the area, members of Wrexham (Chester Street) felt it to be their duty for the advancement of the Kingdom of God to provide for the spiritual needs of a growing population.

A frontage of some eighty feet to Bradley Road was purchased for £148, the object being to build first a Sunday School and ultimately a Chapel in front, but it was then decided to build the Chapel first.

The foundation stones were laid on the 21 October 1898. Stones were laid in the following order:

1. By the Rev. J. H. Thomas, Pastor of Chester Street Chapel.
2. By Mrs. Lyon in memory of her husband Rev John Lyon, a former Pastor of the Church.
3. By Lady Emily Osborne Morgan in memory of her husband the Right Hon. Sir George Osborne Morgan, Bart., QC, MP, for 29 years, and who had served the cause of religious equality in Parliament.
4. By Alderman Simon Jones JP, who had been a faithful officer of the Church for a very long period.
5. By Mr. John Sudlow, the oldest Member of Chester Street Chapel.

In his address on this occasion Alderman Simon Jones urged that "Back to the Scriptures" should be the cry of the Free Churches.

Unfortunately there is no record of the opening of the chapel but it is thought to have been in 1899.

Congregational singing in the Baptist Chapel was encouraged by the Officers of Bradley Road and the

Bradley Road Evangelical Baptist Church

"Psalmody Festivals" were revived with more than ten Churches taking part. At the first service a great surprise was created by announcement that Dr D. E. Jones, Mus. Doc., of Scranton, Pennsylvania, one of America's foremost Welsh musicians, was present. He was given a hearty reception and afterwards gave an interesting address.

When Rev. John Hobson Thomas left Chester Street Chapel in 1899, the Mission at Bradley Road called to the pastorate, Rev. Joseph Beaupré, as its first pastor and he commenced his ministry on 7 July, 1900. He was also responsible for two other English language churches, namely those at Holt and Lodge Brymbo. He did not stay in Wrexham for long as he took up the pastorate at Wincanton, Somerset, the following year. Rev. Charles Nicholas undertook charge of the church for a few months in 1935. Apart from these ministers the church has been under the joint ministry of the mother church at Chester Street until it became an independent church in 1971.

Shortly after the church gained its independence, the building was found to have extensive dry rot and so had to be demolished. A new church building was then erected.

Along with the Chester Street Church the Church joined the North Wales Baptist Union in 1915. As a consequence of the Christological controversy in the Baptist Union it left the Lancashire and Cheshire Association in 1972. The church is now known as Bradley Road Evangelical Baptist Church and it is a member of the Associating Evangelical Churches of Wales.

Ministers

Branch of Chester Street, Wrexham	*c. 1898-1900*
Joint Pastorate with Holt and Lodge Brymbo	*1900-01*
Beaupré, Joseph	7.07.1900-01
Branch of Chester Street, Wrexham	*1901 – c. 1971*
Nicholas, Charles (*Supply*)	1935
Harding, James Leslie	25.09.1976-86
Green, Steven John	1992-97

Bibliography

Primary Sources

John Evans List of Dissenting Congregations and Ministers 1716-1729 (DWL MSS 34.4)

Shropshire Baptist Association Minute Books: 1818-1892; 1892-1912 (SA NO7290)

Circular Letters

Circular Letter of the Elders and Messengers of several Baptist Churches Being Met in Association at Shrewsbury, May 26 and 27, 1801. (Copy in Shropshire Baptist Association Minute Book 1818-1892)

Shropshire Baptist Circular Letters 1809-1823, 1826 (BCRL Church History A 270.08 C12)

Circular Letter of the Shropshire Baptist Association 1862 (RPC) & 1907

Church Books

Unless otherwise indicated the Church Books are in the possession of the Church

Aston on Clun

Church Meeting Book May 1929-June 1964 (SA NO6144/1)

Broseley (Old Chapel)

Broseley Baptist Church Register 1749-1877 (SA NO6144/7)

Donnington Wood

Church Meeting Minutes: January 1899-January 1924; March 1924- July 1951; February 1952 – November 1967; October 1968-September 1992

Deacons' Minutes: May 1949- May 1968; June 1968-November 1970; May 1971-June 1976' August 1976-January 1981

Ludlow

Church Minute Book 1874-1901 (SA NO5033/1) & 1901-1929 (SA NO5033/2)

Market Drayton

Minute Book 1923-1955 (contains photocopies of H. C. Brookes, "History of Market Drayton Baptist Chapel", *Newport and Market Drayton Advertiser*, c. 1890) (SA NO7290)

Minute Books 1970-1980 and 1980-1993 (held by Rev. Dr. John Smith)

Oswestry

Oswestry Baptist Church Records 1803-1990 (SA NO6813)

Pontesbury

Church Book 1852-1869

Sarn

Church Meeting Minutes 1894-1929 & 1931-1982

Shrewsbury

Claremont Church Books 1718-1814 (SA NO 2706/1) & 1819-1846 (SA NO/2706/2)

Welshpool

Church Meeting Minutes 1821-1865 & 1872-1935

Whitchurch

Church Meeting Minute Books 1809-1848 (SA NO6144/5/1), 1848-1887 (SA NO 6144/5/3/1), 1887-1911 (SA NO 6144/5/5/3/2), 1911-1919 (SA NO6144/5/3/4), & 1936-1939 (SA NO6144/5/3/5)

Sermons

"How shall I stand before God?", A Sermon Preached on Lord's-Day Evening, August 4th, 1895, at Birch Meadow Chapel, Broseley, by Mr. Arthur Shinn (Minister), London.

Secondary Sources

Unless stated otherwise London is the place of publication of books and Chapel Histories have been published by the respective churches

General

T. M. Bassett, *The Welsh Baptists*, Swansea, 1977.

David Bogue and James Bennett, *History of Dissenters from the Revolution in 1688, to the Year 1808*, 4 volumes, 1812

Geoffrey R. Breed, *Particular Baptists in Victorian England and their Strict Communion Organizations*, Didcot, 2003.

J. H. Y. Briggs, *The English Baptists of the Nineteenth Century*, Didcot, 1994.

Raymond Brown, *The English Baptists of the Eighteenth Century*, 1986.

Kenneth Dix, *Strict and Particular: English Strict and Particular Baptists in the Nineteenth Century*, Didcot, 2001.

Charles Hulbert (ed.) and Thomas Phillips, *The History and Antiquities of Shrewsbury*, 2nd Edition, Shrewsbury, 1837

John Jones, *The History of the Baptists in Radnorshire, with a sketch of the history of Nonconformity in the County*, 1895.

J. M. Gwynne Owen (ed.), *Records of an Old Association Being A Memorial Volume of the 250th Anniversary of the Midland, now the West Midland Baptist Association*, [Birmingham?], 1905

Dale A. Johnson, *The Changing Shape of English Nonconformity 1825-1925,* New York & Oxford, 1999.

Thomas Phillips, *The History and Antiquities of Shrewsbury*, Shrewsbury, 1779.

Shropshire Sites and Monuments Record (http://www.ahds.ac.uk)

R.F. Skinner, *Nonconformity in Shropshire 1662-1816: A Study in the Rise and Progress of Baptist, Congregational, Presbyterian, Quaker, and Methodist Societies*, Shrewsbury, 1964.

Royal Commission on the Historical Monuments of England, *An Inventory of Nonconformist Chapels and Meeting- Houses in Central England (compiled by Christopher F. Stell),* 1986.

Ian Sellers (ed.), *Our Heritage: The Baptists of Yorkshire and Cheshire 1647-1987,* Leeds, 1987.

William Urwick (ed.), *Historical Sketches of Nonconformity in the County Palatine of Chester,* London & Manchester, 1864.

B. R. White, *The English Baptists of the Seventeenth Century,* Didcot, 2nd Edition, 1996.

W. T. Whitley, *Baptist Association Life in Worcestershire 1655-1926.*

W. T. Whitley, *Baptists of North-West England 1649-1913,* London & Preston, 1913.

Chapels and Meeting-houses

Bridgnorth

A petition to Cromwell, 1 February 1651/2, and *A Further Testimony to the Truth,* October 1659 in Alan Betteridge, "Early Baptists in Leicestershire and Rutland (II) Original Documents: Commonwealth and Restoration, 1650-1661," *Baptist Quarterly,* 25 (April, 1974), 272-285

J. B. [probably James Butterworth of Bromsgrove], "History of the Baptist Church, Bridgnorth, Shropshire," *Baptist Magazine,* 1821, pp. 108-109.

Broseley

Footprints on the Track of Time during Fifty Years: A History of Birchmeadow Sunday School to its Jubilee, 1864.

Denis Mason, *The Old Baptist Chapel, c.* 1991

J. Randall, *History of Broseley and its Surroundings being a Complete History of Broseley, Willey, Barrow, Benthall and Linley,* Madeley, Salop, 1879, pp. 222-226.

Coxall

Patrick J. Baker, *Coxall Baptist Church Centenary 1871-1971,* 1971.

Dawley

Arthur Lester, *Fifty Years: A Jubilee Sketch of the Work and Progress of Dawley Baptist Church 1846-1896,* Reprinted 1999.

H. Mostyn Jones, *Baptist Church Dawley: A Brief Account of 100 Years of Christian Witness,* Reprinted 1999.

W. G. Newell, *Baptist Church Dawley: an Account of the First 150 years* (unpublished MSS)

Knighton

[John Pugh], *Centenary Souvenir Baptist Church Knighton, Rads. 1833-1933,* Knighton, 1933.

D. J. Richards, *Norton Baptist Church Knighton. In Commemoration of one hundred years of worship, witness and work, 1865-1965,* Llandrindod, 1965.

Madeley

[A.S. Clement], *Baptist Church Madeley. Centenary Brochure 1858-1958.*

Pontesbury

The Baptist Church, Pontesbury, Shropshire: Register of baptisms, admissions, exclusions, dismissals and death 1828-1836 together with a history of the establishment of the Church in Pontesbury [PRO ref. RG4/1893], Shropshire Family History Society, 1983.

Frank Houlding, *A History of One Hundred and Fifty Years of Pontesbury Baptist Church 1828 to 1978.*

Shrewsbury

W. H. Compton, *Claremont Baptist Church, Shrewsbury: Tercentenary Souvenir 1920.*

Janice V. Cox, "'Simplicity without Meanness, Commodiousness without Extravagance' The Non-conformist Chapels and Meeting-Houses in Shrewsbury in the Nineteenth-Century", *Shropshire History and Archaeology.* 1997, 72, 52-97.

Janice V. Cox (ed.), *The People of God: Shrewsbury Dissenters 1660-1669,* Shropshire Record Series Vols 9 & 10, Keele, Staffs., 2006-2007

M.M. Thomas and P. Price, *From Dun's Shut to Claremont Street 1620 to 1995: A brief history of Claremont Baptist Church,* Shrewsbury: Claremont Street Baptist Church, 1995.

Stoke upon Tern

Thomas W. Hardy, "Notes on Early Baptists at the Hurst Farm, Stoke upon Tern," *Transactions of the Shropshire Archaeological Society,* 1969-1974, 59, 48-52.

Wellington

Harry Foreman, *Old Dissent in Wellington, Shropshire 1700-1920: The Story of Union Free Church,* 1986.

Wem

A de M. Chesterman, *A Short History of Wem Baptist Church 1815-1965,* 1965

E. Dakin, *A Short History of Wem Baptist Church 1815-1997.*

Wrexham

J. Davis, *History of the Welsh Baptists,* Pittsburgh, 1835 (Reprinted USA, 1982, pp 93-6)

Alfred Neobard Palmer, *A History of the Older Nonconformity of Wrexham and its Neighbourhood,* Wrexham, 1888.

G. Vernon Price, *The "Old Meeting" Its Times, Ministers and People: The History of the Chester Street Baptist Church Wrexham,* Wrexham, n.d. [1930?].

Joshua Thomas (gol. B. Davies), *Hanes y Bedyddwyr yn mhilth y Cymry, Pontypridd, 1885, tt. 295-315*

Bradley Road Evangelical Baptist Church Centenary 1899-1999.

Notes

Unless stated otherwise chapel histories are published by the church and London is the place of publication of books

1. W. T. Whitley, "Radnorshire Baptists 1644-1776", *Transactions of the Radnorshire Society*, 1935, 5, 28-39; T. M. Bassett, *The Welsh Baptists*, Swansea, 1977, p.14; Christopher J. Ellis, *Gathering: A Theology of Spirituality of Worship in the Free Church Tradition*, 2004, p. 47.
2. Thomas Baker and his wife, Elizabeth, of Sweeney Hall, were patrons and benefactors of Independent preachers and dissenters served as family chaplains (R. F. Skinner, *Nonconformity in Shropshire 1662-1816*, p. 16 and Plate VIII).
3. Richard Gough, *The History of Myddle* (ed. David Hey), 1981 (Reprinted The Folio Society, 1983), p. 159.
4. Thomas Crosby, *A History of the English Baptists*, 1738-40 (Reprinted USA, 1978), Vol. 1, pp. 377-78.
5. David Davies, *Vavasor Powell: The Baptist Evangelist of Wales in the Seventeenth Century*, 1896, pp. 95-9; Barbara Coulton, "Vavasor Powell and his Baptist Connections", BQ, 40 (October 2004), 477-87; Edward Hubbard, "Baptismal Tank, Rhual", *The Buildings of Wales Clwyd (Denbighshire and Flintshire)*, 1994, p. 398.
6. *Bwlchysarnau Baptist Church 1828 Ter-Jubilee 1979*, p. 4
7. B. R. White, "John Miles and the Structures of the Calvinistic Baptist Mission to South Wales", *Welsh Baptist Studies*, Cardiff, 1976, pp. 35-76.
8. BMag, 1816, 42; Ieuan Gwynedd Jones and David Williams (ed.), *The Religious Census of 1851 Volume 1 South Wales*, Cardiff, 1976, p. 636; Geoffrey L. Fairs, "The History of the Baptist Church in Hay", *Trafodion Cymdeithas Hanes Bedyddwyr Cymru*, 1975, 37-48.
9. Peter Baines and Govilon Village History Group, *Llanwenarth Baptist Church 1652-2002.*
10. Alfred Neobard Palmer, *A History of the Older Nonconformity of Wrexham and its Neighbourhood*, Wrexham, 1888, pp. 57-94.
11. John Jones, *The History of the Baptists in Radnorshire*, 1885, pp. 135, 155-6.
12. The Independents at Llanbrynmair (Yr Hen Capel) united with the Baptists from Garthfawr to form a new cause known as Capel Newydd. It remained a mixed congregation of Baptists and Independents until 1784 when it became Baptist (Dewi Bach, "Eglwys Y Bedyddwyr Yn Staylittle", *Y Greal*, 1880, 39, 226-9; David Davies, 'An Essay on Llanidloes', *Montgomeryshire Collections*, 61, 1969-70, 97-112).
13. Densil Morgan, "The Baptists" in *The Historical Atlas of Montgomeryshire*, [Welshpool], 1999, pp. 80-2.
14. The plaque on the outside of the chapel says that it was rebuilt in 1815. It was restored in 1905. In 1954 the building caught fire and was burnt down leaving only the walls standing. The chapel was rebuilt and re-opened for worship in 1957. It is likely that the entrance porch and the school room at the rear of the chapel were added to the original building.
15. "Hanes Eglwys Rhydfelain, Sir Drefaldwyn" in Joshua Thomas, *Hanes y Bedyddwyr*, Pontypridd, 1885, tt. 619-20. The usual spelling is 'Rhydfelin' derived from *rhyd*, ford, and *melin*, mill.
16. W. T. Whitley, *A History of British Baptists*, 1923, p. 20; Charles W. Deweese, *Baptist Church Covenants*, Nashville, Tennessee, 1990, p. 23.
17. I am grateful to Rev. Geoffrey H. King for information about the church covenant.
18. E. G. Bowen, "The Teifi Valley as a Religious Frontier", *Ceredigion*, 1972, 7 (1), 13.
19. Evan Davies, *Revivals in Wales: Facts and Letters from the 1859 Revival*, n. p., 1859 [Reprinted 2002].
20. Socinianism arose from the teaching of the Italian theologian Socinius (Lelio Sozzini, 1525-62) and his nephew Fausto Sozinni (1539-1604). It denied the doctrine of the Trinity and appealed to those who were distressed by bitter theological controversy and were looking for a less dogmatic form of Christianity.
21. Raymond Brown, *The English Baptists of the Eighteenth Century*, 1986, pp. 80-2.
22. Ian Sellers, *Our Heritage: The Baptists of Yorkshire, Lancashire and Cheshire*, Leeds, 1987, p. 16.
23. Janice V. Cox, "'Simplicity without Meanness, Commodiousness without Extravagance' The Non-conformist Chapels and Meeting-Houses in Shrewsbury in the Nineteenth-Century", *Shropshire History and Archaeology*. 1997, 72, 52-97.
24. Palmer, *op. cit.*, p. 110.
25. George Gould, *Open Communion and the Baptists of Norwich*, 1860; William Norton, *Baptist Chapel, St. Mary's Norwich: The Suit Attorney-General versus Gould and Others*, 1860.
26. For a recent discussion see Kenneth Dix, *Strict and Particular: English Strict and Particular Baptists in the Nineteenth Century*, Didcot, 2001.
27. [Melvyn J. Reynolds], *A Commemoration of 350 years of Baptist Witness in Nantwich and 20 years of the joint Baptist United Reformed fellowship that is the Market Street Church*, Nantwich, 2003, p. 6
28. E. Elliot (ed.), *A History of Congregationalism in Shropshire*, Oswestry,1898, p. 140
29. A. T. Gaydon (ed.), *A History of Shropshire* (VCH), Vol. 8, 1968, p.140
30. L. G. Champion, "The Preaching Baronet", BQ, 1941,10, 429-33; Barbara Doughty, *Rugby Baptist Church Bicentenary A History of 200 Years of Baptist Worship in* Rugby, 2003, pp. 3-5.
31. "Chapel opened at Ledbury, Hereford.", BMag, 1832, 30.
32. T. Morris, "Lord Teynham", *Y Bedyddiwr*, 1845, 248.
33. Stafford Baptist Church Minute Book. I am grateful to the Church Secretary, Mr. Peter Dwight for this information.
34. See further Seymour J. Price, *A Popular History of the Baptist Building Fund*, 1927.
35. Tim Shenton, *Christmas Evans: The Life and the Times of the One-Eyed Preacher of Wales*, Darlington, 2001, pp. 218-29.
36. E. Ebrard Rees, *Christmas Evans*, [*c.* 1935], pp. 176-9.
37. T. L. Underwood, *Primitivism, Radicalism and the Lamb's War: The Baptist Quaker Conflict in Seventeenth Century England*, New York & Oxford, 1997.
38. Whitley, "Radnorshire Baptists 1644-1776", *Transactions of the Radnorshire Society*, 1935, 5, 28-39 (1935).

39. This information, derived from the leaflet made available to visitors to The Pales, differs from that in the Religious Census of 1851, when it was stated the meeting house was erected in 1745 and re-erected in 1828 (Ieuan Gwynedd Jones and David Williams, *op. cit.*, p. 645).
40. A. G. Matthews, *The Congregational Churches of Staffordshire*, 1924, p.3.
41. Alan Betteridge, "Early Baptists in Leicestershire", BQ, 1974, 275-7.
42. For a recent study of the history and theology of the Catholic Apostolic Church, see Columba Graham Flegg, *'Gathered under Apostles': A Study of the Catholic Apostolic Church*, Oxford, 1992
43. For the importance of Edward Irving as a theologian see C. Gordon Strachan, *The Pentecostal Theology of Edward Irving*, 1973 (Reprinted, Peabody, Massachusetts, 1973); Graham W. P. McFarlane, *Christ and the Spirit: The Doctrine of the Incarnation according to Edward Irving*, Carlisle, 1996.
44. Tim Grass, "'The Restoration of a Congregation of Baptists': Baptists and Irvingism in Oxfordshire", BQ, 1998, 37, 283-97.
45. David Thompson, *"A Book of Remembrance," or a Short History of the Baptist Churches in North Devon*, 1885, pp.23-4.
46. F. Roy Coad, *A History of the Brethren Movement*, Exeter, 1968, pp.69-71.
47. Philip J. Cooke (ed.), *The Worcestershire Association Remembered: A Compilation celebrating the life of the Association 1836-2000*, 2001, n. p., pp. 21-23.
48. "PAYN, DAVID" (Obituary), BH, 1889, p.152.
49. *Baptist Reporter*, 1844, 1 (New Series), 417; B. W. Gamston, *Lichfield Street Baptist Church, Willenhall, Staffordshire, 1862-1962*.
50. Whitchurch Baptist Church, Church Meeting Minute Book 1884-1887 (SA NO6144/5/3/1)
51. Review of Cyprian Thomas Rust, *"The Brethren". An Examination of the Opinions and Practices of the new sect usually denominated "Plymouth Brethren"* in *The Primitive Church Magazine*, 1844, 189.
52. Alan Betteridge, "Early Baptists in Leicestershire and Rutland", BQ, 1974, 25, 272-85, 355-78.
53. William L. Lumpkin, *Baptist Confessions of Faith*, Valley Forge, 1969, pp. 220-35.
54. W. T. Whitley (ed.), *Minutes of the General Assembly of the General Baptist Churches in England*, London, Vol. 1, 1909, pp. 37-54.
55. Joseph Ivimey, *A History of the English Baptists*, Vol. 1, 1811, p. 206.
56. Bassett, *The Welsh Baptists*, Swansea, 1979, p.337.
57. Seymour J. Price, "The Early Years of the Baptist Union", BQ, 1928, 4, 53–60, 121–31, 172–78.
58. Brian Stanley, *The History of the Baptist Missionary Society*, Edinburgh, 1992, p.29.
59. Douglas C. Sparkes, *The Constitutions of The Baptist Union of Great Britain*, Baptist Historical Society, 1996.
60. W. Hanson, *"A Reason for the Hope that is in you," or What Baptists Believe, and Why*, [1879], pp. 67-71.
61. Thomas Steadman, *Memoir of the Rev. William Steadman, D. D.*, 1838, pp. 227-8.
62. Dale A. Johnson, *The Changing Shape of English Nonconformity 1825-1925*, New York & Oxford:, 1999, p. 31
63. For the development of Ministerial Accreditation see Douglas C. Sparkes, *An Accredited Ministry*, Baptist Historical Society, 1996.
64. Bassett, *op. cit.*, p. 378.
65. BU Directory, 1973-74, pp. 40-1.
66. E.g. Paul S. Fiddes, Roger Hayden, Richard L. Kidd, Keith W. Clements, and Brian Haymes, *Bound to Love: The Covenant Basis of Baptist Life and Mission*, 1985; Anthony Clarke (ed.), *Bound for Glory? God, Church and World in Covenant*, Oxford, 2002.
67. W. T. Whitley, *Baptists of North-West England 1649-1913*, London & Preston, 1913, pp. 121, 349.
68. H. Owen and J. B. Blakeway, *A History of Shrewsbury*, Vol. 2, 1825, p. 484.
69. Skinner, *op. cit*, p.117.
70. "An Essay on Llanidloes 1861" *Montgomeryshire Collections*, 61, 1969-70, 97-112; John Jones, *The History of Baptists in Radnorshire*, 1895, p.111.
71. T.H. Price and J. P. Pugh, *A Brief History of the Beginning and Growth of Nantgwyn and Beulah Baptist Churches*, Revised Edition, 1966, p. 5. John Creasey, *Index to the John Evans List of Dissenting Congregations and Ministers in Dr. Williams's Library*, 1964, p. 28, incorrectly identified 'Blaneglay' as Blaenglesyrch.
72. Alan Betteridge, personal communication.
73. William Steadman, "Memoir of the Late Rev. John Palmer, of Shrewsbury," BMag, 1823, 317-24, 367-73.
74. Seymour J. Price, *A Popular History of the Baptist Building Fund*, 1927, p. 57.
75. E. Elliot, *A History of Congregationalism in Shropshire*, Oswestry, 1898, p. 137.
76. Raymond Brown, *op. cit.*, p. 123.
77. John Rippon, *Baptist Annual Register*, 1801, Vol. 3, p. 30.
78. Philip Cooke, *op. cit.*, p. 1.
79. Church Book Baptist Church Shrewsbury 1720-1814 (SA NO 2706/1)
80. Janice V. Cox, *art. cit.*
81. Registration of Places of Worship, PRO RG31/17 Salop, No. 191.
82. *Ibid.*, PRO RG31/7 Salop, No. 192.
83. Skinner, *op. cit.*, p. 28.
84. M. M. Thomas, *From Dun's Shut to Claremont Street 1620-1970*, pp. 8,15; Steadman, *art. cit.*
85. BMag, 1815, 480; Shropshire Baptist Association Circular Letter 1815.
86. BMag, 1809, 79.
87. *Greal y Bedyddwyr*, 1828, 2, 161-162.
88. *The Journals of Thomas Brocas*, pp. 57-60 (SA 5492/2). I am grateful to Frank Law for drawing my attention to this. The views of Thomas Brocas were also published in *The nature and extent of the atonement made by Jesus Christ, discussed in a public disputation held in Zion chapel, Lane End, Staffordshire, by Mr. S[haw] Baptist Minister, and T. B. To which is annexed a brief discourse delivered extempore at the close of the dispute, in defence of infant baptism*, 1811

89. For the story of Baptist Home Mission see Charles Brown, *The Story of Home Missions*, 1897, and Douglas C. Sparkes, *The Home Mission Story*, Didcot, 1995
90. Geoffrey L. Fairs, *Annals of a Parish: A Short History of Hay-on-Wye*, Hay-on-Wye, 1994, pp. 65-66; Patrick Goodland, *The Greening of Wild Places: English village life over two centuries-The Story of Gorsley Baptist Church, 1800-2002,* 2002, pp. 8-9
91. "Tenbury Museum. Goff's Free School", http.// www.worcs.org/tenburymuseum/goffs.html.
92. BMag, 1828, 375.
93. Barrie Trinder, *The Industrial Revolution in Shropshire*, London and Chichester, 1981, p.302.
94. W. H. Compton, *Claremont Baptist Church, Shrewsbury Tercentenary Souvenir 1920*, p. 10.
95. *The Church Book of the Baptists at Oswestry 1806-1992*, pp. 55-6 (SA NCO 6813)
96. John D. Gay, *The Geography of Religion in England*, 1971, p. 122.
97. Clive D. Field (ed.), *Church and Chapel in Victorian Shropshire: Returns from the 1851 Census of Religious Worship* (Shropshire Record Series Vol. 8), Keele, Staffordshire, 2004.
98. J. Edwin Orr, *The Second Evangelical Awakening in Britain*, London & Edinburgh, 1949, pp. 58-77.
99. Kenneth S. Jeffrey, "Making Sense of the 1859 Revival in the North-East of Scotland" in Andrew Walker and Kristin Aune (editors), *On Revival: A Critical Examination*, Carlisle, 2003, pp. 105-20; Kathryn Theresa Long, *The Revival of 1857-8: Interpreting an American Religious Awakening*, New York, 1998.
100. Orr, *op. cit.,* p.89.
101. *Ibid*., p. 133.
102. D. C. Cox in *A History of Shropshire (VCH)*, Vol. 11 (ed. G, C. Baugh), 1985, p. 245
103. Harry Foreman, *Old Dissent in Wellington, Shropshire: The Story of Union Free Church*, 1986.
104. Cymro Bach [Benjamin Price], "Bywgraffiad Y Diweddar Barch. John Jones, Drefnewydd, Swydd Drefnewydd", ["Biography of the late Rev. John Jones, Newtown, Montgomeryshire"], *Greal y Bedyddwyr*, 1831, 5(57), 256-61; "Memoir of the Rev. John Jones, Late Pastor of the Baptist Church, Newtown, Montgomeryshire", BMag, 1831, 472-78.
105. "New Wells Baptist Chapel" in Elaine English (ed.), *A Collective History of the Communities of Llandyssil, Abermule, Llanmerig*, Llandyssil Community Council, Powys, 1999.
106. Densil Morgan, *art. cit.*
107. Registration of Places of Worship, PRO RG31/1 Montgomery No. 170.
108. John Rippon, *Baptist Annual Register*, Vol. 3, 1798, p. 42. His name is not given among the list of Pastors in Dilwyn Jones, *The Rhydfelin Story 1791-1991.*
109. Jones, *op. cit*., pp. 102-4. Jones employed the anglicized spelling 'Llangunllo'. The church at Gravel was first listed in BMan in 1857.
110. His was the only name listed in the entry for Plumbers, Decorators and Glaziers in *Pigot & Co. Directory North Wales, 1829.*
111. *Chirbury Particular Baptist Chapel, Shropshire: Register of Births 1828-1835* (PRO ref. RG/2796), Shropshire History Society.
112. John Williams, the first pastor of Shrewsbury, Coleham, moved to Holyhead where he worked as a mercer (Indenture dated 11th December 1862, PRO Chancery Records C54/16057 10763. I am grateful to Mrs. Janice Cox for drawing my attention to this Indenture.
113. Cymro Bach, *Greal Y Bedyddwyr*, 1831, 5(57), 257-61; BMag, 1831, 472-78.
114. Jones, *op. cit*., p. 91.
115. R. E. Chadwick, *Sacred Ground, High Tradition Salendine Nook Baptist Church 1743-1993*, 1993, p.17.
116. The school ran from 1836 to 1839 (Patrick Goodland, Personal Communication).
117. John Pugh, "ROWSON, THOMAS" (Obituary), BH, 1936, p. 353.
118. George Yuile (ed.), *History of Baptists in Scotland*, Glasgow, 1926, pp. 79, 99.
119. "THORNE, GEORGE" (Obituary), BH, 1886, pp. 135-36
120. "The Rev. D. L. PUGHE" (Obituary), BMan, 1855, p. 54
121. *The Journals of Thomas Brocas* (SA 5492).
122. Sarn National School Register of Admission, Progress and Withdrawal, Book No. 1 (1867-93).
123. Jones, *op. cit*., p. 102.
124. "Memoir of Mrs. Wycherley", *Primitive Church Magazine*, 1844, pp. 124-125.
125. Jones, *op. cit*., p. 118.
126. Peter Francis, Jane Price and Kim Yapp (compilers), *Never on a Sunday: Memories of a Stiperstones Mining Community*, Bucknell, 2000, p.31
127. Skinner, *op. cit*., pp. 25-6. *The Salopian Zealot or The Good Vicar in a Bad Mood* was reprinted with notes by J. A. Jones of Mitchell Street, London, in 1837 (see GH, 1837, 5, 208-9)
128. Bassett, *op. cit*., p. 73.
129. [Abraham Booth], *The Principles of Antipædobaptism ... Completely Consistent in Answer to the Arguments and Objections of Mr. Peter Edwards in his Candid Reasons, The Preface and Notes by James Dore*, 1795. Reprinted in Abraham Booth, *Paedobaptism Examined, with replies to the objections of Dr. Williams and Mr. Peter Edwards,* 1829, Vol. 3, pp. 389-460
130. Review in *Primitive Church Magazine*, 1, 1841, 186, of W. Hawkins, *Essays on the Prominent Doctrines of the Gospel and the Constitution of the Christian Church*, Shrewsbury & London.
131. Janice V. Cox, *art. cit.*
132. Claremont Baptist Church Minute Book 1816-1846, p. 137 (SA NO2706/2)
133. G. V. Price in A. H. Dodd (ed,), *A History of Wrexham Denbighshire*, Wrexham, 1957, pp. 199-200.
134. Shropshire Baptist Association Circular Letter 1809.
135. James Ford, " A Historical Sketch of the Midland Baptist Association" in J. M. Gwynne Owen (ed.), *Records of an Old Association*, [Birmingham?], n. d. [1905]. p. 110.

136. BMag, 1816, 295-96. This article seems to be the source of references to the 'Shropshire and Cheshire Association' in several publications (e.g. M. M. Thomas and P. Price, *From Dun's Shut to Claremont Street 1620-1995*, p. 21, and J. H. Y. Briggs *The English Baptists of the Nineteenth Century*, Didcot, 1994, p. 204).
137. Midland Association Circular Letter 1801.
138. BMag, 1810, 531. The Baptist church at Newbridge (Bontnewydd) is in the parish of Cefn Mawr. Thomas Davies of Cefn Bychan was a frequent preacher at Northern Association meetings between 1805 and 1818 (Ellis Evans, *Greal y Bedyddwyr,* 1828, 2(20), 225-227).
139. BMag., 1815, 220.
140. Richard Morgan, *A Study of Radnorshire Places-Names*, Llanwrst, 1998, p. 13
141. J. Randall, *History of Broseley and its Surroundings being a Complete History of Broseley, Wiley, Barrow, Benthall, and Linley, Madeley*, 1879, pp. 222-6.
142. "PRYCE, RICHARD" (Obituary), BH, 1866, p. 130.
143. Owen Thomas *The Atonement Controversy in Welsh Theological Literature and Debate 1707-1841* [Translation by John Aaron of the background material on theological controversies from *Cofiant John Jones, Talysarn*, Wrexham, 1874], Edinburgh, 2002, pp. 76-77, 249-51, 378
144. BMag, 1809, 39.
145. *Ibid,* 1825, 218
146. EV, 1871, 27, 191.
147. Indenture dated 11th December 1862, PRO Chancery Records C54/16057 10763.
148. M. M. Thomas, *From Dun's Shut to Claremont Street 1620-1970: A Brief Survey of Baptist Work and Witness during Three and a Half Centuries*, p. 12
149. Michael Watts, *Why did the English stop going to Church?*, 1995.
150. W. H. Compton, *Claremont Baptist Church, Shrewsbury Tercentenary Souvenir 1920*, p. 13.
151. "DAVIES, DAVID MORGAN" (Obituary), BH, 1928, p. 306
152. R. Tudur Jones, *Faith and the Crisis of a Nation Wales 1890-1914*, Cardiff, 2004, pp. 76-77.
153. *Y Greal*, 1896, 76.
154. S. P. Edwards, "Dr. Gordon a'i Freuddwyd [Dr. Gordon and his Dream]", *ibid*., 1896, 1-4. See also A. J. Gordon, *How Christ came to the Church A Spiritual Autobiography*, 1895.
155. A. J. Gordon, *The Ministry of the Spirit*, 1895, p. 68
156. *Montgomery County Times*, Saturday, April 14, 1900
157. J. Edwin Orr, *The Flaming Tongue: Evangelical Awakenings 1900-*, Chicago, 2nd Edition, 1975, p. 1.
158. Radnorshire and Montgomeryshire Baptist Association Circular Letter, 1903.
159. Orr, *The Flaming Tongue*, pp. 2-3; Kevin Adams and Emyr Jones, *A Pictorial History of Revival: The Outbreak of the 1904 Welsh Awakening*, Farnham, 2004, pp. 38-9.
160. John Llewellyn Bowen, Presidential Address in Radnorshire and Montgomeryshire Baptist Association Circular Letter, 1951.
161. *West Midland Baptist Association Year Book*, 1916, pp. 18-23, 28-30.
162. George Roberts, MSS *A History of Baptist Places of Worship in Shropshire*
163. RCHME, Nonconformist Chapels and Meeting-houses in Central England, 1986, p. 195 (No. 44)
164. Field, *op. cit*, No.90
165. "MATHEWS, MATTHEW" (Obituary), BH, 1907, 469
166. *Baptist Messenger*, 1868, 247.
167. Indenture dated 11th December 1862, PRO Chancery Records C54/16057 10763.
168. Information for the period 1929-64 is taken from *Aston-on-Clun Minute Book* (SA NO6144/1)
169. Skinner, *op. cit.,* p.28.
170. Richard Moore-Colyer, *Welsh Cattle Drovers*, Ashbourne, 2002, p. 143.
171. Jones, *op. cit*., pp 102-4.
172. In the Circular Letters of the Old Welsh Baptist Association the name was first spelt as 'Velindre', then from *c.* 1869 until 1888 as 'Velindref', and thereafter as 'Felindre'.
173. Applications for Licences for Dissenting Places of Worship, Shropshire County Quarter Sessions (PRO RG 31/7 265 & 268)
174. Baptist churches in Wales held a second meeting after the evening service. This was known in English as the 'society meeting' and in Welsh as *Y Gyfeillach*. All non-members left after the first meeting at which news of the Fellowship was shared. If a non-member stayed behind for the second meeting, it was taken as a sign that he/she wished to become a member. Members were asked to stand and it was taken as a sign that they wished to become church members. The person who had stayed behind always remained for the second meeting having once indicated his/ her desire to become a member. Baptism might not take place for several weeks or even months. He/she would be treated as a member, although not allowed to vote at a church meeting or partake of communion. Many Welsh-language Baptist churches still hold *Y Gyfeillach.*
175. Jones, *op. cit*., p.78.
176. *Ibid*., p. 51.
177. Field, *op. cit.,* No. 648.
178. Alan Wilson (in John Leonard and Alan Wilson, "Bettws-y-Crwyn" in *The Gale of Life: Two Thousand – Years in South-West Shropshire,* South-West Shropshire Historical and Archaeological Society, 2000, p.137) thought that the Baptist Chapel had originally been built by the Primitive Methodists but in conversation with the author (19 January 2007) he said that he now thought that it was the Baptists who built Black Mountain Chapel).
179. John Pugh, "ROWSON, THOMAS" (Obituary), BH, 1936, p. 353.
180. Jones, *op. cit*., p.184.
181. "MANSFIELD, WILLIAM GEORGE" (Obituary), BH, 1912, 494-5; Old Association Circular Letter, 1892, pp. 9, 11.
182. Road improvements mean that the chapel [Ordnance Survey ref. 123829) is no longer on the road to Newtown.

183. Squatting, i. e., the occupation of former common land was a marked feature of the expansion of rural population in Wales during the early nineteenth-century. The traditional way of claiming a parcel of land was by building a *tŷ unnos* (literally a one-night house). It was believed that if a person built himself a house on common land between sunset and sunrise he acquired a freehold right to the property. The first house, often of turf, would then serve as a cow shed. It was replaced at leisure by a more substantial cottage.
184. Clarice Thomas, *A History of Cwmgwyn 1900-2000: A Chapel and its People,* 2005, pp. 14-1,
185. *The Montgomeryshire Express and Radnor Times*, June 19, 1906
186. *Ibid.,* January 31 1905, March 28 1905, April 11 1905.
187. Personal Communication, David Meredith, Church Secretary, Felindre Baptist Church.
188. "Baptist Chapel Re-opened", *Montgomeryshire Express and Radnor Times*, Saturday, October 13, 1956. The Memoir of Rev. D. J. Richards (UBCLL, 1980, pp. 82-83) does not mention his work at Bettws-y-Crwyn and I am grateful for information provided by Rev. Patrick J. Baker.
189. Applications for Licences for Dissenting Places of Worship, PRO RG31/7 Salop, No. 191
190. Alan Betteridge, "Early Baptists in Leicestershire and Rutland", BQ, 1974, 35, 275-277.
191. C. F. Gwilt, *The Port and Bridgnorth including the Chapel on the Bridge*, p.16. I am grateful to Rev. Ray Gill for this reference.
192. *Zion's Trumpet*, 1840, 8, 128-133.
193. Gwilt, *op. cit.*
194. C. S. Hall, *The Church Book 1654-1798 of Messiah Baptist Chapel, Netherton, Cinderbank, Worcs.,* p. 40
195. Alan Betteridge, Personal Communication.
196. Skinner, *op. cit.*, p.27.
197. J. B. [probably James Butterworth], "History of the Baptist Church, Bridgnorth, Shropshire", BMag, 1821, 106.
198. James Kenworthy, *History of the Baptist Church at Hill Cliffe*, Baptist Tract and Book Society, London, n.d. [1887?], reprinted in the USA 1987, pp. 68-70.
199. Ralph F. Chambers, MSS *The Strict Baptist Chapels of England. The Chapels of the North and Lincolnshire.*
200. "History of the Baptist Church, Bridgnorth, Shropshire", *art. cit.*
201. George Roberts, MSS *A History of Baptist Places of Worship in Shropshire.*
202. Field, *op. cit.*, No. 168.
203. "PAYN, DAVID" (Obituary) , BH, 1889, 152
204. RCHME, *Nonconformist Chapels and Meeting-houses in Central England*, p. 191 (No.5).
205. Field, *op. cit.*, No. 166.
206. "The Late Mr. James Boyd Warren of Irthlingboro'," EV, 1894, 50, 303-5; W. Jeyes Styles, "WARREN, JAMES BOYD" (Obituary), BH, 1895, pp. 159-160
207. James Ford in Gwynne Owen (ed.), *op. cit.*, p. 94; W. T. Whitney, *Baptist Association Life in Worcestershire 1655-1926*, n.d. [1926], p. 18.
208. Information from Brockton Baptist Church Minute Book (photocopies provided by Mr. Gordon Andrews).
209. "BURTON, ARTHUR" (Obituary), BH, 1954, 322-3
210. Broseley Baptist Church Register 1749-1877 (SA NO 6144/7)
211. T. Phillips, *The History and Antiquities of Shrewsbury*, Shrewsbury, 1779, p. 112.
212. Joshua Thomas, *op. cit.*, p. 205; Geoffrey F. Nuttall, "Joshua Thomas' History of the Baptist Association in Wales", *Trafodion Cwmdeithas Hanes Bedyddwyr Cymru*, 1985, 3-12.
213. J. M. Gwynne Owen, *op. cit.,* pp.81, 86, 108, 109; Geoffrey Nuttall, *art.cit.*
214. RCHME, *Nonconformist Chapels and Meeting-houses in Central England*, p. 192 (No. 8).
215. Nikolaus Pevsner, *The Buildings of England Shropshire,* 1958, p. 86
216. "Broseley Jubilee", EV, 1854, 10, 256-7.
217. Denis Mason, *The Old Baptist Chapel*, n. d. [*c.* 1991].
218. "Broseley Jubilee", *art. cit.*
219. Randall, *op. cit,*, pp. 222-226.
220. Skinner, *op. cit.*, p. 32.
221. "The Rev. JOHN THOMAS" (Obituary), BMan, 1850, p.44
222. "The Rev. JAMES THOMAS" (Obituary), BMan, 1859, p. 55.
223. Harry Lathey Hemmens, "THOMAS, HERBERT JAMES" (Obituary), BH, 1943, p. 294.
224. Randall, *op. cit.*, pp. 224-225; BH 1890.
225. Field, *op. cit.*, No. 228.
226. Mason, *op. cit*
227. Skinner, *op. cit.,* p. 28
228. "A Visit to Broseley, and to the Ven. Thos. Jones", EV, 1880, 36, 163.
229. "The Late Mr. Thomas Jones of Broseley, Staffs.[*sic.*]", EV, 1883, 39, 231-5; S. K. Bland, "Memoir of Mr. Thomas Jones, Baptist Minister, late of Broseley", GH, 51, 234-7 & 338-40; *idem*, "JONES, THOMAS" (Obituary), BH, 1884, 293-4.
230. BMag, 1825, 218.
231. Geo. Banks, " Birch Meadow Chapel and the late Mr. Thos. Jones, Broseley, Salop", EV, 1885, 41, 31.
232. "Broseley, Shropshire Recognition Services [of Arthur Shinn]", EV, 1888, 44, 251-2, 284-5.
233. Arthur Shinn, "How shall I stand before God?, A Sermon preached on Lord's-Day evening, August 4th, 1895, at Birch Meadow Chapel, Broseley".
234. *Primitive Church Magazine*, 1841, 1, 302-3.
235. "Broseley – Sabbath School Jubilee", EV, 1864, 20, 287-8.
236. *Footprints on the Track of Time during Fifty Years: A History of Birchmeadow Sunday School to its Jubilee,* 1864
237. Field, *op. cit.*, No. 229.
238. *Baptist Reporter*, 1841, 151
239. Skinner, *op. cit,*, p, 28
240. Edward Mogg, *Patterson's Roads*, Eighteenth Edition London, 1841, p. 237.

241. Unless otherwise stated the information about the history of Baptist work in Burslem is taken from Barbara Young in *The History of the County of Stafford* (VCH), Vol. VIII, pp. 282-3, and John Briggs, *One hundred years and more: Baptists in Newcastle-under-Lyme*, [1972].
242. BMag, 1828, 327
243. Whitley, *Baptists of North- West England*, p. 171
244. *Lancashire and Cheshire Association of Baptist Churches Circular Letters*, 1844-46.
245. J. Cecil Whitaker in J. M. Gwynne Owen, *op. cit.*, pp.187-88
246. Boase, Vol. 5, column 830.
247. Arthur S. Langley, "The Churches of the North Staffordshire District", in J. M. Gwynne Owen, *op. cit.*, pp. 173-75.
248. Whitley, *Baptists of North-West England*, p. 330.
249. *Ibid.*, p. 46.
250. "The History of Ebenezer Baptist Church, Chester", http://www.ebcc.org.uk
251. Whitley, *Baptists of North- West England*, 1913, p. 331.
252. Kenworthy, *op. cit.*, p. 33.
253. Whitley, *Baptists of North- West England*, 1913, pp. 125, 155
254. William Urwick (ed.), *Historical Sketches of Nonconformity in the County Palatine of Chester,* London & Manchester, 1864, pp. lxiv-lxv.
255. Whitley, *Baptists of North- West England*, p. 155
256. See ref. 20.
257. Urwick, *op. cit.*, pp. 39-40; Christopher Stell, *Nonconformist Chapels and Meeting-houses in the North of England*, 1994, p. 6. (Nos. 24 & 25).
258. Joseph Jenkins, *The Right of improvement on Divine Judgment. A Sermon occasioned by a dreadful Explosion of Gunpowder at Chester, November 5th 1772*, Wrexham, 1772. (translated into Welsh by Rev. Benjamin Evans, of Llanuwchllyn, under the title *Pregeth ar y achlysur chwythiad Powdwr-gwn yn Nghaerlleon Gawr*, Wrexham, 1773).
259. Joshua Thomas, *op. cit.*, p. 307.
260. John Mellor was a plumber as well as a hosier at Chester (Palmer, *op. cit.*, p. 106 Note 24).
261. Palmer, *op. cit.*, p. 159
262. *Ibid.*, p. 161.
263. Whitley, *Baptists of North- West England*, pp. 155, 331.
264. Dix, *op. cit.*, pp. 42-43.
265. "The Rev. SAMUEL STENNETT" (Obituary), BU Proc, 1842, 31
266. BMag, 1815, 393-394.
267. Whitley, *Baptists of North- West England*, p.192.
268. "PRICE, PAUL" (Obituary), BH, 1899, 220.
269. "The History of Ebenezer Baptist Church, Chester", http://www.ebcc.org.uk
270. Whitley, *Baptists of North- West England*, p. 331.
271. Information about the Scotch Baptist Church and the building in Pepper Street is taken from "THE REV. – SIMM" (Obituary), BU Proc, 1841, 37; Whitley, *Baptists of North-West England*, 1913, pp. 165, 332; Sellars, *op. cit.*, p. 26; Minute Book of Grosvenor Park Baptist Church, Chester.
272. Information from the Minute Book of Grosvenor Park Baptist Church (supplied by Mr. Colin Dyke, Church Secretary, Upton Baptist Church); "History of Upton Baptist Church, Chester", http://www.ubc.org.uk
273. Pastor David Carson, private communication.
274. Information about Hoole Baptist Church was supplied by Mrs. Ruth Ludgate.
275. "HALL, JOHN" (Obituary), BH, 1886, p. 116.
276. BMag, 1831, 23, 387.
277. *Ibid.*, 1834, 26, 483.
278. *Chirbury Particular Baptist Chapel, Shropshire: Register of Births 1828-1835.*
279. Information supplied by Mrs. Doreen Thomas, whose great-grandfather, James Reece Bennett, was one of those who built the chapel.
280. Skinner, *op. cit.*, p. 28.
281. "An Essay on Llanidloes 1861" *Montgomeryshire Collections*, 61, 1969-70, 97-112.
282. "SMITH, JOSEPH" (Obituary), BH, 1870, p. 204.
283. John Piper and John Betjeman, *Shropshire: A Shell Guide,* [1951], p. 16.
284. At the Old Association Conference in June 1877 the Coxall church was received into membership. However, the church was still listed as belonging to the Shropshire Association in the Association Minute Book in 1881.
285. *Montgomeryshire and Radnor Times*, February 21, 1905.
286. Patrick J. Baker, *Coxall Baptist Church Centenary 1871-1971.*
287. John Pugh, "Baptist Church, Coxall" in *Baptist Church, Knighton, Rads. Centenary – Souvenir 1833-1933,* 1933, p. 29.
288. Nikolaus Pevsner, *The Buildings of England Shropshire*, 1958, p. 115.
289. Information supplied by Margaret Garfitt, Craven Arms Library.
290. See ref. 165.
291. *Baptist Reporter*, 1845, 251.
292. Ieun Gwynedd Jones (ed.), *The Religious Census of 1851. A Calendar of the Returns Relating to Wales, Vol. 2 North Wales*, Cardiff, 1981, p. 44.
293. *Montgomeryshire Express and Radnor Times*, Tuesday, November 2, 1897, p.8.
294. The information about Baptist work at Dawley Bank is principally taken from Arthur Lester, *Fifty Years:* A. J. Lester, *Fifty Years: A Jubilee Sketch of the Work and Progress of Dawley Baptist Church, 1846-1896*, Wellington, 1896; H. Mostyn Jones, *Baptist Church Dawley: A Brief Account of 100 Years of Witness*, Wellington, 1946; and W. G. Newell, *Baptist Church Dawley: An Account of the first 150 years* (unpublished MSS).
295. BMag, 1818, 237-238.
296. A. J. L. Winchester in *A History of Shropshire (VCH)*, Vol. 11 (ed. G. C. Baugh), 1985, p. 131; Field, *op. cit.*, No. 209.
297. RCHME, *Nonconformist Chapels and Meeting-houses in Central England*), p. 193. (No. 21).
298. It is for this reason that in S. C. Clifford, *Sources of Shropshire Genealogy*, Shropshire Family History Society, 1963 the chapel is called Lawley Bank Chapel.

299. PRO RG 31/7 Salop, No. 283
300. PRO RG 31/7, Salop, No. 315.
301. PRO RG 31/7 Salop, No. 331.
302. BM, 1830, 528
303. The plaque can no longer be read.
304. Pevsner, *op. cit.*, 122
305. R. Whillock, *Sights in the Pit and Peeps in Glory Included in a Sketch of the Life, Vision, and Death of Mary Rider, Late of Donnington Barracks, Donnington, Salop*, Dawley Bank, 1861
306. Field, *op. cit.*, No. 618.
307. "MORELL, CORNELIUS" (Obituary), BH, 1878, p. 350.
308. Alan Betteridge, "Early Baptists in Leicestershire and Rutland", BQ 1974, 279-82.
309. Richard Gough, *op. cit.*, p. 170.
310. Skinner, *op. cit.*, p. 28.
311. See ref. 310.
312. Gaydon, *op. cit.*, p. 85.
313. The information about Baptist work at Hadley is taken from G. C. Baugh (ed.), *A History of Shropshire. (VCH)*, Vol. *9*, pp. 264-5.
314. Field, *op. cit.*, No.595.
315. *Baptist Messenger*, 1859 (January-June), 109.
316. BMag, 1828, 336.
317. *Seren Cymru*, 1894, 143. For a description of the building see RCAHMW Data Base ref. NPRN 7638.
318. Ieun Gwynedd Jones, *op. cit.*, p. 147.
319. Skinner, *op. cit.*, p. 28.
320. Shropshire Baptist Association Circular Letter, 1819.
321. George Roberts, *op. cit.* The Memorial Inscriptions are no longer legible.
322. *Baptist Reporter*, 1844, 393.
323. *Ibid,*, 1847, 448.
324. Samuel Manning, M. A., became minister of Sheppard's Barton, Frome, Somerset, in 1848.
325. Congregational records give his name as Samuel Minshall (G. R. Breed, personal communication).
326. Field, *op. cit.*, No. 524
327. R. J. Gresty and T. W. Hardy, *Memorial Inscriptions Mossfield Baptist Chapel Ightfield, Shropshire*, Shropshire Family History Society (SA 624/4).
328. Skinner, *op. cit.*, p. 28.
329. The information is principally taken from John Jones, *op. cit.* pp. 86-94; John Pugh, *op. cit.;* and D. J. Richards, *Norton Street Baptist Church, Knighton In commemoration of one hundred years of worship, witness, and work, 1865-1965*, Llandrindod Wells, 1965.
330. Bassett, *op. cit.*, p. 49.
331. Along with Rev. T. Harvard and Rev. N. Gould, Velindre, he conducted the ordination service for Rev John George at Gravel and he preached at Mr. George's first baptismal service (Jones, *op. cit.*, pp. 79-80, 184).
332. *The Church*, 1867, p. 345.
333. W. S. Mayo, "Letter to the Editor", EV, 1871, 27, 90.
334. "Baptist Minister's Tragic Death", *Montgomeryshire and Radnor Times*, November 11, 1919, p. 8.
335. "Former Baptist Chapel (The Old Workshop), Station Road, Knighton", RCAHMW Data Base ref. 97073.
336. Field, *op. cit.*, No. 549.
337. Indenture dated 17th November 1810 conveying land at Sarn Wen to the Ministers and Deacons of the Baptist Societies in Shrewsbury, Oswestry and Wellington (Oswestry Baptist Church Records SA NO 6813).
338. George Roberts, *op. cit.*
339. Frances E. Bomford, *A History of the Baptist Church at Atch Lench 1825-1925,* p. 15.
340. "The Rev. WILLIAM OWEN" (Obituary), BMan, 1851, 47.
341. Ieun Gwynedd Jones, *op. cit.*, p. 75.
342. BMag, 1830, 395.
343. Oswestry Baptist Church Records (SA NO 6813)
344. Mrs. Maureen Wilde gave the newspaper cutting to the Author, but he has been unable to trace the date or source of the article.
345. BMan, 1850, 38.
346. The information about the history of Lord's Hill is principally taken from an address given by Rev. J. L. Bowen at the Centenary Services on 15 June 1933. The spelling 'Lord's Hill' was used in the 19th century but the more usual spelling today is 'Lordshill'.
347. RCHME, *Nonconformist Chapels and Meeting-houses in Central England*, p. 206 (No. 116); SSMR ID-SALOPSMR-15812.
348. Ivor J. Brown, *West Shropshire Mining Fields*, Stroud, Glos., 2001, p. 22; Barrie Trinder, *A History of Shropshire*, Chichester, 1998, p. 84
349. "EVANS, Rev. Edw." (Obituary), BH, 1873, 257.
350. *The Church*, 1866, 168.
351. *Ibid.*, 1866, 196
352. See ref. 349
353. Field, *op. cit.*, Nos. 662 & 663.
354. Peter Francis, Jane Price and Kim Yapp, *op. cit.*, p. 32
355. Gladys Mary Coles, *Mary Webb*, Bridgend, 1990, pp. 70-71.
356. A video describing the making of the film. called *Hollywood comes to Shropshire: The Making of Mary Webb's Gone to Earth*, was produced by QV Productions with financial assistance from Wrekin Council.
357. Alan Betteridge, "Early Baptists in Leicestershire and Rutland", BQ, 1974, 25, 279-83.
358. Claremont Baptist Church Minute Book 1720- , p. 118 (SA NO2706/1)
359. Shropshire Baptist Association Circular Letter, 1812.
360. Information for the period 1874-1929 is taken from the Church Minute Books.
361. Baugh in *A History of Shropshire Vol. XI Telford*, p. 71
362. See also RCHME, *Nonconformist Chapels and Meeting-houses in Central England*, p.194 (No. 24)
363. G. C. Baugh, *op. cit.*, p. 71.
364. The information about Maesbrook is taken from "Maesbrook Baptist Chapel Centenary Services", *The Border Counties Advertizer*, August 30, 1944; Field. *op., cit.*, No. 369A and 369B; *Oswestry Church Book* 1806-1892 (SA NO6813)

365. For the early history of Market Drayton Baptist Church the Author is indebted to articles by H. C. Brookes, "History of Market Drayton Baptist Chapel" published in *Newport and Market Drayton Advertiser* (*c.* 1890).
366. Ernest Elliott, *A History of Congregationalism in Shropshire*, Oswestry, 1898, p. 121.
367. BMag, 1818, 327-38.
368. Ralph F. Chambers, *The Strict Baptist Chapels of England,* Vol. 4, *The Industrial Midlands*, 1963, pp. 16-18, pp. 70-71; *idem*, unpublished MSS, *The Strict Baptist Chapels of England, The Chapels of Bunyan's Land: Beds, Bucks, Berks and Oxon*, p. 76; *idem*, unpublished MSS, *The Strict Baptist Chapels of England, The Chapels of East Anglia* [*art.* on Lakenheath]; Ernest S. Marriott, *A History of Gower Street Chapel, London*, 1921, pp. 11-12.
369. S. K. Bland, "Fifty Years Ago", GH, 1883, 51, 77. The details of Littleton's ministry are obscure. He was converted through the ministry of Dr. Robert Hawker (1753-1827) and became pastor of a church in Bath at the age of 21. He then served at Market Drayton; Chester; Edward Street, London; Bethel, Cheltenham and Chippenham. Six of his sons became Gospel Standard ministers. See E. Littleton, *A Jubilee of Ministerial Mercies; or 55 Years' Labour in the Vineyard, Being The Autobiography of Mr. E. Littleton,* 1908
370. Elliot, *op. cit.*, p. 137.
371. BMag, 1818, 237-38.
372. *The Montgomeryshire and Radnor Times*, Tuesday, June 1, 1897.
373. *Ibid.*, Tuesday, June 29, 1897.
374. *The Montgomery County Times*, Saturday, June 23, 1900.
375. Skinner, *op. cit.*, p. 28.
376. Skinner, *op. cit.*, p.28.
377. Field, *op. cit.*, No. 539.
378. *Baptist Messenger*, 1869, 274; D. C. Stamper in *A History of Shropshire (VCH),* Vol. 11, 1985, pp. 301-302
379. James Ford in J. M. Gwynne Owen, *op. cit.*, p. 110.
380. John Aitken (editor), *Census for Religious Worship, 1851 The Returns for Worcestershire*, Worcestershire Historical Society, 2000, p. 2 (No. 10).
381. Ralph F. Chambers, *The Strict Baptist Chapels of England Vol. 4 The Industrial Midlands*, 1963, p. 43
382. Field, *op. cit.*, No. 557.
383. Information from The Church Book of the Baptists in Oswestry 1806-1892 (SA NO 6813)
384. William Cathrall, *The History of Oswestry*, Oswestry, 1855, p. 155; Claremont Baptist Church Book, p. 82 (SA NO2706/1)
385. BMag, 1818, 238.
386. Field, *op. cit.*, No. 408.
387. I am grateful for information about the church which was supplied by Mr. Tony Peake.
388. The Church Book of the Baptists in Oswestry 1806-1892, March 1860, p. 82 (SA NO 6813)
389. Isaac Watkin, *Oswestry, with an Account of its old houses, shops, etc., and some of their occupants*, London & Oswestry, 1920, p. 169.
390. *A History of Shropshire* (VCH), Vol. 8, 1968, p. 292.
391. See Frank Houlding, *A History of One Hundred and Fifty Years of Pontesbury Baptist Church 1828-1978*, 1978.
392. BMag, 1828, 375.
393. *Ibid.*, 1828, 524.
394. Field, *op. cit.*, No. 280.
395. Field, *op. cit.,* No. 279.
396. Skinner, *op. cit.*, p.28.
397. Field, *op. cit.*, No. 170.
398. "Maesbrook Baptist Chapel Centenary Services". *The Border Counties Advertizer*, August 30, 1944
399. Shropshire Baptist Association Circular Letter, 1818; BMag, 1818, 238.
400. Claremont Baptist Church Minute Book 1816-1841, 26 July 1819 (SA NO 2706/2)
401. Skinner, *op. cit.*, p. 28.
402. St. Davids Diocesan Records, NLW, SD/QA/183; E. Rowley-Morris, "History of the Parish of Kerry", *Montgomeryshire Collections*, 1892, 26, 112-115.
403. St. Davids Diocesan Records, NLW, SD/Misc. B/73
404. Cymro Bach, *Greal Y Bedyddwyr*, 1831 5(57), 257-61; BMag, 1831 472-78.
405. *Montgomeryshire Records No. MR/MI/ 66 Parish of Sarn Memorial Inscriptions*, Montgomeryshire Genealogical Society, 2004
406. *Montgomeryshire and Radnor Times*, Tuesday, September 25, 1906, p.2.
407. His Memoir (BH, 1930, 319) states that he was baptized at Grange Road, Darlington, in his 19th year but this is probably incorrect. He was presumably the author of the Memoir of his father (BH, 1926, 320) in which he stated that he was baptized by his father in the brook where Charles Joseph was baptized.
408. Will of Reverend Thomas Harrisson, Baptist Minister of Beckbury, Shropshire, 16 October 1810 (PRO B 683 11/1515. I am grateful to Mr. Frank Law for this reference.
409. BMag, 1814, 132.
410. "Aston Street Chapel, Shifnal", *Bye-Gones relating to Wales and the Borders*, April 26 1906, 284; Aug. 22 1906, 284.
411. "The Rev. WILLIAM HUMPHRIES" (Obituary), BMan, 1846, 45-6.
412. Lichfield Diocesan Record Office BA/A/12ii. I am grateful to Dr. Sylvia Watts for this reference.
413. James Ford in Gwynne Owen (ed.), *op. cit.*, p. 94; W. T. Whitley, *Baptist Association Life in Worcestershire 1655-1926*, p. 19
414. BMag, 1811, 393.
415. *Ibid.,* 1820, 337.
416. Field, *op. cit.*, No. 193.
417. See ref. 409.
418. *Baptist Reporter*, 1844, 1 (New Series), 177.
419. Field, *op. cit.*, No. 194.
420. Alan Betteridge, personal communication.
421. I am grateful to Mr. Richard Pidduck for transcribing these Memorial Inscriptions.
422. M. M. Thomas, *op. cit.*, p. 6
423. H. Owen and J. B. Blakeway, *op .cit.*, 1825, p. 484.

424. T. Phillips, *The History and Antiquities of Shrewsbury*, Shrewsbury, 1779, p.112
425. Janice V. Cox, personal communication.
426. Whitley (1909), pp. 37-54.
427. Owen and Blakeway, *op. cit.*, p. 485; Jones, *op. cit.*, p. 153; Bassett, *op. cit.*, 65. The Cwm church is believed to have met at Cwmfaerdy, a farm situated just off the road from Crossgates to Abbeycwmhir.
428. The word 'shut' seems to imply a closed alleyway or thoroughfare. The origin of the word is obscure, although there are also shuts in Wellington, Ellesmere and Oswestry (A Scott-Davies & R. S. Sears, *Shuts and Passages of Shrewsbury*, Shropshire Libraries, p. ii)
429. Cox, *art. cit.*, 64
430. John Davis, *A History of the Welsh Baptists, from the year sixty-three to the year one thousand seven hundred and seventy*, Pittsburgh, 1835 (Reprinted USA 1982), p.120.
431. Davis, *op. cit.*, p. 137.
432. Claremont Minute Book 1718-1814 (SA NO 27061/1).
433. Skinner, *op. cit.*, p.32.
434. Michael A. G. Haykin, *One Heart and One Soul: John Sutcliff of Olney, his friends and his times*, 1994, pp. 64-66. 85-91.
435. Seymour J. Price, *A Popular History of the Baptist Building Fund*, 1927, p. 57.
436. "Mrs. Penney of Calcutta, and Mrs. Palmer of Shrewsbury, Sisters" , BMag, 1831, 287-9; "Mary Penney" in W. H. Carey (ed.), *Oriental Christian Biography*, Vol. I, Calcutta, 1850, pp. 456-460.
437. Claremont Baptist Church Minute Book 1816-46, 21 November 1821 (SA NO 2706/2)
438. "William Rushton, Jun.", *Gospel Herald*, 1838, 125. *A Defence of Particular Redemption* was reprinted in 1839 and a Welsh translation was published in 1832. The 4th American Edition was published in 1973.
439. Arbitration Award, July 10, 1836 (Claremont Baptist Church Minute Book 1816-46, p. 93 (SA NO 2706/2)
440. Field, *op. cit.*, No. 350.
441. RCHME, *Nonconformist Chapels and Meeting-houses in Central England*, p. 201 (No. 90).
442. Cox, *art. cit.*, 71-2.
443. *Idem, art. cit.*, 75; BMag, 1828, 223.
444. Field, *op. cit.*, No. 349.
445. EV, 1849, 5, 226.
446. GH, 1837, 5, 99; J. A. Jones, *The Mutual Requirements of Pastor and People*, 1837 [GH, 1837, 5, 209].
447. Ralph F. Chambers, *The Strict Baptist Chapels of England Vol. 4 The Industrial Midlands*, 1963, pp. 44-46.
448. *Baptist Messenger*, 1864, 167.
449. EV, 1872, 28, 338.
450. *Ibid.*, 1873, 29, 132
451. Janice Cox, *art. cit.*, 88-89 cited 'Information provided by the librarian, Dr. Williams's Library, London,' which appears to be based on information given in BH, 1861 & 1862.
452. *Shropshire Chronicle*, Friday, 21 August 1863; *Eddowes's Shrewsbury Journal*, 19 August 1863.
453. "VERNON, CHARLES FREDERICK" (Obituary), BH, 1889, 159-60.
454. BYB, 1866, p. 18.
455. *Baptist Messenger*, 1868, 303.
456. "SATCHWELL, WALTER" (Obituary), BH, 1917, 398.
457. A temperance organization characterized by a blue ribbon worn in the button hole.
458. Thomas W. Hardy, "Notes on Early Baptists at Hurst Farm, Stoke upon Tern", *Transactions Shropshire Archaeological Society*, 59, 1969-74, 48-52.
459. Joseph Ivimey. *op. cit.*
460. G. Lyon Turner, *Original Records of Early Nonconformity under Persecution and Indulgence*, London & Leipsic, 1911, Vol. 1, p. 55.
461. M. H. Ridgeway, "Anabaptists in Shropshire and Cheshire in the Eighteenth Century", *The Cheshire Sheaf*, Notes 2, 4 (January 1966), 6 (February 1966).
462. Field, *op. cit.*, No. 235.
463. Oswestry Baptist Church Minute Book, January 1831; RCHME, *Nonconformist Chapels and Meeting-houses In Central England*, p. 198b (No. 69)
464. BMag, 1838. 213; GH, 1837, 5, 306.
465. G. C. Baugh, *op. cit.*, p. 243; Harry Foreman, *op. cit.*
466. "Former Chapel, Portway House", SSMR 16566.
467. The church records do not refer to the pastorate of Rev. Richard Pryce and so Harry Foreman (*op. cit.*) thought that Rev. William Keay was the first minister.
468. Field, *op. cit.*, No. 594.
469. "Former Baptist Chapel, King Street, Wellington", SSMR 3129.
470. *Baptist Reporter*, 1845, 147.
471. Field, *op. cit.*, No. 450.
472. Roger Jary, personal communication. Ellenydd was previously known as Burton House [Ion Trant (ed.), *The Changing Face of Welshpool*, Welshpool, 1986, p.12].
473. BMag, 1821, 214.
474. *Ibid.*, 1828, 278.
475. Seymour J. Price, *A Popular History of the Baptist Building Fund*, p. 161.
476. BMag, 1836, 455
477. *Ibid.*, 1842, 368.
478. Old Association Circular Letter, 1843.
479. *Baptist Reporter*, 1844, 23, 132, 205.
480. *Ibid.*, 1845, 278.
481. Address by Rev. D. Jones at the funeral of the late George Thorpe in *The Montgomeryshire Express*, Tuesday, 25 August, 1885.
482. "THORNE, GEORGE" (Obituary), BH, 1886, 135.
483. The church was reopened by G. Thorne and not by W. T. Thorne as claimed in "Welshpool Baptists Centenary", *Montgomery County Times*, Saturday, October 14, 1911, p. 5.
484. Arthur Lester, *op. cit.*, p. 21.
485. A. de Chesterman, *A Short History of Wem Baptist Church 1815-1965*; E. Dakin, *A Short History of Wem Baptist Church 1815-1997.*

486. "Independent Chapel, Chapel Street, Wem", RCHME, *Nonconformist Chapels and Meeting-houses in in Central England*, p. 204 (No. 109).
487. Field, *op. cit.,* No. 482.
488. Alexander Carson, *Baptism its modes and subjects*, Edinburgh, 1831, enlarged edition 1844
489. Joseph Bryant Rotherham, *Reminiscences extending over a period of more than seventy years, 1828-1906*, (c. 1910), pp. 22-30
490. BMag, 1815, 394; "Mr. John Bayley" (Obituary), *ibid.,* 1823, 466
491. Application for Licence for Dissenting Places of Worship, PRO RG31/7 Salop 321, 13 July 1813.
492. BMag, 1814, 132.
493. Field, *op. cit.,* No. 533.
494. "Baptist Chapel, Whitchurch", SSMR 3401.
495. BMag, 1809, 337.
496. Field, *op. cit.,* No. 55.
497. A. T. Gaydon. *op. cit.*, p. 292
498. Joshua Thomas, *op. cit.*, pp. 295-308; John Davis, *op. cit.*, pp. 93-6; Alfred Neobard Palmer, *op. cit.;* G. Vernon Price, *The "Old Meeting Its Times, Ministers and People: The History of the Chester Street Baptist Church Wrexham, idem,* "English Nonconformity and the Toleration Act (1689)" in A. H. Dodd (ed.) *A History of Wrexham*, Wrexham, 1957.
499. John Davis, *op. cit.*, p.143.
500. Geoffrey F. Nuttall, "Joshua Thomas' History of the Baptist Association in Wales", *Trafodion Cwmdeithas Hanes Bedyddwyr Cymru*, 1985, 6.
501. John Davis, *op. cit.*, p. 96.
502. "Rev. Thomas Barraclough, of Wrexham" , BMag, 1812, 186-191
503. [Ordination of Rev. George Sayce and a brief history of Wrexham Baptist Church], BMag, 1822, 68-71.
504. Ieuan Gwynedd Jones, *op. cit.,* p. 157.
505. G. Vernon Price, *op. cit.*, p. 272.

Index of Names

Following the practice of *The Baptist Handbook* Strict Baptist ministers referred to as 'Rev.'. Obituary notices are listed where they are known. Details of pastorates are given where these details are not given in their memoirs. An asterisk indicates that the minister's name is included in 'The Register of Covenanted Persons Accredited for Ministry' in BU Directory, 2004-2005.

ADAMS, Rev. John Swancott (1863-90); BH, 1892, 115 **33, 108**

AINSWORTH, Henry (1571-1622); ODNB, 1, 501-4 **101**

AITKEN, Rev. Robert Wilson; last listed in BU Directory, 1982-83, 115 **88**

ALCROFT, H. T., builder of chapel at Newton (Craven Arms), 1872 **57**

ALCROFT, J. D., living at 108 Lancaster Gate, London in 1884 **57**

ALFORD, Rev. James Drewitt (1831-97) BH, 1898, 178 **105**

ALLCOCK, Rev. Andrew John* **60**

AMERY, Hannah, of Chester (d. 1709) **52**

ANDREWS, Mrs. Ann, wife of Gordon **46**

ANDREWS, Gordon, elder, Brockton Christian Centre **46**

ANGLIN, Rev. Harry Thomas (d. 1956, aged 68); see CYB, 1957, 367 **103**

ANGUS, Rev. Henry; Bradford College, 1844-48; Rugby, Warks., 1848-67; Claremont Street, Shrewsbury, 1867-72; Ernest Street, Church, Accrington, Lancs. 1873-78; last listed in BH, 1883 **97**

APPLEBY, Rev. Eric Corrigan (1916-87); URCYB, 1988-89, 134 **103**

APPLETON, Mr., of Shrewsbury, preacher at the opening of Osbaston Chapel, 1803 **89**

ARCHER, Rev. George (1856-1922); BH, 1923, 274 **84**

ARCHER, Rev. William Elisha (1815-1903); BH, 1904, 211 **51**

ARMINIUS, Jacobus; Protestant theologian (1560-1609) **9**

ARNESBY, Rev. George (1799-1861); BH, 1863, 112 **25, 98**

ARNOLD, Rev. W. J.; Market Drayton, 1919 **79**

ASHFORD, Joseph, Senior; deacon Welshpool, fl. 1833 **104**

ASHFORD, Rev. Joseph, Junior (*c.* 1790-1853); Welshpool, 1820-29; Kensington, Brecon (E.), 1829-30; Donnington Wood, 1830-31; Brettle Lane, Staffs., 1831(?)-8; Burton Latimer, Northants, 1842-51 **22, 27, 62, 68, 103, 104, 105, 106**

ASHWORTH, Rev. Abraham (1831-85); BH, 1886, 102 **111**

ASHWORTH, Prof. Graham William (1935-) **59**

ASTON, Rev. James (d. 1830); see Kenneth Dix, *Strict and Particular* (2001), 42-43 **53**

BACH, Rev. Albert Ernest (1873-1936); BH, 1937, 335 **52**

BAILEY, Charles George, trustee of Penuel. Oswestry, 1872 **85**

BAINES, Rev. John Leslie; see *The Baptist Who's Who*, n. d. (1933), 32 **46, 80**

BAKER, Rev. Frederick Arthur (1887-1975); BU Directory, 1975-76, 265 **61, 73, 76, 91**

BAKER, Rev. Patrick John* **67**

BAKER, Rev. Stephen James (1863-1944); last listed in BH, 1901, 386; emigrated to the USA in 1903; see Robert S. Johnston, *Stephen's Story* (Spurgeon's College Archives) **91**

BANKS, Kevin, Highley (Lay), 1981-83 **63, 64**

BARKER, John, author of *Shrewsbury Free Churches* (1916?) **94**

BARKER, Rev. William (1824-91); BH, 1892, 118 **52**

BARNETT, John; his house at Donnington Wood registered for worship, 1814 **60**

BARRACLOUGH, Rev. Thomas (1782-1811); BMag, 1812, 187-91 **110, 111**

BASSETT, Rev. Brinley (d. 1979, aged 71); BU Directory, 1981-82, 286 **105**

BATH, John Alexander Thynne, 4th Marquis of, (1831-96) **28, 70**

BAUGH, Rev. Timothy; see Breed, 324 **49, 50, 61, 62, 92, 98**

BAYLEY, Mrs. Elizabeth, wife of John Bailey **77, 107**

BAYLEY, John (*c.* 1744-1823); BMag, 1823, 466 **77, 107**

BEAN, George; registered his house at Fitz for worship in 1779 **62**

BEAUPRÉ, Rev. Joseph (1870-1917); last listed in BH, 1912, 302; South African ministry, 1912-17 **112**

BEETHAM, Rev. John; Burslem, 1817 **51**

BELL, Rev. Samuel M.; Welshpool, 1848-49 **105**

BENFIELD, Rev. George Ernest; Bridgnorth, 1941-44; last listed in BH, 1966, 238 **45**

BENNETT, Mrs. Ann, widow, fl. 1877 **72**

BENNETT, Rev. James (1774-1862); ODNB, 5, 133 **23**

BENETTT, James Reece, builder of Chorley Chapel, 1878 **120 (ref. 279)**

BENNETT, Rev. William; last listed in BH, 1970, 254 **107**

BENYON, Rev. John Jones (1787-1853), Independent Minister, Dorrington & Lyth Hill, Salop; CYB, 1855, 207-08 **86**

BERRY, Rev. John James (1832-1904); BH, 1905, 402, 405 **9**

BIRCH, Mr., of The Rolly Farm, Osbaston, 1803 **89**

BIRD, Rev. William; Chirbury 1834-40 **27, 54, 55**

BLACKBURN, Thomas, fl. 1833 **96**

BLACKLIDGE, Rev. Amos Alfred (1884-1962); BH, 1963, 356 **32, 34**

BLACKMORE, Rev. Samuel (d. 1880, aged 83); Kington, Herefs., 1820-44 **66**

BLACKSTOCK, Rev. Edward (d. 1849/50); Market Drayton, 1822-25; Potton, Beds., 1826-35; John Street, Wolverhampton, Staffs., 1835-38, Temple Street, Wolverhampton, 1836; Lakenheath, Suffolk, 1838-39; Providence, Leicester 1840-41 (*Supply*); Gower Street, London, 1842-47; Watford, Herts.,1847; Riding House Lane, London, 1849 **77, 79**

BLAKEWAY, Rev. John Brickdale (1765-1826), ODNB, 6, 135-6 **93**

BLAND, Rev. Samuel King (1822-1908); BH, 1909, 441-3 **49**

BODENHAM, Rev. J., Birch Meadow, Broseley, 1870; possibly to be identified with John Bodenham, who according to the 1881 Census, was a retired baker and confectioner living at St. John, Worcester, Worcs. **50**

BOGUE, Rev. David (1750-1825), ODNB, 6, 433-4 **23**

BONNER, Rev. William Harding (d. 1869); Donnington Wood, *c.* 1838 & Schoolmaster at Broseley; Breed, 325 **62**

BONSER, Rev. William (1857-1937); BH, 1938, 336 (His Memoir does not mention pastorate at Burslem 1882-83) **51, 52, 82**

BONTEMS, Rev. William; Whitchurch, Salop 1848-55 **25, 108**

BOOTH, Rev. Abraham (1734-1806); ODNB, 6, 597-8 **28, 70**

BOOTH, Rev. Jonathan; Highley, 1974-80 **63, 64**

BOTTOMLEY, Rev. W. C.; Hamilton Place, Chester, 1826-28 53

LAWRENCE, Rev. Henry; Stepney College -1847; Lewes, Sussex, 1848-54; Dawley, 1854-55; Truro, Cornwall, 1856-58, St. John's Hill, Shrewsbury, 1858; not listed in BMag 1859 Supplement or in BH 1861 **60, 74, 98**

LEDSHAM, Mr. W., member of Whitchurch, Salop fl. 1898 **93**

LENG, Rev. William; Stockon-on-Tees, 1823-69 **106**

LEIGH, Rev. John Samuel* **76**

LEIGH, Rev. Sir Egerton, Baronet, (1762-1818); DEB, 683 **16**

LEITCH, Rev. Alexander (d. 1972, aged 87); Dunoon Baptist College; Ackhill, Rads., 1909-20; Bleddfa, Rads., 1919-1920; Glasbury and Penyheol, Brecs., 1920-29; Duckpool Road, Newport, Mon., 1929-49; East Usk, Newport, Mon., *c.* 1946-49; Felindre, Rads. (*Honorary*), 1963-66; Aston-on-Clun (*Oversight*), 1963 -70(?) **40**

LESTER, Rev. Arthur (1866-1940); BH, 1941, 338 **60**

LEWIS, Rev. Anthony James Leonard; last listed in BU Directory 1990-91, 216 **84**

LEWIS, Rev. Benjamin (1863-1941); Penuel, Oswestry (Student), 1888-89; BH, 1941, 339 **34, 85**

LEWIS, Rev. David (1843-1913); Knighton, 1871-73; BH, 1914, 484 **66**

LEWIS, Rev. David; Pontesbury, 1856-57 **88**

LEWIS, Rev. David John (1888-1961); BH, 1963, 369; UBCLL, 1963, 121-2 **67**

LEWIS, David Richard (d. 1955); Market Drayton (Lay), 1953-55 **79**

LEWIS, Rev. George (1763-1822); ODNB, 33, 610; DWB, 552-3 **30**

LEWIS, William; Lodge (branch of Welshpool), assistant preacher, 1831 **27**

LIDDLE, Mr.; Shropshire Itinerant, fl. 1820-29 **86**

LITTLETON, Rev. Thomas (1753-1849); Ministry commenced in Bath 1714/15; York Street, Bath, *c.* 1822-24; Market Drayton, 1825-33; Hamilton Place, Chester, 1833-; Edward Street, London; Bethel, Cheltenham, Glos.; Old Baptist Chapel, Chippenham, Wilts., 1845-46 (It has not been possible to identify 'Edward Street, London') **23, 53, 77, 79**

LLAWDDEN, see HOWELL, Rev. David

LLEWELLYN, Rev. Lewis (c. 1841 -); Huntingdon, Union Church (assistant) 1867-72; Harvey Lane, Leicester, 1872-80; Wyle Cop, Shrewsbury, 1880-83; Sandhurst, Kent, 1884-87; Immanuel, Castle Road, Southsea, Hants., 1887-91 **99**

LLOYD, Charles; Maesyrhelem, Rads., assistant preacher, 1831 **27, 41**

LLOYD, George, of Cwm House, Bettws-y-Crwyn, 1851**41**

LLOYD, Rev. Isaac; Briarcliffe, Lancs., -1879; Whitchurch, 1879-93; Ryde, Isle of Wight, 1883- **108**

LOCKWOOD, Rev. J. B.; Nantwich, 1864-65; Infirmary Street General Baptist, Bradford, 1865- **16, 70**

LOVELL, Rev. Edward Ebenezer (1856-1931); BH, 1932, 325 **108**

LOWE, Mr., son of Rev. Thomas Lowe, fl. 1669 **101**

LOWE, Rev. Thomas (1634-95); see G. Vernon Price, *The "Old Meeting" Its Times, Ministers and People*, 127-8 **17, 100, 101**

LUCAS, William, of Tyn-y-vron, Bettws-y-Crwyn, 1809 **40**

LYCETT, Rev. Ronald Edwin*; Crowmoor Mission, Shrewsbury (Lay), 1972-76; Crowmoor, Shrewsbury (Lay), 1976-89 (His entry in the BU Directory 2004-2005 does not mention his lay pastorate at Crowmoor as he was not then an ordained minister) **99, 100**

LYON [*née* Sibree, daughter of Rev. Peter Sibree, of Birmingham], m. Rev. John Lyon during his ministry at Chester, Street, Wrexham, 1861-65 **111**

LYON, Rev. John (d. 1881, aged 46); Chester Street, Wrexham, 1861-65; qualified as a surgeon and worked for Liverpool Medical Mission **111**

M'CARTHY [McCARTHY], Mr.; supply at Madeley, 1856 74

M'CAW [McCAW], Rev. Trevor Martin; see BU Directory, 2006-2007, 278 **111**

MACGOWAN, Rev. John (1726-80); ODNB, 35, 957-8; DEB, 718 **44, 45**

MACLAREN [McLAREN], Rev. Alexander, DD (Edinburgh 1877) (1826-1910); BH, 1911, 490-2; ODNB, 35, 719-21 **107**

MCHAFFIE, Rev. James (1915-90); BU Directory, 1991-92, 326 **92**

MCKAY, Rev. David William (1869-1930); BH, 1931, 325 **46**

MCLEOD, Rev. J. L. Keith; Wem, 1910; Earlscourt Baptist Church, Toronto, Canada **107**

MCMILLAN, Rev. Peter; Whitchurch, Salop 1920 **108**

MAGILL, Sister Daisy Joan (1916-1973); BU Directory, 1974-75, 292 **34, 73**

MANN, Rev. Isaac (1785-1831); BMag, 1832, 307 **51**

MANNING, Rev. James; St John's Hill, Shrewsbury, 1871-72 **98**

MANNING, Rev. Samuel, LLD, (1821-81); BH, 1882, 307 **65, 98**

MANSFIELD, Rev. William George (1867-1910); BH, 1912, 494-5 **41, 42, 43**

MANTLE, D.; Maesyrhelem, Rads., assistant preacher,1843 **27**

MAPP, William, of Cwm Micon, Bettws-y-Crwyn, fl. 1810 **40**

MARCH (later Rev.) Roger Edgar; see *FIEC Directory* 2005 **100**

MARSTON, Rev. John (d. 1778); Broseley, 1770-78 **49**

MATTHEWS, Rev. Matthew (1826-1906); BH, 1907, 469 **39, 40, 57**

MAURICE, Rev. William (1850-1925); BH, 1926, 325 **82. 97**

MAYBERRY [MAYBURY, or MEABRY or MEABURY], Rev. W.; evangelist, Shropshire Itinerant & pastor of Minsterley, fl. 1817-19 **22, 58, 65, 79, 86**

MAYO, W.S., currier of Knighton, fl. 1833-71 **66**

MEABURY, Mr. (see MAYBERRY, Rev. W.)

MEDLEY, Rev. Samuel (1738-99); ODNB, 37, 693-4 **28**

MELLOR, John, Chester, member of Chester Street, Wrexham, dismissed to form Common Hall Lane, Chester, in 1779 & 1782 **53**

MELLOR, Mary, member of Chester Street, Wrexham, dismissed to form Common Hall Lane, Chester, in 1779 & 1782 **53**

MESSAGE, Rev. Hugh; Donnington Wood, 1978-81 **62**

MINSHALL, Rev. Samuel (1789-1861); CYB, 1901, 604 **65**

MINSHULL, Samuel (see MINSHALL)

MONKLEY, Rev. Douglas Reginald* **59, 60, 76**

MOODY, Philip Geoffrey; Woodside, Telford, 1979-83; Whitehall Evangelical Free Church (FIEC), Bordon, Hants.; currently (2005) Adult Carers Support Worker for Montgomeryshire (Powys Carers Service) **109**

MOORE, Miss Dorothy (1913-64) **75**

MOORE, Mrs. Emma (Emmie) (1901-71) **75, 100**